BRITAIN AT THE PO... ...2

Britain
at the Polls
1992

ANTHONY KING
IVOR CREWE
DAVID DENVER
KENNETH NEWTON
PHILIP NORTON
DAVID SANDERS
PATRICK SEYD

CHATHAM HOUSE PUBLISHERS, INC.
Chatham, New Jersey

BRITAIN AT THE POLLS, 1992
Chatham House Publishers, Inc.
Post Office Box One
Chatham, New Jersey 07928

Publisher: Edward Artinian
Production supervisor: Katharine Miller
Jacket and cover design: Lawrence Ratzkin
Composition: Bang, Motley, Olufsen
Printing and binding: Arcata Graphics/Fairfield

LIBRARY OF CONGRESS CATALOGING-IN-PUBLICATION DATA

Britain at the polls, 1992 / Anthony King ... [et al.].
   p. cm.
   Includes index.
   ISBN 0-934540-96-9. — ISBN 0-934540-95-0 (pbk.)
   1. Great Britain. Parliament—Elections, 1992. 2. Elections—Great
Britain. 3. Great Britain—Politics and government—1979–
I. King, Anthony Stephen.
JN956.B742 1993
324.941′0859—dc20
                                    92-33413
                                        CIP

MANUFACTURED IN THE UNITED STATES OF AMERICA
10 9 8 7 6 5 4 3 2 1

Contents

The Contributors

Ivor Crewe is professor of government at the University of Essex and elections analyst for *The Times*.

David Denver is senior lecturer in politics at Lancaster University and author of *Elections and Voting Behaviour in Britain*.

Anthony King is professor of government at the University of Essex and elections analyst for the BBC and the *Daily Telegraph*.

Kenneth Newton is professor of government at the University of Essex and executive director of the European Consortium for Political Research.

Philip Norton is professor of politics at the University of Hull and author of numerous books and articles on the Conservative party.

David Sanders is reader in government at the University of Essex and author of *Losing an Empire, Finding a Role: British Foreign Policy since 1945.*

Patrick Seyd is senior lecturer in politics at the University of Sheffield and author of *The Rise and Fall of the Labour Left*.

Preface

British national elections are among the best documented in the Western world. Ever since 1945 Nuffield College, Oxford, has sponsored a study of each election as it happens under the general title *The British General Election of* ———. The first volume was written by R.B. McCallum and Alison Readman, the second by Herbert Nicholas. The remainder have all been written by David Butler either alone or with a collaborator. Butler's book on the 1992 election will shortly appear, and he and Dennis Kavanagh have already agreed to work together on the 1996–97 volume.

The Nuffield studies are indispensable works of reference. Their statistical appendices and their substantive chapters on such matters as the press, television, the opinion polls, and the social and political backgrounds of parliamentary candidates are required reading for all students of British electoral politics. But the Nuffield studies are mainly concerned with presenting "the facts." Their authors for the most part consciously eschew analysis and interpretation. This volume, the first in a projected series on British general elections, seeks to complement the latest Nuffield study by presenting, to be sure, a considerable number of facts, but also by offering a series of interpretations of the election and its outcome.

The first chapter considers the political legacy of Margaret Thatcher, who, although she did not herself contest the election, haunted it like some hyperactive ghost. The next three are concerned with the evolution of the three main political parties between 1987 and 1992. The fifth deals with what turned out to be the longest election campaign since the mid-1960s. The sixth seeks to explain why, despite a deep recession, the Conservative government was again returned to power. The concluding chapter discusses the implications for the British political system as a whole of the Conservatives' continuing electoral dominance.

The events of April 1992 deserve particularly close study. The governing party won against heavy odds. The principal opposition party lost despite the equally heavy odds in its favour. It may be that the 1992 election was a signal that the long historical era in which the two major parties in Britain alternated reasonably frequently in office had finally come to an end. If so, it was an extraordinary election in the literal meaning of that word.

ANTHONY KING

The Thatcher Legacy

Ivor Crewe

John Major was first elected to Parliament in May 1979, when Margaret Thatcher became prime minister, and he succeeded her as prime minister over eleven years later in November 1990. In most people's view, the Britain Thatcher bequeathed him underwent a more profound transformation in those eleven years than in any other period since World War II.

Most observers, whether supporters or detractors, agreed that "Thatcher's revolution" involved four main changes. The first was in the way Britain was governed. Direction and leadership replaced negotiation and compromise; government by conviction replaced government by consensus. Thatcher reasserted the authority of the core executive over organised interests and the public sector, and within the executive she stamped her personal authority over the cabinet and the civil service. The second change was in the economy. A broadly corporatist economy was turned into a broadly market economy: Most state-owned industries and services were privatised; subsidies to private industry ceased; economic planning was scrapped; and large swathes of economic activity, notably finance, were deregulated. A third change was social and communal. Partly by accident, partly by design, the gap between Disraeli's "two nations" widened. More people than before, especially in the South and the Midlands, owned their own homes, bought shares, and acquired consumer luxuries; but more people than before, especially in the North and Scotland, were unemployed and in poverty. The fourth change was cultural. Not only in the media but among ordinary people the old values of class loyalty, national planning, and welfare seemed out of tune with the times; the new accent was on the individual, choice, and "getting on." To supporters, the changes represented a welcome shift from a dependency culture to an enterprise culture; to critics, a dismaying shift from caring to acquisitive values.

Not everyone agreed that all these changes had in fact occurred or that those that had occurred amounted to a "revolution," let alone one to which Thatcher herself could lay claim. Some of the changes may have been illusory or skin deep, and others would have occurred under any government. But most politicians and commentators believed both that major transformations had taken place and that they had enduring consequences for the party system. Social trends were moving irrevocably in the Conservatives' favour. The electorate's values and preferences had undergone an ideological sea change. The opposition parties had had to tack hard to the right. Or so they had assumed.

Thatcher's Governmental Legacy

Margaret Thatcher held an austerely centralist conception of the role of government: It should rule untrammeled by organised interests or by other governments, whether local or European; and within government the prime minister should be unimpeded by doubting ministers or officials. "It must be a conviction government. I could not waste time having any internal arguments," she told a journalist.[1] This view sprang partly from a willful and crusading personality; but it also reflected her contempt, shared by most Conservative politicians, for the way preceding governments (including the 1970–74 Heath administration) had kowtowed to trade unions and bankrupt companies and lost control of public expenditure. It would not be allowed to happen while she was in charge.

WHITEHALL AND WESTMINSTER

In one sense the political system of 1992 hardly differed from that of 1979. Most of the changes Thatcher introduced were changes of style and procedure rather than of structure. She was skeptical about institutional solutions to problems, being instinctively suspicious of public organisations. Her preferred way of dealing with obstructive institutions was not to reform them but to abolish or bypass them, unless they were so weak that she could ignore them.

Thus parliamentary institutions hardly changed. A system of backbench select committees, roughly one for each department, was introduced into the House of Commons in 1979, but their powers and resources were too limited to enable them to embarrass the government. They published reports that occasionally made a splash, but they could not change departmental policy or call ministers to account, as became evident when the Select Committee on Defence tried but failed to investigate Thatcher's role in the Westland affair (see chapter 2). A more significant innovation, introduced in 1988, was the televising of the House of Commons. What most frequently made the news bulletins was the prime minister's question time, a stylised battle of wits between the opposition leader and the prime minister, each flanked by ministers and cheered on by backbenchers. It reinforced the popular view of party competition as a gladiatorial combat between the Conservative and Labour leaders.

In Downing Street the structure stayed intact, but the style changed. Thatcher resisted the idea urged on her by her more radical advisers of establishing a prime minister's department. But decision making steadily became less collegial and more concentrated in the person of the prime minister or her private office. The cabinet met less frequently and for shorter periods. It was not so much chaired by the prime minister as led: Thatcher would state her views from the outset rather than sit back and invite discussion. The number of cabinet committees was reduced, and on some key issues and crises—such as the Falklands War and the 1984 miners' strike—Thatcher bypassed the cabinet committee system and worked through informal groups of trusted officials, politicians, and outsiders.[2] Over the years she came to rely increasingly on a small number of personal staff, notably one of her private secretaries, Charles Powell, her press secretary Bernard Ingham, and her economic adviser Alan Walters. The breakdown of her relations with some senior cabinet ministers in 1989 and 1990 precipitated her own downfall in November 1990. Under John Major, the sense of government as a working team returned: cabinet meetings were more consensual, relations between the prime minister and departmental ministers more relaxed.

Whitehall, too, changed its ethos more than its structure. The number of civil servants was cut by 20,000 during the first two governments, and by larger numbers after 1987 through the Next Steps programme of contracting out professional and technical services, such as Her Majesty's Stationery Office and the Vehicle Inspectorate, to private agencies. A "Financial Management Initiative" established principles of management efficiency—clear lines of managerial authority, financial accountability at every level, the costing of services—which served as a model for the rest of the public sector (such as the National Health Service) in the course of the decade. But there was next to no merging or splitting of departments,[3] and very few outsiders were brought in at senior level. What did change was the relationship between ministers and officials. Civil servants were required to serve. Ministers expected them to find ways of implementing the government's radical programme, not to find reasons for warning against it. Their traditional role as policy advisers was called on much less. And they were required to serve with absolute loyalty. Those like Clive Ponting or Peter Wright (the "spycatcher"), who believed that as servants of the crown they were entitled to leak documents in the "public interest," were vigorously prosecuted.

Thatcher herself was instinctively suspicious of senior officials as a breed. Until proved otherwise, they were assumed to be unimaginative, negative, unmanagerial, and overpensioned members of the consensus establishment. She was sometimes accused of "politicising" Whitehall. In the sense of promoting or recruiting senior officials on partisan grounds, this was untrue; but she did intervene more than her predecessors to arrange for the accelerated promotion of younger, "can-do" officials who, in her words, "bring me solutions, not problems." Many civil servants believed the charge of partisanship to be true, however, with the result that some chose to be politically more guarded in their relations and more reluctant to "speak truth unto power."

THE HUMBLING OF THE UNIONS

The impact of Thatcher's "statecraft" in Westminster and Whitehall was largely invisible to the general public. Its impact on the government's relations with outside bodies, however, was very clear. The most dramatic example was the humbling of the unions.

In the 1970s the trade unions played a central role in British government. The public regarded trade unions as more powerful than Parliament and trade union leaders as more powerful than cabinet ministers. For some years, trade union leaders had been given the trappings of power; the senior ones could expect peerages on retirement and every royal commission or official banquet had its trade union quota of places. But they wielded real power too. Full employment, legal immunities from damages, the growing interdependence of the national economy, and the development of effective "secondary" picketing gave trade unions unprecedented powers of disruption. In 1971 the trade union movement successfully defied the Heath administration's Industrial Relations Act, the undertaking of a Conservative manifesto commitment that proposed to make agreements between unions and employers legally enforceable. In 1973–74 an all-out miners' strike against a policy of statutory wage controls precipitated an early election, which the Conservatives lost. The trade unions were treated as an Estate of the Realm. But they appeared to act as a power above Parliament and the courts. By the mid-1970s there were growing fears, especially on the right, that Britain was "ungovernable."

Partly as a consequence, trade unions were increasingly involved in day-to-day policy making. They were automatically given places alongside business and government officials on national economic forums, industrial sector working parties, and Whitehall committees; they were consulted by ministers as a matter of routine. They became even more closely involved with the 1974–79 Labour governments, which, desperate to control runaway inflation, agreed to a series of legislative measures on matters of employment as well as to price and rent controls in return for tacit wage restraint. When the agreement broke down in the late fall of 1978, crippling strikes broke out in the public sector (the "Winter of Discontent"), which led to the Labour government's defeat in the May 1979 election.

Rarely, if ever, has a major organised interest group lost power and status as rapidly and thoroughly as the trade unions did between 1979 and 1990. By 1991 trade unions were a shadow of their former selves, and nobody talked any longer about Britain being ungovernable. Trade union membership slumped. In the 1970s recruitment had steadily risen; but between 1979 and 1991 the unions lost 3 million members, a quarter of their total number.[4] The main reasons were the rise in unemployment and the shift in the economy from manufacturing to services and from large plants to small; but the trade unions' evident ineffectiveness in defending their members also played a part.

The unions' diminishing power took three forms. The first was an immediate exclusion from the corridors of government. The tripartite machinery of economic consultation was largely dismantled. Invitations to beer and sandwiches at Number 10 to help resolve disputes became a thing of the past. On the only occasion that Thatcher received a delegation of trade unionists (to protest against the trade union ban at GCHQ, the national defence communication centre) the delegates' leader, Len Murray, came out complaining "she just wouldn't listen to us." The only trade union peerage went to an ex-communist turned anti-Labour.[5]

The second element in the marginalising of the unions was legislation. The Thatcher government's approach was piecemeal but relentless: a series of employment acts—seven in all between 1980 and 1990—systematically stripped trade unions of their powers and immunities. Secondary picketing and political strikes were made illegal. Prestrike ballots and a period of delay before the strike were made compulsory. The traditional immunities from damages in the course of an illegal strike were swept away. The closed shop was effectively made unenforceable: an individual worker not wishing to join a union or, if a union member, to participate in a dispute was legally protected. Union officials had to be elected by secret ballot. Approval by postal ballot was needed to set up or maintain a political fund.

The third and crucial part in the humbling of the unions was played by the government's success in resisting the prolonged strikes that broke out in the early 1980s. Every set-piece confrontation with the government (and employers) was lost. The fourteen-week steel workers' strike in 1980 failed to stop planned employment cutbacks in the industry; a Trades Union Congress (TUC) Day of Action in May 1980 was a humiliating flop; the civil servants' 1981 strike against a clear government breach of faith petered out. And in the longest and most bitter confrontation of all, the miners' strike led by Arthur Scargill in 1984–85 collapsed after twelve months, leaving the union humiliated, split, and bankrupt and the employers' programme of pit closures intact. The defeat of the miners was of the utmost political importance. If the mighty miners, scourge of the 1970–74 Heath government, could not beat the government, no one could. It was a historic turning point, comparable to the rout of the Chartists at Kennington Common in 1848. Thereafter, the number and length of industrial disputes steadily declined. In 1991 the number of stoppages was the lowest since statistics began to be compiled a century ago.[6] Not surprisingly, the issue of strikes, which dominated the 1970s, was completely absent from the 1992 campaign.

BRINGING LOCAL GOVERNMENT TO HEEL

The unions were the Thatcherites' first *bêtes noires*. Local councils were the second. Profligate, inefficient, self-important, and in some Labour cases subversive, they were the one sector of government that the Thatcher administration sought to overhaul thoroughly. An increasingly frantic cat-and-mouse game was played between central and local government. By the end of the 1980s the government had markedly reduced (and redistributed) its central grant to local authorities; imposed tight controls over capital spending and stopped it altogether on housing; excluded local government from urban development, technical training, and other functions and jurisdictions; abolished the metropolitan authorities, including the Greater London Council (in 1986); prohibited certain categories of local authority employee from standing for local election; given schools and council housing associations strong incentives to opt out of local authority control; and "capped" the rates (the local property taxes) where they were set above a government-defined maximum. The campaign against local government culminated in Thatcher's abortive attempt to impose a flat-rate community charge (the "poll tax") on all citizens in place of the rates, which effectively were paid only by heads of owner-occupied households. The game may have been cat-and-mouse; but, except in the case of the poll tax, the cat always won.

THE ASSAULT ON THE LIBERAL ESTABLISHMENT

One other set of institutions was the target of Thatcherite assaults: the "liberal establishment." From World War II until the late 1970s, the leaders of the great public institutions of Britain—the armed forces, the civil service, the judiciary, the Church of England, the BBC, Oxford and Cambridge universities—thought of themselves, and were thought of by others, as belonging in a loose way to one establishment. They worked together on committees and commissions; they mixed socially in clubs and country houses. Most of them were Conservatives, but liberally minded Conservatives. They believed that they served the public interest and that the government thought that they served the public interest. They believed that their structures and procedures were basically sound and that the government agreed. There were routine conflicts with the government over funding and structure, but these were kept private, relations were generally warm, and the government treated them with respect. They were all on the same side.

These cozy assumptions were shattered in the Thatcher years. The only public institutions of which Thatcher and her ideological allies thoroughly approved were the armed forces and the police. The others were all suspect to varying degrees. The Church of England, for example, earned their displeasure for its "soft" attitude on social problems, for its ambivalence about nuclear weapons, for the archbishop of Canterbury's accent on reconciliation at the thanksgiving service after the Falklands War, and for its apparent obsession with the issues of homosexual and women clergy. But government action in this case amounted to little more than poisonous asides to friendly journalists.

Universities got rougher treatment. They were seen as badly managed and overprivileged ivory towers, insensitive to the needs of business and the rights of the taxpayer. The government sharply cut central grants, squeezed salaries, abolished academic tenure, and steadily deflated the amount of student support.

The government's most consistent target, however, was the BBC. Conservatives regarded it as a grossly overstaffed public bureaucracy, grown fat on the licence fee required of every television owner. They also convinced themselves that it was colonised by left-wingers who conspired to run down the Thatcher government at every opportunity.[7] The government froze the television licence fee, packed the BBC Board of Governors with political sympathisers, and put pressure on the corporation to withdraw programmes that were implicitly critical of government policy. Between 1985 and 1988, for example, the Home Office requested the BBC to withdraw its "Real Lives" documentary on Northern Ireland (which it had not seen); sanctioned a police raid on the BBC's Glasgow studios to confiscate material relating to the Zircon defence project; issued an injunction to prevent the broadcasting of a Radio 4 series about espionage, "My Country, Right or Wrong"; and used its powers under the 1981 Broadcasting Act to ban all radio and television interviews with members of the Irish Republican Army (IRA) and allied organisations (the BBC dubbed in actors' voices instead). During the same period, the Conservative party chairman, Norman Tebbit, launched a more openly partisan campaign against "left-wing bias" in the BBC, choosing its news coverage of the U.S. bombing of Libya in 1986 as his *cause célèbre.* The BBC's charter gave it formal independence, but most observers believed that by the late 1980s the BBC was in some ways running scared of the government.

One of Thatcher's legacies, therefore, was the breakup of the old establishment and the alienation of institutions that, while not at the centre of the political system, influenced the political culture. An early sign was Oxford University's very public refusal in 1983 to accord Thatcher an honorary degree, breaking the tradition of honouring every prime minister who was an Oxford alumnus. Liberal institutions looked on the Thatcher government as the enemy, hijacked by a new breed of Conservative who disparaged their achievements, misunderstood their purposes, and imposed on them unworkable "reforms." By the end of the 1980s, very few of these institutions' leading figures wanted the return of a fourth Conservative government.

THE IMPACT ON THE ELECTORATE

The impact of Thatcher on the electorate was more complex. Ordinary voters were unbothered by the changes in Whitehall and Downing Street, if they were aware of them at all. The attacks on the liberal establishment registered a little louder, but failed to arouse either applause or anger. For example, only a small minority detected any political bias in the BBC, and most of them thought the bias was anti-Labour.[8] But a majority supported the ban on interviews of IRA members. Deep fears about an erosion of civil liberties under the Thatcher governments were confined to a narrow stratum of liberal activists.

The running battle between central and local government had more impact on voters, but the party political outcome was mixed. It enabled the Labour party to cast itself in the role of defender of local autonomy and public services against interference and cuts from London. But it enabled the Conservatives to offer themselves as the champion of the hard-pressed tax and rate payer against extravagant Labour councils; the Conservatives made particular play of the grants given by "loony-left" councils in the big cities to ethnic, homosexual, and feminist groups. Voters tried to square the circle, as they always do on taxes versus spending issues. In local elections the Conservatives steadily lost ground over the 1980s; by 1991 they had lost control of every major city in the country.

Local electors were happy to vote for parties that promised to maintain local services (especially if they did not have to pay local rates) and anyway used local elections as a means of registering their dissatisfaction with the government's overall performance.

Moreover, the poll tax, which came fully into effect in 1990 (although earlier in Scotland) was exceptionally unpopular, less because of the inequity of a per capita flat rate than because for many people it involved a sudden and huge increase in the payment they had to make. (See a further discussion of the poll tax in chapter 2.) It led in 1990 to nonpayment campaigns in the big cities, serious rioting in London, and protest demonstrations in hitherto sleepy market towns like Newbury and Windsor. But the conflicts over central government helped reinforce the association of Labour with high spending and the Conservatives with low taxation. Even in the "poll tax" local elections of 1990, voters' ambivalence about taxing and spending was apparent. Generally the Conservatives did badly, but where Conservative control was likely to lead to a low poll tax (e.g., in some London boroughs) or Labour control was likely to lead to a high poll tax, there was a swing to the Conservatives.[9] The poll tax was hated and was blamed on the Conservatives; but when it came to voting, fears and hopes about taxes appeared to trump fears and hopes about services.

As for Thatcher's style of government in general, people were fairly evenly divided, as a set of questions in the BBC's 1983 and 1987 election surveys revealed.[10] Voters were asked whether it was better for governments to stick firmly to their beliefs or to meet opponents halfway; whether it was better for governments to be tough or caring; whether governments by themselves could do much to create prosperity; whether governments should involve major interests in making decisions or keep them at arm's length; and whether it was better for Britain to stick resolutely to its own position or meet other countries halfway. There was certainly no consensus for Thatcherite statecraft: anti-Thatcherites were in a slight majority in 1983, which widened in 1987. But Thatcher's style did influence the way people voted and was an important component in vote switching. Conservative defectors between 1979 and 1983 disapproved of Thatcher's style of governing by a large margin, whereas recruits from Labour approved of it by almost as large a margin.

The impact of Thatcher herself on the voters was the subject of many myths. She was widely believed, by the left as well as the right, to be an exceptionally popular prime minister whose extraordinary personality and instinctive feel for the British people won three successive elections for the Conservatives. Many commentators thought that these election victories demonstrated that her crusading style of politics was a model for other party leaders to follow. In fact, the long-standing "satisfaction" ratings in the monthly Gallup poll show that she was the second *least* popular prime minister since the war, surpassed (and only just) by Edward Heath.

The truth is a little more complicated. Thatcher's image among voters was unusually sharp edged. Most political leaders in Britain get middling scores across a range of attributes. She was different; she obtained notably high scores for her "warrior" qualities—determination, courage, the ability to earn respect abroad—but notably low scores for such "healing" qualities as compassion, capacity to compromise, and the ability to unite the country. To this unbalanced repertoire of leadership qualities, the British electorate responded with both intensity and ambivalence. Like Britain's other peacetime warrior prime minister, Lloyd George, she polarised opinion: fervently admired by her supporters, she was loathed by her detractors. And many in between had contradictory views. Not much liked as a human being, she was widely if grudgingly respected as a leader. The net benefit to the Conservative vote was modest: negative in 1979; positive in the wake of the Falklands War in 1983, when the Conservatives would have won anyway; and neutral in 1987. Thatcher's style of leadership was one way for a party to win elections. But it was certainly not the only way.

Whatever the reality, the myth of Thatcher the "Iron Lady" took hold. "Strong leadership" caught on, especially after the Falklands War. It spread to other cabinet ministers and then to industry, where there was much talk of the "manager's right to manage" and some well-publicised, and widely applauded, examples of "tough bosses" such as Michael Edwardes of British Leyland and Rupert Murdoch of Times International "taking on the unions." The popular press was mesmerised by the phenomenon. Eventually it infected the opposition parties. The warrior style baffled and repelled Michael Foot and Roy Jenkins, who led the Labour party and the Social Democratic party (SDP) in the early 1980s, and would have been incapable of practising it even if they wished to. But it had a profound effect on their successors, Neil Kinnock and David Owen. Thatcher's domination of the House of Commons fascinated them. It also appealed to the sizable *macho* streak in their personalities. They were convinced that an image of decisiveness and toughness won votes and had been an important factor in the Conservatives' landslide election victory in 1983; and they blamed the internal troubles of their own parties on the feeble leadership of their predecessors. Their emulation of Thatcher's style came out in trivial ways, such as Neil Kinnock's transparent efforts to assume a military bearing on public occasions, but also in more serious ways, such as their method of party management.

Within their respective parties, both Owen and Kinnock chose to lead from the front. They confronted problems, set objectives, took clear positions, and sidelined or bullied opponents. Both of them accumulated power in their own hands by building up their private offices and creating ad hoc committees of personal allies to bypass their parties' official decision-making structures. In Owen's case this approach eventually led to the disaster of the SDP split over the issue of merger with the Liberals (see chapter 4). In Kinnock's case, it was an almost unqualified success. By 1990 his leadership was unchallenged and his party had moved, institutionally and ideologically, in exactly the direction he wanted.

Thatcher's Economic Legacy

Thatcher adopted a centralist style of governing in order to transform the British economy. Her economic strategy was rooted in the conviction that only a return to the "disciplines of the market" would restore competitiveness and thus prosperity to the British economy. Her main instrument was the money supply, which she attempted to control by major cuts in public expenditures. This in turn required slimming down the public services, reducing the real value of welfare benefits, restoring the nationalised industries to profitability (and, later, privatising them), and ending government subsidies to private companies. This was not as radical a break from past policy as some Thatcherites claimed. The process began in 1976 when, at the prompting of the International Monetary Fund, the Labour government under James Callaghan replaced Keynesian demand management by monetarism. But it was taken much further by the first Thatcher government.

THE RETURN TO UNEMPLOYMENT:
AN ELECTORAL NONEVENT

The economic consequences of Thatcher's strategy (which are fiercely contested)[11] concern us here only to the extent that they affected the political system. One such consequence was the return in the early 1980s to mass unemployment. From 1945 to 1979, governments of both parties were committed to maintaining full employment in precedence over other economic objectives, such as price stability and international competitiveness. The reason was political. After Labour's decisive election victory in 1945, which was widely attributed to voters' fears of a return to the "dole queues" of the 1930s if the Conservatives were elected, the Conservative opposition believed that anything less than a pledge to maintain postwar levels of employment was electoral suicide. Until 1979, almost every British politician was convinced that no government could preside over mass unemployment and survive electorally. Indeed La-bour's defeat in 1979 was partly blamed on the rise in unemploy-ment—from a mere 2.7 to a still modest 5.7 percent—during its period of government.

The Thatcher years punctured assumptions about the electoral sig-nificance of unemployment. In the early 1980s the monetarist strategy took its toll in spiraling bankruptcies. Unemployment doubled to 11.4 percent in the space of two years and touched 14 percent in 1983. It ex-ceeded 25 percent in some centres of heavy industry in the North, Wales, and Scotland and among school leavers. The problems of devastated communities, of youth unemployment, and of the long-term unemployed received massive publicity in the media. Every Friday, for example, ITN's "News at Ten" listed the week's layoffs on an "unemployment map." Unemployment was a major contributor to the serious inner-city riots of summer 1981. It was overwhelmingly cited in the polls as the most im-portant issue, and Labour was always the "preferred" party to deal with it. Yet the Conservatives were returned with a hugely increased majority in 1983. By 1987, unemployment had diminished, but only to 10 or 11 percent, and voters still regarded it as far and away the most serious po-litical issue; but the Conservatives again won comfortably. The lesson was plain. Governments could let unemployment rip and still get re-elected. And it was a lesson not lost on politicians. By 1992, the unem-ployment rate had returned to 13 percent, but the issue hardly featured in the election campaign.

The reasons that unemployment did the government so little elec-toral damage illuminated various facets of electoral politics in the 1980s. First, even in the depths of the recession the unemployed were a rela-tively small minority: 14 percent of the labour force but only 9 percent of the electorate. There was indeed an electoral backlash against the gov-ernment in unemployment black spots such as Glasgow and Merseyside. But the vast majority of British people who wanted jobs had jobs and were affected in much larger numbers and more directly by prices, taxes, and interest rates. Those with jobs, moreover, saw their living standards rise, albeit modestly; the burden of the recession was largely borne by the long-term unemployed and welfare dependents. Second, the typical outlook of the unemployed was one of resigned skepticism rather than organised anger, cynicism about politics in general rather than hostility to the government in particular. They were less likely than others to be on the electoral register;[12] and if they were registered, they were less likely to vote.[13] Third, the unemployed who did vote were concentrated in safe Labour seats where an anti-Conservative swing would have no impact on the result.

There was a more important reason, however, why the Conservative government suffered so little from the rise in unemployment. The Labour party lacked credibility on the issue. Both the public and the unemployed themselves placed the main blame for unemployment in the 1980s on the "world economy"[14] rather than the government. Partly as a result, people were profoundly skeptical that a Labour government could do much better in the short term. For most electors, unemployment was a problem, not an issue; they saw Labour as the most concerned and "caring" about the problem, but not necessarily as the most competent. In the 1940s and 1950s the spread of Keynesian ideas and memories of the wartime economy persuaded voters that Labour's commitment to full employment was credible. In the 1980s, after a Labour government that had presided over a doubling of unemployment, Labour's reliance on old Keynesian nostrums was less plausible. It paid the price for past failures of government and for the left's bankruptcy of ideas. It was a telling instance of the Labour party's crisis of credibility.

THE NEW ELECTORAL GEOGRAPHY

A leading sociologist of Britain summarised the social and economic trends of the Thatcher years as follows:

> A pattern has emerged of a more unequal society with a majority securely attached to a still prosperous country and a minority in a marginal economic and social position, the former moving into the suburbs of the new economy of a "green and pleasant land," the latter tending to be trapped in the old provincial industrial cities and their displaced fragments of peripheral council housing estates.[15]

These inequalities were reflected in the electoral geography of the Thatcher years. Until the 1980s, the whole of the country moved in the same direction at elections: it responded as one nation. But both the 1983 and 1987 elections were "two nations" elections. The Conservatives advanced where there was prosperity and growth but retreated where there was deprivation and decline. Broadly speaking, the economy was most dynamic in the southern and eastern regions, most sluggish in the northern and western regions. As the geographical axis of economic growth tilted, so did that of party support. The country as a whole swung by 2.4 percent from Labour to the Conservatives between 1979 and 1987. But the swing was much bigger in high-growth regions of East Anglia (6.2 percent), the South East (5.3 percent), and the East Midlands

(5.8 percent), whereas voters swung to Labour in the depressed regions of the North (by 2 percent), the North West (3.5 percent) and Scotland (4.2 percent). Within the regions the Conservatives gained most in the suburbs, small towns, and countryside and least in the large towns, inner city, and outer-fringe council estates.

This geographical pattern rapidly accelerated a long-term trend that went back to 1959, with two important consequences for the party system. The first was that in the 1980s the Conservative and Labour parties ceased to be national parties in the sense of representing the full range of Britain's social and geographical spectrum. In the 1960s and 1970s most Conservative MPs came from the shires, suburbs, and seaside resorts, but a sufficient minority was elected from the big cities of the North to keep their party in touch with the realities of industrial decline. In 1959 the northern cities of Glasgow, Edinburgh, Liverpool, Manchester, Newcastle, Bradford, Leeds, Sheffield, and Hull elected twenty-eight Conservative MPs; in 1979 they elected twelve; but in 1987 they elected a mere five. Old industrial Britain was one world, the Conservative party another. There was a parallel in the Labour party. It had always represented the inner-city smokestack towns and council estates, but in the 1960s and 1970s a sufficient minority was elected from the New Towns and other parts of the urban South to keep the party in touch with the changing expectations of the more affluent working class. In 1959 nineteen Labour MPs were elected from the southeastern third of Britain (excluding London); in 1979 the number was fourteen, by 1987 only three. Prosperous Britain was one world, the Labour party another. Each party had become the almost exclusive representative of only one of the historic two "nations."

The new electoral geography of the 1980s had a second, more technical, consequence for the party system—one of enormous significance. In the Thatcher years the Conservatives improved most where they were already strong, and Labour retreated least, if at all, where it was already strong. This reinforcing relationship of economic growth/decline, geographical region, and prior party strength dried up the supply of marginal, or "swing," seats. By the standard definition, the number declined from 157 in 1959 to 108 in 1979 and to 88 in 1987. This meant that the number of seats changing hands on a 1 percent swing halved from seventeen in 1959 to nine in 1987.[16] Thus the exaggerative properties of Britain's electoral system—its capacity to convert a small shift of votes into a larger turnover of seats and thus manufacture single-party government from a small plurality of votes—became seriously weakened. As a result, Labour's task became more difficult. In 1964 Labour could have overturned the Conservative party's parliamentary majority of 100 with a 3 percent national swing—and did. In 1992 Labour could only have over-turned the Conservatives' majority of 102 with a swing of 8 percent —and did not.

Thatcher's Social Legacy

The Thatcher administration was far more determined than previous Conservative governments had been to reshape the social structure. The government's first priority was to spread individual property ownership more widely than before, in the name of individual "self-sufficiency" and "responsibility." The motive was mainly ideological, but the anticipated economic and partisan side benefits played an important part too. The two main means of extending property were the sales of shares of stock in the newly privatised utilities and industries such as British Telecom and British Gas and the sale of council houses (i.e., houses rented from local authorities) to long-standing tenants at a discount on their market value.

Privatisation was not part of the original Thatcherite project. It rated barely a mention in the Conservative party's 1979 manifesto and played little part during Thatcher's first term. The 1983–87 government stumbled across privatisation as an effective, quick means of cutting the public-sector borrowing requirement (i.e., the budget deficit), and it packaged it as "popular capitalism"—a means of spreading wealth and the ownership of industry. Before the 1980s, stock ownership was confined to small numbers of the monied middle classes and was the opposite of "user friendly." The privatisation share issues were therefore specially tailored for the modest investor. Inducements included payment by installments, vouchers to pay telephone and gas bills, entitlements to buy very small packages of shares, and, probably, a deliberately discounted issue price so that quick profits could be made. These were backed up by a massive advertising campaign directed at "Sid," the man in the street, and by countless articles in the popular press.

The campaign was effective. Over a fifth of the public (22 percent) bought shares in at least one of the privatisation issues, and the total number of shareholders more than trebled from 7 percent in 1979 to 25 percent in 1991.[17] If indirect owners of shares through private pension schemes are added, at least a third of the electorate by 1991 had a personal stake in share values.[18] First-time share buyers, moreover, were drawn fairly evenly from across the entire social spectrum. Exactly half were in the skilled manual and semi- and unskilled manual classes.[19]

When Thatcher became prime minister, trade unionists outnumbered shareholders in the electorate by four to one; when she left Downing Street, shareholders outnumbered trade unionists by five to four.

The electoral significance of the privatisation issues, however, turned out to be small. First-time share buyers were drawn disproportionately from Conservative ranks in the first place and swung to Labour between 1983 and 1987 in line with the national average.[20] This was hardly surprising. Most of them bought small quantities of shares, which made up only a tiny part of their assets (and many quickly sold them for a windfall gain). But the bare voting figures probably underestimate the political importance of the growing numbers of shareowners, for they might have voted differently had the Labour party threatened the value of their holdings. The Labour manifesto carefully assured voters that the "special new securities" to which British Telecom and British Gas shares would be converted "would be bought and sold in the market in the usual way."[21] The Labour party could no longer risk any hint of renationalising the industries that had been privatised. When Bryan Gould at the 1987 Labour party conference aired the idea of a "socialist" share-owning democracy in which workers and consumers would own shares in the privatised industries, he was immediately forced to retract by the Labour leadership.[22] The privatisation programme of the 1980s permanently scuppered the Labour party's historic commitment, still enshrined in its constitution, to the public ownership of industry.

Housing, of course, represents a much larger investment for most people. In the 1930s Herbert Morrison, the Labour leader of London, promised to "build the Tories out of London" by planning large council estates in the London suburbs. Thatcher's aim was to march the Conservatives back in again by selling the estates to their tenants at a substantial discount on their market value.

Between 1980 and 1990, over 1.2 million council houses were sold. Nothing more perfectly encapsulated Thatcherism's appeal to the aspiring, modestly affluent working class, and it yielded electoral dividends for the Conservatives. As in the case of shares, the tenants who bought were more likely to be Conservative than those who did not; but in the early years especially, the Labour tenants who bought were much more likely to have stopped voting Labour by the time of the next election than those who continued to rent. In 1987 the impact of council house purchases was weaker than in 1983 but was nonetheless to the disadvantage of Labour: buyers swung by 2 percent from Labour to Conservative (against the national trend), whereas the continuing renters swung by 5.5 percent from Conservative to Labour.[23] To this extent, the Conservative government has legislated away part of Labour's electoral base. But one should not exaggerate the overall impact. Sales affected only 7 percent of the whole electorate and about 8 percent of manual workers. Their political significance was symbolic as much as substantive.

Council house sales, however, merely accelerated a steady, long-term growth of homeownership in Britain. The mid- to late 1980s in particular witnessed a new housing boom, fueled by the entry of the high-street banks into the home-loan market (following the deregulation of the financial services industry) and by relatively low interest rates. People borrowed to the hilt to step onto the housing ladder or up to a higher rung. New housing estates and DIY (Do It Yourself) superstores sprouted up on the outskirts of every city. In 1979 just over half (52 percent) of all households owned their homes, either outright or through a loan ("mortgage"); by 1989, two-thirds (66 percent) did, including the majority (56 percent) of manual workers. Over the same period the proportion renting from a local authority fell from a third (34 percent) to a quarter (24 percent).[24]

The spread of homeownership in the 1980s undoubtedly helped the Conservatives; at a rough estimate, it produced a 2 to 3 percent swing from Labour to the Conservatives between 1979 and 1991[25]—the equivalent of twenty to thirty seats. The Conservatives benefited from being historically associated with low rates and mortgage tax relief (the tax exemption on home-loan interest), while Labour was associated with high rates and an ambivalent attitude to mortgage tax relief. Labour may have suffered from the fragmentation of formerly homogeneous council housing estates into buyers and nonbuyers. It was noticeable, for example, that buyers soon created status distinctions by adding porches, dormer windows, and other extensions to their houses. The departure of the more affluent and skilled manual workers to private housing estates deprived the Labour party of the elite of neighbourhood activists who had mobilised the Labour vote in the past; as council estates have increasingly been occupied by a residual "underclass" of welfare dependents, their electoral turnout has declined.

It would nevertheless be misleading to say that the private housing boom in the Thatcher years gave the Conservatives an electoral advantage that was permanent and automatic, for that would depend on homeowners continuing to regard the Conservative party as their friend and the Labour party as their enemy. By the late 1980s, they no longer did. Their gratitude quickly wore thin in the 1989–92 recession, as home-loan interest rates soared, the housing market collapsed, and building societies and banks increasingly resorted to the repossession of loan defaulters' homes. The opinion polls showed that by 1990 Labour was the preferred party both of mortgagees and outright owners, although Labour had lost that position by the 1992 election when, as we see in chapter 6, interest rates had come down again.[26]

The mortgage rate problems in the late 1980s represented the electoral downside of Thatcher's social engineering—and then only part of it. Between 1981 and 1990, outstanding debt *excluding mortgages* more than doubled both in real terms and as a proportion of household expenditure.[27] The credit booms of 1982–83 and 1986–88, fueled by lowering interest rates and the wealth illusion of rising house prices, swung more voters to the Conservatives than share issues or house buying. The real symbol of social change in the Thatcher years was not the stock certificate or property title deed but the credit card.

The spread of home loans and consumer credit had an important consequence for the party system. In the course of the 1980s the electoral touchstone of government competence became the management of interest rates. In the 1970s governments believed—and were probably correct in believing—that to be reelected they had to keep inflation and unemployment down. Interest rates mattered less because savers outnumbered debtors, and mortgagees, being higher up the social scale, were mainly committed Conservatives. By 1990, interest rates directly affected the living standards of much larger numbers, many of them working-class voters with fickle party preferences. Econometric models of public support for the government in the late 1980s estimated that interest rates and inflation were the key determinants of the vote, but that interest rates were by far the more important. Roughly speaking, for every percentage point drop in inflation (assuming constant interest rates) support for the government increased by .2 points, whereas for every percentage point drop in interest rates (assuming a constant inflation rate), support for the government increased by 1 point.[28] Ironically, at just the time that interest rates became electorally crucial, the Conservative government entered the European exchange rate mechanism, which effectively took away its freedom to manipulate them for electoral purposes.

Thatcher's Cultural Legacy[29]

One of the elements that distinguished the newly elected Conservative government of 1979 from previous reforming administrations was that its ambitions extended beyond a programme of institutional reforms. Thatcher's objective was nothing less than a cultural revolution. The public had to be persuaded to lower its expectations of, and dependence on, the state; the social democratic consensus had to be replaced by a new neoliberal consensus.

The 1980s provided almost perfect conditions for creating such a new consensus. Unlike most prime ministers, Margaret Thatcher possessed a coherent set of core principles that shaped her views on a wide range of specific subjects. Not since William Gladstone had Britain been led by such an opinionated and evangelical prime minister.[30] Moreover, she was granted considerably more time and greater powers than most elected leaders are to reshape the public consciousness. Few party leaders are elected to the helm of a centralised, unitary state for an unbroken eleven years, with no serious institutional opposition and with the following wind of an enthusiastically partisan press. The only parallel abroad, dictatorships excluded, was Charles de Gaulle's eleven years as president of the fledgling Fifth Republic.

Many observers believed that precisely such a shift in cultural values took place. Airy generalisations abounded. Pointing to the oversubscribed privatisation share issues and near-elimination of strikes, Thatcherites talked of "the end of the old class war" and the "new mood on the shop floor"; pointing to the growth of begging and homelessness, anti-Thatcherites talked of the new "uncaring society." In truth, a plausible case could be made for almost any thesis about how the values of the British had changed, with the aid of some selected statistics and a few casual impressions. The fallacy was to confuse the distinctive with the representative. The Porsche-driving yuppie, the council tenant turned homeowner, the one-union no-strike deal, and British Gas's "Sid" were all distinctive to the Thatcher decade. But they were all exceptional too. Most council tenants went on renting; most large companies continued to recognise more than one union; most people did not own shares of stock, let alone drive Porsches. The Porsche drivers symbolised the Thatcher decade, making up its tone and style, but they did not add up to a cultural revolution.

This is illustrated by an opinion poll conducted in March 1989, almost ten years after Thatcher came to power (see table 1.1, p. 20). In large to overwhelming proportions, the public's image of the state of Britain was close to the Thatcherite idea. Britain was perceived as a mainly capitalist society in which private interests and free enterprise prevailed, in which the creation of wealth was more highly rewarded than caring for others, in which efficiency took precedence over keeping people at work, in which individuals were encouraged to look after themselves, and in which people were permitted to make and keep as much money as they could.

But in fact this was a long way from the British people's ideal. Asked to choose between a "Thatcherite" and a "socialist" society, respondents opted for the Thatcherite model on only two out of five di-

TABLE 1.1
"THATCHERITE" VERSUS "SOCIALIST" IDEALS

Question: "People have different views about the ideal country. In each of the following alternatives, which comes closest to the ideal for you and your family?"

	All	*Conserva-tives*	*Non-Conser-vatives*
A country in which private interests and a free market economy are more important	30%	46%	21%
or			
A country in which public interests and a more managed economy are more important	62	48	69
A country which emphasises the social and collective provision of welfare	54	34	65
or			
A country where individuals are encouraged to look after themselves	37	61	25
A country which emphasises keeping people at work even if this is not very profitable	59	44	67
or			
A country which emphasises increasing profitability even if this means people losing jobs	29	44	21
A country which allows people to make and keep as much money as they can	48	65	40
or			
A country which emphasises similar incomes and rewards for everyone	43	29	50
A society in which the creation of wealth is more highly rewarded	16	25	7
or			
A country in which caring for others is more highly rewarded	79	71	87

SOURCE: First four pairs of statements: MORI poll, *Independent,* 4 May 1989 (fieldwork March 1989). Fifth item: MORI, *British Public Opinion,* July/August 1988, 4.

mensions and then by slender majorities. They preferred a free society "which allows people to make and keep as much money as they can" (53 percent) to an egalitarian society that "emphasises similar incomes and rewards for everyone" (43 percent). And they chose efficiency (50 percent) in preference to "keeping people in work even where this is not very efficient" (42 percent). Yet a small majority preferred "a mainly socialist society in which public interests and a more controlled economy are most important" (49 percent) to a "mainly capitalist society" (43 percent), and a larger majority opted for a society "which emphasises the social and collective provision of welfare" (55 percent) over one in which "the individual is encouraged to look after himself" (40 percent). And by a massive 5–1 ratio, the respondents preferred a society in which "caring for others" (79 percent) is more highly rewarded than "the creation of wealth" (16 percent). In other words, efficiency is necessary, and the inequalities that accompany it are acceptable; but untrammeled free enterprise and individual acquisitiveness are not. After a decade of Thatcherism, the public remained wedded to the collectivist, welfare ethic of social democracy—or so they said.

Nor was there evidence that the ethic of self-reliance, Thatcher's favourite "Victorian virtue," grew during the Thatcher years. In 1984 Gallup asked voters whether they thought the government's most important job was to provide good opportunities for everyone to get ahead or whether its job was to guarantee everybody steady employment and a decent standard of living. At that time only 30 percent said they were content with good opportunities; 65 percent wanted a government guarantee. The proportion believing in self-reliance had actually been higher when the identical question was put, after six years of war, under Clement Attlee's government in 1945.[31] Asked in 1987 whether the unemployed have usually themselves to blame for their condition, only 13 percent agreed; 87 percent disagreed. Thatcher's self-help doctrines seemingly fell on deaf ears.

Did more people in fact become self-reliant in the 1980s? The picture is mixed. The number of self-employed, having remained constant throughout the 1970s, rose from 1.9 million in 1979 to almost 3.2 million in 1990, a 67 percent increase as a proportion of the total labour force.[32] But the proportion of the population depending on income support and one-parent benefits grew from 3.4 million in 1981 to 5.6 million in 1988—almost the same rise proportionately as that for the self-employed.[33] As for frugality, household saving (excluding life insurance) steadily declined as a percentage of household income after 1980, turned negative in 1985, and went on deteriorating until 1990. By the end of the Thatcher decade, total household expenditures exceeded total household income—hardly the economic behavior of the people of Thatcher's child-hood in Grantham.[34]

This refusal to embrace broad Thatcherite values was paralleled by a growing rejection of more specific Thatcherite positions. For example, at regular intervals the Gallup poll has asked people whether, if forced to choose, they would prefer tax cuts—even at the cost of some reduction in government services such as health, education, and welfare—or the extension of these services, even if this means some tax increases. In May 1979 there were equal numbers of tax cutters and service extenders. By 1983, there were twice as many service extenders as tax cutters; by 1987, six times as many; by October 1989, seven times as many.[35]

Public attitudes to trade unions provide a second example. As we have seen, the employment acts of the 1980s stripped unions of many of their legal immunities and disruptive powers and aimed to shift power within unions from leaders to members. These changes were overwhelmingly supported by the public, including trade union members. But Thatcherism failed in its more ambitious aim of persuading the electorate that trade unions are undesirable or unnecessary institutions. The most straightforward evidence is provided by Gallup's annual question of thirty years' standing: "Generally speaking, and thinking of Britain as a whole, do you think that trade unions are a good thing or a bad thing?" Throughout the decade a majority answered positively, despite the sharp decline in trade union membership, and that majority increased after 1985.[36] Thus the electorate's response to Thatcherite policies on trade unions was entirely pragmatic. It welcomed the elimination of obvious abuses without embracing any principled objection to the collectivism of trade unions.

Privatisation provides a third example. The Thatcher governments spent large sums of public money and much political energy trying to persuade the public of the virtues of privatisation, but to little avail. Thatcher came to power when the public was already firmly in favour of it; between 1979 and 1983, the majority preferring privatisation to nationalisation hovered around 20 percent. By 1987, the majority was a mere 4 percent, and the proportion believing that nationalised industries were less efficient than private companies steadily declined during the Thatcher decade.[37] Once again, Thatcherism appears to have paid the price of its own achievement: as loss-making nationalised industries become almost a thing of the past, the negative connotations of public ownership faded from the public mind, and people became aware of the large profits being made by some of the privatised monopolies.

Thus the Thatcher governments failed to alter public attitudes; if anything, British people edged further away from Thatcherite positions as the decade progressed. Thatcher transformed the political economy, reshaped the social structure, and overturned the political debate; but this was done without a cultural counterrevolution in the thinking of ordinary people.

But public opinion was only part, and the less important part, of the larger picture. Among opinion formers, rather than opinion followers, the crumbling of the social democratic consensus in the face of Thatcherism's neoliberal onslaught was more obvious. One piece of evidence was the conspicuously greater intellectual vitality of the right than the left. Intellectuals of the right were confident; history was on their side, and leftwing ideas were in retreat both in Britain and throughout the world. Intellectuals of the left, by contrast, were defensive, and in the case of many Marxists, half admired the New Right's radicalism and theoretical muscle. Right-wing think tanks such as the Institute for Economic Affairs, the Adam Smith Institute, and the Centre for Policy Studies expanded their influence, while their only counterpart on the left, the Fabian Society, made little impact on informed opinion.[38] Magazines on the centre–left declined: in 1987 *New Society* had to merge with the *New Statesman,* and in 1991 the *Listener* and *Marxism Today,* the liveliest of them all, closed down. On the right, by contrast, the neoliberal *Economist* and high Tory *Spectator* flourished.

An even more telling indicator of Thatcher's intellectual impact was the rapid, massive, and continuing shift to the right taken by the opposition parties. In 1974 Sir Keith Joseph had complained of a "socialist ratchet" in British party politics. In the 1980s the ratchet was capitalist.

The brief life and times of the Social Democratic party (SDP) are instructive. It began in 1981 as a Labour party Mark II, with the nasty socialist bits left out, but a party of the social and economic left for all that. It believed in spending Britain's way out of the recession, in a statutory incomes policy, in a high-tax/welfare economy and, on defence, in scrapping the Trident submarine programme. Six years later, under David Owen, it stood for a low-tax/low-expenditure economy, had abandoned incomes policy as a counterinflationary instrument, proposed internal markets within the public sector, accepted the advantages of privatisation (while insisting on more competition and regulation), and had done an about-turn on Trident. It ended up as a Conservative party Mark II, without the nastier Thatcherite bits.

The progression of Labour party policy followed the same path, but a few steps behind. Its 1989 Policy Review[39] (see chapter 7) amounted to a wholesale abandonment of its 1983 and 1987 programmes and was the least socialist policy statement published in the history of the party. It included a 180-degree reversal on most major policy areas, including the discarding of price and import controls; the dropping of the wealth tax; the commitment not to return to penal rates of personal taxation; the refusal to restore the trade unions' former legal immunities; the embracing of the European exchange rate mechanism; and, most spectacular of all, the rejection of unilateral nuclear disarmament. But it went further: it adopted Thatcher's language of markets and individualism. Acknowledging the advantages of markets in an unprecedented way, it referred to the "strengths" and "vital role" of free markets: "the economic role of modern government is to help make the market system work properly where it can, will and should and to replace it or strengthen it where it can't, won't or shouldn't." Gone were any references to "the working class"; instead, the review talked of "consumers" and "users." Even socialism was redefined in terms that a Thatcherite could accept: "socialism," the Policy Review said, "is about diffusing power and giving people more control over their lives." In effect the Labour party had jettisoned socialism in all but name. It had turned into a party of private enterprise and the free market.

The Labour party's policy transformation was of course brought about by electoral and practical considerations. After its decisive defeat in 1987, when the professionalism of Labour's campaign could not be faulted, the Labour leadership believed that only a clean break from the party's ideological past would make it electable. Moreover, much of the Thatcher government's record was irreversible. A new Labour government simply could not afford to renationalise privatised industries or risk a run on sterling from overspending. Certainly ordinary voters, including Labour voters, were not demanding a reversal of the Thatcherite programme (except for the poll tax). Nor was there stomach for it among the Labour leadership. They had sincerely opposed the privatisation programme, yet its success was undeniable; most of the privatised companies were making profits and by all accounts giving their customers better service. Labour leaders had sincerely opposed the trade union reforms; but in truth industrial relations had improved immeasurably (to Labour's electoral advantage) without workers' wages and conditions suffering. They could hardly admit it, even to themselves, but most of the Labour leadership had been converted. Thatcher had won the political argument.

Thus Thatcher failed to induce a cultural counterrevolution among the general public but succeeded among the political classes. Her cultural legacy was a new two-party consensus. Until 1975, the "public philosophy" differed little from the days of Attlee. There was cross-party agreement on the desirability of Keynesian demand management, a large public sector, trade union immunities and self-government, full employment, and state help for industry. By 1990, the public philosophy was liberal capitalist. There was cross-party acceptance of monetary discipline, privatisation, legally regulated and less powerful unions, the inevitability of unemployment, and laissez-faire. It was her ambition, Thatcher once declared, to "kill socialism." She did.

Thatcher's Legacy: The Balance Sheet

On the night of Thatcher's resignation as prime minister, the editor of *The Times* said on television, "Thatcherism died in six hours." How enduring was Thatcher's legacy?

The part of Thatcher's "revolution" that was wholly bound up with her personality departed with her. This applies in particular to the way she played the roles of prime minister and Conservative party leader. She made no provision for institutionalising her prime ministerial style so that it could, or would have to, continue with her successor. And she failed to groom an ideological heir to succeed her as party leader. It is true that John Major was her preferred choice as successor and received the support of most Thatcherites in the parliamentary Conservative party. But Major was never the "son of Thatcher," as his opponents initially claimed and his Thatcherite supporters hoped. His social background was very different—insecure, *déclassé,* metropolitan, and secular; hers was secure, petit bourgeois, provincial, and Methodist. He shared her passion for sound money, but for little else. None of his first cabinet's senior positions went to committed Thatcherites. And in style he is as different from Thatcher as imaginable. She was a visionary, abrasive and confrontational; he is a manager, emollient and disarming. Thus, on 27 November 1990, when Major became prime minister, the face of the Conservative government was transformed overnight. Voters believed there had been a change of government, not just a change of prime minister, and they went on believing it until the 1992 election.[40]

Yet much of Thatcher's legacy is irreversible in the foreseeable future. Those changes that ran with the grain of underlying social and demographic trends, or that Major's government would anyway wish to preserve, are as permanent as political change can be. It is almost impossible to imagine the trade unions returning to their former political role or to envisage the circumstances in which a government would renationalise the privatised industries. It seems unlikely that the injection of more financial accountability and responsibility into public institutions will not endure. The evolution of the social structure, which the Thatcher years accelerated, will continue in the same direction, to the

Labour party's disadvantage, although the pace may slow down. The habit of owner occupation will spread further, people will go on migrating from north to south, and increasing numbers will supplement their welfare entitlements and rights to public services with private provision.

The paradox of Thatcher's legacy, therefore, is that it had a more enduring impact on the opposition parties than on the Conservative party. Without the devastating defeats of 1983 and 1987, the forced pace of social change, and the Thatcher governments' irreversible measures, the Labour party would not have moved to the ideological centre. If Thatcher had established an ideological dynasty in the Conservative party, it too would not have moved to the pragmatic centre ground. In the event, the 1992 election was the first to be fought since 1966 by three centrist parties; arguably there were fewer policy differences between the Conservative and Labour parties than at any time in this century. But the centre ground has shifted: the new consensus is not the old postwar settlement of welfare Keynesianism within the Atlantic Alliance but the "social market" within the European Community, in which the state's role is limited to the supply side of the economy and to selective, targeted welfare. It is not, perhaps, the legacy that Thatcher wanted to bequeath but it certainly represents a significant and probably permanent change in the British political scene.

Notes

1. *Observer,* interview, 25 February 1979.
2. Peter Hennessy, "The Secret World of Cabinet Committees," *Social Studies Review* 1 (November 1985): 7–11.
3. The exceptions were Trade and Industry (remerged in 1983) and Health and Social Security (broken up in 1988). The Central Policy Review Staff, the policy "think tank," was abolished in 1983.
4. Richard Hyman, "Trade Unions and Industrial Relations," in *Contemporary Britain: An Annual Review 1992,* ed. Peter Catterall (Oxford: Blackwell, 1992), 254–63.
5. Frank Chapple, leader of the electricians and plumbers, who broke away from the Trades Union Congress.
6. Hyman, "Trade Unions and Industrial Relations," 254–63, at 256.
7. See, for example, Norman Tebbit's description of his participation in the BBC's 1983 election night coverage: "The atmosphere in the studio was terrible—almost everyone on the staff seemed to be in mourning, with no attempt to conceal their regret that their side had lost." Tebbit, *Upwardly Mobile* (London: Futura, 1989), 261.
8. Barrie Gunter, Michael Svennevig, and Mallory Wober, *Television Coverage of the 1983 General Election* (Aldershot: Gower, 1986), 84–85.

9. Colin Rallings and Michael Thrasher, "The Electoral Impact of the Poll Tax: Evidence from the 1990 Local Elections in England and Wales," in *British Parties and Elections Yearbook 1991,* ed. Ivor Crewe, Pippa Norris, David Denver, and David Broughton (Hemel Hempstead: Harvester Wheatsheaf, 1991), 145–58.

10. See Ivor Crewe, "Has the Electorate Become Thatcherite?" in *Thatcherism,* ed. Robert Skidelsky (London: Chatto and Windus, 1988), 25–49, tables 8, 9.

11. See, for example, Ken Coutts and Wynne Godley, "The British Economy under Mrs. Thatcher," *Political Quarterly* 60 (April–June 1990): 137–51; and other articles in the same issue.

12. See Jean Todd and Bob Butcher, *Electoral Registration in 1981* (London: Office of Population Censuses and Surveys, 1982), 23, table 10.

13. In 1987 the official turnout rate was 84 percent among those not in the labour market, 83 percent among those in paid work, but 73 percent among the unemployed. See Anthony Heath et al., *Understanding Political Change: The British Voter 1964–1987* (Oxford: Pergamon Press, 1991), 165–68.

14. A fall 1982 survey of the unemployed found that only 24 percent put the main blame on the government, whereas 47 percent blamed "nobody" or the "world economy" and another 14 percent "politicians generally." See "Britain's Jobless," *The Economist* 4 (December 1982): 23.

15. A.H. Halsey, *British Social Trends Since 1900* (London: Macmillan, 1988), 33.

16. See John Curtice and Michael Steed, "Appendix 2: Analysis" in *The British General Election of 1987,* David Butler and Dennis Kavanagh (London: Macmillan, 1988), 316–62, at 354.

17. Central Statistical Office, *Social Trends 22* (London: HMSO, 1992), 102–3.

18. The growth of private pension schemes was a third form of popular capitalism and possibly more significant in terms of the number of people and amount of money involved. The long-term political consequences are difficult to discern at present. Arguably the outbreak of City scandals will turn the regulation of financial services into a partisan issue.

19. BBC/Gallup election survey, 10–11 June 1987.

20. Heath et al., *Understanding Political Change,* 123.

21. Labour Party, *Britain Will Win* (London: Labour Party, 1987), 5.

22. Colin Hughes and Patrick Wintour, *Labour Rebuilt* (London: Fourth Estate, 1990), 44.

23. See Ivor Crewe, "Labor Force Changes, Working Class Decline, and the Labour Vote: Social and Electoral Trends in Postwar Britain," in *Labor Parties in Postindustrial Societies,* ed. Frances Fox Piven (Oxford: Polity Press, 1991), 20–46, at 34.

24. See Heath et al., *Understanding Political Change,* 106–7, 206–7; and Government Statistical Service, *OPCS Monitor SS 90/3 (General Household Survey)* (London: Government Statistical Service, 1990), 4, table 5.

25. This is based on applying Heath et al.'s estimate of a 4.8 percent swing between 1964 and 1987 pro rata to the 1979–91 period. The association be-

tween housing tenure and vote has been very steady since 1964. See Heath et al., *Understanding Political Change*, 206–7.

26. In March 1990 the swing to Labour since the 1987 general election was 18 percent among mortgagees compared with 14.5 percent among council tenants. See Ivor Crewe, "Centre of Attraction," *Marxism Today*, May 1990, 14–17.

27. Central Statistical Office, *Social Trends 22*, 113.

28. See David Sanders, "Government Popularity and the Next General Election," *Political Quarterly* 62 (April–June 1991): 235–61, esp. 248.

29. Parts of this section are revised extracts from Ivor Crewe, "The Policy Agenda: A New Thatcherite Consensus?" *Contemporary Record* 3 (February 1990): 2–7.

30. See Anthony King, "Margaret Thatcher: The Style of a Prime Minister," in *The British Prime Minister*, 2d ed., ed. Anthony King (London: Macmillan, 1985).

31. *The Economist*, 25 May 1985, 22.

32. Central Statistical Office, *Social Trends 22*, 75.

33. Central Statistical Office, *Social Trends 19* (London: HMSO, 1989), 91; and Central Statistical Office, *Social Trends 18* (London: HMSO, 1988), 86.

34. Central Statistical Office, *Social Trends 22*, 115.

35. Crewe, "Policy Agenda," 4.

36. Ibid.

37. Ibid., 5.

38. The Institute for Public Policy Research was established in 1988 "to provide an alternative to the free-market think tanks," and Charter 88, a left-of-center pressure group, was founded in the same year to campaign for a wide range of constitutional reforms. It is too early to judge their influence.

39. Labour Party, *Meet the Challenge, Make the Change* (London: Labour Party, 1989).

40. On the day of the 1992 election, the Harris exit poll asked voters who was to blame for "the present state of the British economy." Nearly half (47 percent) blamed "world economic conditions" and almost as many (46 percent) "Mrs. Thatcher's government." Only 5 percent blamed "John Major's government"—even though the majority of its cabinet served under Thatcher and Major was her chancellor of the exchequer.

2

The Conservative Party from Thatcher to Major

Philip Norton

On 11 June 1987, Margaret Thatcher achieved a distinction without precedent in the history of mass politics in Britain: she led her party to a third consecutive election victory. Leading the party to victory is a powerful reinforcement of a leader's political position.[1] Doing it three times in a row—being returned on the third occasion with a three-figure majority—creates a perception almost of invulnerability. As she stood on the steps inside Conservative Central Office acknowledging victory, Margaret Thatcher was at the zenith of her political power.

On the morning of Thursday, 22 November 1990, just over three years and five months after her triumphal return to Downing Street, Thatcher read a short statement to her cabinet. It was then released to the press. "Having consulted widely among colleagues, I have concluded that the unity of the party and the prospects of victory in a general election would be better served if I stood down to enable cabinet colleagues to enter the ballot for the leadership. I should like to thank all those in cabinet and outside who have given me such dedicated support."[2] Six days later, she ceased to be prime minister.

Often portrayed as the most powerful of modern prime ministers, Margaret Thatcher had failed to maintain the support of her parliamentary party. The "Iron Lady" had been laid low by her spear carriers. What had happened in those three years and five months to wreak such a transformation in Margaret Thatcher's fortunes? And how did her successor differ from her in substance and style?

On the face of it, the loss of leadership is almost inexplicable. The thesis of prime ministerial government—propounded by Richard Crossman and others[3]—dictated that Thatcher was impregnable. She enjoyed good health—indeed, she appeared to thrive on hard work—and her party had a large overall majority in the House of Commons. She appeared to epitomise what Lord Hailsham in 1976 characterised as an "elective dictatorship."[4] She dominated her cabinet; institutions that got in her way were "handbagged."[5] She had a clear goal, embodied in the eponymous philosophy of Thatcherism, and she was not going to be deflected from achieving it. She crafted a Thatcherite party and carried all before her. Thatcherism appeared to triumph in three successive elections. There seemed nothing to stop her from carrying out her declared intention of "going on and on."

On the basis of this analysis, there was nothing that could have toppled Margaret Thatcher from the leadership of the Conservative party. The problem lies in the fact that it is a flawed analysis. It fails to appreciate or incorporate the nature of Thatcherism, the electorate, the parliamentary Conservative party, and the changes that had taken place in the method of electing the party leader. The changes that allowed Thatcher to grasp the leadership in 1975 were to be the basis of her downfall.

Thatcherism

Margaret Thatcher is the only British prime minister to have an "ism" named after her. "Thatcherism" was seen as the hallmark of her government. Nevertheless, it was never a coherent philosophy; Thatcher led her party to victory in three elections despite Thatcherism and not because of it; and despite the fact that the parliamentary party was dominated by Thatcher, it was itself never a Thatcherite body. Neither was the Conservative party in the country.

MARGARET THATCHER AND THATCHERISM

Margaret Thatcher was elected leader of the Conservative party in 1975. She was elected for one principal reason: she was not Edward Heath. She offered to lead the party in a new direction. At the time of her election, she was associated with the neoliberal, or free market, strand of Conservative thought, but there was no philosophy associated exclusively with her. As leader of the party in opposition, she sought to bring together different strands within the party. Not until she was ensconced in office—following the general election of 1979—did she begin to unleash a range of policies that marked out her approach to public policy as essentially novel. Thatcher as party leader thus predated Thatcherism by several years.

Thatcherism itself had three distinct elements. One was economic:

the commitment to a free market economy. Thatcher emphasised the liberating effects of market capitalism. The market was seen as necessary for wealth creation. Competitive market forces, it was argued, were also essentially democratic because they allowed individual consumers the opportunity to register preferences with every purchase. Government intervention was considered harmful and illegitimate. According to Sir Keith (now Lord) Joseph, Thatcher's mentor in the 1970s, "there are limits to the good which governments can do to help the economy, but no limits to the harm."[6]

What flowed from this approach in structural terms was a strengthening of the state. If the old collectivist forms of government were to be dismantled, and other power sources restrained, the centre had to be strengthened. A strong centre was essential to hold and police the ring in which market forces could operate. Hence the seeming paradox summed up in the title of Andrew Gamble's book on the subject, *The Free Economy and the Strong State.*[7]

What flowed from this approach in policy terms was an emphasis on combating inflation and on ridding the individual of the shackles of state control. This led to reductions in direct taxation (shifting the burden to indirect taxation), to attempting to control public spending and the money supply (the first relatively more successfully than the second), and to adhering to free collective wage bargaining as an alternative to subsidies and pay norms. It also produced later, almost by accident, the privatisation of various public utilities. During Thatcher's premiership, more than twenty utilities, including gas, steel, water, and electricity, were returned to private ownership. There was a pervasive emphasis on ownership—home and share ownership increased significantly during the Thatcher premiership—and on curbing the power of the trade unions.

The second element of Thatcherism was not economic but moral. Thatcher was keen not only to laud and re-create the economic liberalism of the Victorian era but also to laud and restore Victorian morality. There was, consequently, an emphasis on moral values and on the maintenance of public and educational standards. The permissive society of the 1960s was deemed to be excessive and to have undermined the very fabric of society. Parental responsibility had been undermined and needed to be restored. If individuals broke the law, the fault was that of the individual and not of society. There was thus a strong emphasis on giving greater power to parents in the sphere of education, on requiring school pupils to be taught about sex in the context of family values and responsibility, and on law and order. Though there was never a parliamentary majority to restore the death penalty for murder, Thatcher was consistent in voting for its restoration.

These two elements of Thatcherism, the economic and the moral, were not always compatible. Indeed, taken to its logical conclusion, a free market philosophy is essentially amoral. (Under the free market philosophy, everyone is equal and equally vulnerable—for example, to unemployment—and therefore no one is to blame.) The two caused tensions within Thatcher's approach to public policy, but only rarely.[8]

The third, and in many respects the most important, element of Thatcherism was one of style. That style was a combative and aggressive one. Thatcher and her supporters were prepared to proclaim publicly and confidently the values they espoused and to take on all those who dared to challenge them. Thatcher had no hesitation in using the public arena to articulate her personal credo and, if necessary, in mobilising support for it. She also used the public arena to damn her opponents and fainthearted friends in her own party. Colleagues who lacked her rigour and her philosophy were derided as "wet." The more visible "wet" members of her cabinet were removed from office, especially in the years between 1981 and 1983.

Thatcher's combative style was as apparent on the international stage as on the domestic. She hectored fellow heads of government at European Community summits. During the Falklands crisis in 1982, she reduced Ronald Reagan to whimpering acquiescence after he dared to suggest, in a telephone conversation, that British forces might stop fighting before they had retaken the islands' capital, Port Stanley. It was this style that established Thatcher's reputation, both nationally and internationally.

This style became confused with the philosophy of Thatcherism. The philosophy and the style combined in the one person. For the purposes of analysis, however, it is important to distinguish one from the other. For Thatcher and her followers, the support that the Conservative party attracted in the years after 1979 was attributable to the philosophy of Thatcherism. In practice, the empirical evidence suggests that inasmuch as any aspect of Thatcherism contributed to the party's electoral success, it was the style and, concomitantly, the conviction with which Thatcher held her beliefs, not the beliefs themselves.

THATCHERISM AND THE ELECTORATE

Despite the impact that Thatcher had on British politics in the 1980s, she did not manage to bring about a significant shift in attitudes. There was no mass conversion to Thatcherism among electors.

This hypothesis is borne out by survey data. Trends in public opinion analysed by Ivor Crewe and Donald Searing reveal that on only one of ten issues did the attitudes of the electorate become "more Thatcher-

ite" between 1974 and 1987 (see table 2.1). On the remaining nine issues, electors became "less Thatcherite," in some cases markedly so.
There was a shift away from free market to more welfare-oriented positions. "Asked to choose between tax and social service cuts or tax and
social service increases, the public was evenly divided—37 percent apiece
—when the Conservatives came to office in May 1979. By 1983 service
increasers outnumbered tax cutters by 52 percent to 24 percent, and by
May 1987 they did so by the even greater margin of 64 percent to 13
percent. Thatcher may have triumphed in 1987, but Samuel Smiles did
not."[9] These findings were reinforced by those of the 1988 British Social
Attitudes Survey, which found that, given a choice between holding
down inflation or unemployment, only 23 percent of respondents favoured holding down inflation; 73 percent preferred to hold down unemployment.[10] As inflation came down, popular concern with the growing
numbers of unemployed became more pronounced.

Insofar as any element of Thatcherism contributed significantly to
election victory it was, as I have suggested, the style and not the substance. The Conservative party is essentially a party of governance.[11] It is
concerned with holding office and demonstrating its competence to govern. Thatcher conveyed a sense of purpose, of knowing what she wanted
to achieve and how to achieve it. In the first two Parliaments of her government, she gave the impression of firm leadership. When the party fal-
tered in the opinion polls, it was because that sense of leadership fal-
tered—as during the Westland crisis at the beginning of 1986 (see later
in the chapter). At other times, the capacity to convey a sense of leadership, coupled with the nature of the party's opponents,[12] ensured a lead
in the opinion polls.

THATCHERISM AND THE PARLIAMENTARY PARTY

As prime minister, Thatcher was able to dominate her party in Parliament. But she did not convert it to her particular brand of Conservative
thought.

The Conservative party is a coalescence of different strands of Conservative thought.[13] An analysis of the 374 Conservatives sitting in the
House of Commons in 1989 identified seven identifiable groupings.[14]
Three of these could be grouped under the umbrella heading "Thatcherite": (1) *the neoliberals:* 16 in number, believing in the rigourous applica-
tion of market forces; (2) *the Tory right:* 22 in number, stressing moral
issues, with a strong attachment to discipline and maintaining law and
order; and (3) *pure Thatcherites:* 30 in number, combining a commitment to market forces with a strong law-and-order emphasis (supporting, unlike the neoliberals, capital punishment). Combined, this pro-

TABLE 2.1
SUPPORT FOR THATCHERITE POLICY POSITIONS, 1970–87

Issue	1970	1974	1979	1983	1987		Trend[a]
Privatisation of nation-alised industry	33%	24%	40%	42%	—%	1974–83	+18%
Death penalty	81	—	75	63	—	1970–83	−18
Abortion (gone too far)	—	43	44	32	—	1974–83	−11
Abortion (restrict)	41	42[b]	36[c]	—	—	1973–80	−6
Pornography	—	64	66	64	—	1974–83	—
Repatriation of immi-grants	—	43	34	—	—	1974–79	−9
Equal opportunity for blacks	—	27	30	20	—	1974–83	−7
Trade union power	73	81	83	74	—	1974–83	−7
Illegitimacy of trade unions	29	33	41	28	25[d]	1974–86	−8
Prices vs. jobs		60[e]	56[c]	27	14[d]	1976–86	−46
Profits vs. taxes to create jobs		—	74	61	53	1979–87	−21
Welfare benefits	—	34	50	20	—	1974–83	−14
Tax cuts vs. social services	—	—	37	24	13	1979–87	−8

SOURCE: I. Crewe and D.D. Searing, "Ideological Change in the British Conservative Party," *American Political Science Review* 82, no. 2 (June 1988): 376.

NOTE: "Don't know"s excluded from percentage base.

a. Plus = more Thatcherite; minus = less Thatcherite.   b. 1973.   c. 1980.   d. 1986.   e. 1976.

duced a Thatcherite wing of 72 MPs, less than 20 percent of the parliamentary party.

This leaves four remaining groupings, accounting for four out of every five Conservative MPs. Of these four groups, two can be combined under the umbrella heading of "critics": those of *the wets,* 27 in number (about 7 percent of the party) believing in a role for government intervention in economic and social affairs and committed to the Disraelian concept of "one nation"; and *the damps,* 40 in number (about 11 percent of the party), generally sympathetic to government intervention but not adopting such a rigid and consistent stand as the wets. The critics thus mustered almost as many supporters as the Thatcherites. Both Thatcherites and the critics combined (a total of 139), however, still accounted for less than 40 percent of Conservative MPs.

To these have to be added *the populists,* reflecting popular attitudes on policy issues: generally left-wing on social issues but right-wing on law and order. They were few in number: 17 members, less than 5 percent of the party. This leaves the final, and most numerous group: *the party faithful.* This group constituted those MPs whose loyalty was principally to the party itself, and to its electoral success, rather than to any particular strand of thought within the party. Loyalty does flow to the leader, but usually on a qualified basis.[15] As long as the leader provides competent and successful leadership, loyalty follows; if the leader falters, the party faithful start to waver. More than half (58 percent) of the parliamentary party, 217 members, fell into this category.

A number of these groupings, especially the Thatcherites and the critics, were associated with organised bodies within the party (see figure 2.1) and hence in a position to mobilise supporters if government policy veered away from their particular predilections. Margaret Thatcher was thus unable to assume an unquestionably loyal parliamentary party. Nor was she able to assume an underlying Thatcherite trend. New Conservative MPs—those first returned in the general elections of 1979, 1983, and 1987—were not predominantly Thatcherite in disposition; indeed, the new entrants in 1987 were overwhelmingly identifiable as falling into the category of the party faithful.[16] Support for the party leader was thus contingent, not certain.

ELECTING THE LEADER

Adding to Thatcher's potential vulnerability was the fact that she was the first leader of the Conservative party to be subject to annual election. Before 1964, the leader of the party was not elected but simply "emerged." There was usually an heir apparent—as in 1955, for example, when Sir Anthony Eden succeeded Sir Winston Churchill. On occasion, however,

FIGURE 2.1

GROUPINGS WITHIN THE PARLIAMENTARY CONSERVATIVE PARTY

Stance	Party faithful	Thatcherites		Populist	Wet	Damp	Party faithful
		Tory Right	Neoliberal				
Organisations		——— 92 Group ——— Monday Club	Selsdon Group ——— "No Turning Back"		Centre Forward ——— — Tory Reform Group ——— ——— C.A.R.E.		
Positions on specific issues 1987–88		——— anti-EC ——— — critical of race relations law —	pro–open government antihanging	———— Opposed to Community Charge ———— ———— Opposed to Health Charges ————	pro–open government ——— antihanging ——— support for —— Child Benefit		
Notable figures		G. Gardiner Sir R. Boyson Teddy Taylor	J. Biffen Sir R. Body N. Budgen I. Gow	N. Winterton Dame J. Knight A. Beaumont- Dark	E. Heath Sir I. Gilmour N. Scott P. Walker	M. Heseltine W. Waldegrave Mrs. L. Chalker	

SOURCE: P. Norton, "Choosing a Leader: Margaret Thatcher and the Parliamentary Conservative Party, 1989–90," *Parliamentary Affairs* 43 (1990): 251.

NOTE: Broken line indicates a number of exceptions.

the succession was far from clear. In 1911 the party narrowly avoided a ballot of MPs to choose between Walter Long and Austen Chamberlain. (Both withdrew in favour of a compromise candidate, Andrew Bonar Law.) In 1957 and again in 1963 there was no undisputed successor and, as the party was in office, the choice fell to the Queen. Though the Queen took advice on whom to send for, both occasions dragged the monarch into political controversy. The choice in 1963 proved particularly controversial, both because of the process involved (disputed soundings of MPs and ministers) and the outcome (a member of the unelected House of Lords becoming prime minister).[17]

In order to prevent a repetition of such embarrassments, the leader and the parliamentary party agreed in 1964 to a new procedure under which the leader was to be elected. The electorate was to be made up solely of Conservative MPs. But the leadership was to remain freehold, not leasehold; in other words, once elected, the leader remained leader until death or voluntary retirement intervened. The new procedure, first employed in 1965, resulted in the election as leader of Edward Heath.

The freehold element was to prove short lived. Edward Heath's leadership came under criticism from Conservative MPs in 1972 and 1973. Sudden changes in policy, coupled with an autocratic style of leadership, left Heath unpopular with an increasing number of backbenchers.[18] Discontent with his leadership reached new levels following two general election losses in 1974.[19] At the end of 1974 the parliamentary party decided on a change in the rules for electing the leader, inserting a provision for annual election. Believing he would have little difficulty in gaining reelection, Heath agreed to the change. The first contest under the new rules was held in February 1975, resulting in the election of Margaret Thatcher.[20] The result took most commentators, and Heath, by surprise.

Margaret Thatcher thus established her power base: the parliamentary party. Under the old method of "emergence" she would never have become leader. Yet the basis of her strength was also her potential weakness. The rule providing for annual election was not confined to periods when the party was in opposition. Thatcher could thus be challenged for the party leadership after she entered Downing Street. In the event of mutterings on the back benches, she could always challenge critics to put up a candidate against her. That would be one way of helping silence them. But there was always the danger that a candidate would run against her. The threat alone could prove a serious embarrassment. And in the event of her falling foul of her backbench supporters, there was always the danger—remote, but still there—of a contest being somewhat more than an embarrassment.

Margaret Thatcher thus led a parliamentary party that was not committed to her brand of political thought and that could ultimately determine her fate. The weapons in her prime ministerial armoury were formidable. But the ultimate weapon lay in the hands of Conservative MPs.

The Fateful Years, 1987–90

At the time of the 1987 general election, Margaret Thatcher had been leader of the party for twelve years and prime minister for eight. Her power as prime minister had been variable.

At times, she had been in a weak position. On three occasions in particular, her leadership had been under threat. In 1981 the country was in a recession and a new political party, the Social Democratic party (SDP), had been formed. Support for the new party in alliance with the Liberal party at one point forced the Conservatives into third place in the opinion polls. Some of Thatcher's critics in the parliamentary party actually contemplated running a candidate against her for the leadership. A challenge did not materialise, but the prospect of it served to some extent to undermine Thatcher's position.

The second occasion was brief but serious. Immediately following the Argentinian invasion of the Falkland Islands in April 1982, the position of the prime minister and her government was precarious. Had a task force not been dispatched to retake the islands—and its dispatch announced to the House of Commons when it assembled in special session on Saturday, 3 April—the government would probably have fallen.[21] In the event, the vigour with which the prime minister prosecuted the military action restored her support and, indeed, raised it to new heights.

The third occasion was in 1986. A dispute between two members of the cabinet—the defence secretary, Michael Heseltine, and the trade and industry secretary, Leon Brittan—over the future of Britain's last remaining helicopter company, Westland, developed very quickly into a major public battle. Thatcher proved unable to rally a cabinet majority in order to restrain the defence secretary. When she did move eventually to restrict his activities, he resigned and publicly attacked the prime minister's style of government. The affair also resulted in Brittan's resignation after it was found that the leaking of a confidential letter from the attorney general to Heseltine had come from Brittan's department. The prime minister's handling of the affair resulted in a major debate in the House of Commons, the outcome of which was considered uncertain, not least by Thatcher herself. In the event, she was saved by a disastrous speech by Neil Kinnock, the leader of the opposition.[22]

These three occasions demonstrated that Thatcher could not take her support in Parliament for granted. Nevertheless, the periods were exceptional. She was prime minister and prepared to use the considerable powers of the office to get her way. She weeded out several "wets" from the cabinet, starting with Norman St.John-Stevas in 1981. Remaining members were not usually prepared to stand up to her; indeed, one was to concede that they did not know how to deal with a female leader.[23] Her position was strengthened enormously by the military success in the Falkland Islands in 1982, by her determination to face down the National Union of Mineworkers during a national coal strike in 1984–85, and by improvements in economic indicators. By the time of the 1987 election, unemployment and inflation rates were falling, the latter more significantly than the former. Though the Westland crisis had weakened her position in the cabinet,[24] she was clearly the dominant—and dominating—figure in government and in British politics. It was virtually impossible to think of British politics without thinking of Thatcher. When she led her party to victory in 1987, her position appeared unassailable.

Yet within two years her position was far from unassailable and within three years it was extremely vulnerable. There is no single explanation for this change in her fortunes. Rather, Thatcher's fall from power can be attributed to five variables and their historical coincidence. The prime minister was the victim of the "London bus syndrome": no major problems for ages and then several come along at the same time. The five variables were those of style, developments in three key policy areas (Europe, the poll tax, and the economy), and political mismanagement. None by itself was sufficient to topple Thatcher. In combination, they were to prove fatal.

STYLE

Style, as we have seen, was an important element of Thatcherism. For most of Thatcher's premiership, it was a political plus; but it was also a potential danger. In his analysis of presidential character in the United States, James David Barber identified rigidification as a feature of his "active-negative" characters.[25] Margaret Thatcher demonstrated such rigidification on particular policy issues. As we shall see, it became pronounced on the issues of Europe and the poll tax.

Her style also had a wider and more pervasive impact prior to the eruption of Europe and the poll tax as issues threatening her leadership. She was essentially concerned with policies rather than personalities. She knew what she wanted to achieve. The management of people was essentially secondary to achieving those goals. Consequently, her handling of her ministers and her parliamentary supporters was often less than sensitive. This lack of sensitivity became more pronounced the longer she was in office.

In the early years of her premiership, Thatcher did make some effort to maintain close contact with her parliamentary supporters. She met regularly on a rota basis with the officers of backbench committees. She took time to be seen in the Commons' tea and dining rooms.[26] Her parliamentary private secretary (PPS), Ian Gow, proved effective as her "ears and eyes" among backbenchers. When there was disquiet on the back benches, concessions were made; worried supporters received letters from the prime minister.[27] It proved effective in ensuring that Thatcher's power base, the parliamentary party, remained solidly behind her.

The relationship was less close in the second Parliament. The prime minister's time was increasingly occupied with matters of state. In the wake of the 1983 general election, there were more than eighty new MPs on the Conservative benches. The prime minister had little time to develop close links with them. Ian Gow was promoted to ministerial office, and his successors as the prime minister's PPS lacked his political antennae as well as his ability to speak plainly to Thatcher. On a number of issues the government appeared out of touch with its supporters and, despite the largest Conservative majority in the House since 1935, experienced some embarrassments in the division lobbies.[28] Though Thatcher was described by one of her backbenchers as remaining "a good listener,"[29] the link between her and her natural constituency was notably less strong than before.

Whereas the backbenchers provided the prime minister with her natural constituency, the cabinet did not. In her first cabinet, she included a number of leading party figures associated with the leadership of her predecessor, Edward Heath. Starting in 1981, she began to remove her critics. The manner of their departure attracted critical comment, including from some of those who were dismissed. (One, Sir Ian Gilmour, wrote a particularly damning letter.) In the wake of the 1983 election, she dismissed the foreign secretary, Francis Pym, a man with supporters on the back benches, and in the wake of the 1987 election dismissed another popular minister, the Leader of the House, John Biffen.

The most damaging effect of her poor management of her ministers, however, was to result not from those she removed from the cabinet but from those who removed themselves. The resignations of Leon Brittan and Michael Heseltine in 1986 damaged her. More significantly, so did the resignations of the chancellor of the exchequer, Nigel Lawson, in October 1989, and of the Leader of the House, Sir Geoffrey Howe, on 1 November 1990. The latter set in train the events that led to Thatcher's fall. Lawson resigned after Thatcher refused to dismiss Sir Alan Walters as an adviser on economic affairs. Howe resigned because of her stance on the issue of Europe, though his resentment with her leadership had clearly been simmering since his unexpected removal from the Foreign Office in 1989. Both objected to the style as well as the substance of her leadership. She variously made it clear that she did not intend to change. "She simply could not admit there was a problem with her style. In interview after interview she said it was her way and she wouldn't change."[30]

The unwillingness to change encompassed policy as well as style. That did not matter too much if the policies were successful. When they proved politically damaging, the position of the prime minister was threatened. Intransigence on the issues of European union and the poll tax severed the prime minister's links with the party faithful.

EUROPE

Membership in the European Community (EC) has been an issue that has divided the Conservative party since the Community was first formed. A section of the party has always harboured suspicions of it, preferring instead to look westward to the United States or more globally to the Commonwealth. For some within the party, membership in the EC actually constituted a betrayal of traditional links with Commonwealth countries. For others, membership constituted a threat to the British constitution, undermining the sovereignty of Parliament.

Opponents of EC membership within the parliamentary party expressed their opposition at the time of Britain's two bids for membership in the 1960s and again in 1971 and 1972 following the successful completion of the negotiations for membership.[31] During the 1970s, they pressed for Britain's withdrawal from membership. A referendum in 1975 produced a substantial "yes" vote for remaining within the Community.[32] Thereafter, the debate changed in nature. The question was no longer whether or not Britain should remain a member of the Community but what role it should play within it.

A number of Conservative MPs remained opponents of membership in the late 1970s and 1980s. They may be termed anti-Europeans. There was also a body that emerged that supported the principle of a single market—and hence supported EC membership—but was opposed to the concept of political and economic union. For them, the goal was a single market and no more. They opposed moves towards any centralisation of power within the Community other than those necessary for completion of the single market. They came to be known as "Euro-skeptics." Those members of the party who were wholeheartedly in favour of moves towards political and economic union were dubbed "Euro-fanatics." The rest, probably a majority of the parliamentary party, can be considered

Euro-agnostics, those accepting the reality of entry and prepared to utilise Britain's membership as seemed appropriate in Britain's interests.

As a member of the Heath cabinet, Margaret Thatcher voted loyally in support of membership in 1971 and 1972. As the new leader of the Conservative party, she campaigned in 1975 for a "yes" vote in the referendum. Once returned to office in 1979, however, she quickly emerged as a Euro-sceptic. She battled with other European heads of government for a reduction in Britain's contribution to the Community budget. She was often a minority of one and enjoyed poor relations with a number of other leaders.

By the mid 1980s the issue was not a prominent one on the political agenda. The prime minister had achieved her goal, getting back from the Community some of what she termed "our money." In 1986 she approved the Single European Act—as did Parliament under the provisions of the 1986 European Communities (Amendment) Act—in order to ensure that decisions could be taken centrally to speed up the process of achieving a single market. The single act achieved little coverage in the mass media and did not impinge significantly on parliamentary attention. Partly as a result, the issue of European union did not figure prominently in the 1987 election campaign.

The situation changed significantly within months of the Conservative election victory. Margaret Thatcher began to march in one direction, while her chancellor and foreign secretary began to march in another. The prime minister had not fully appreciated the implications of the single act. The act strengthened the decision-making capacity of the council of ministers in the EC. Under the provision of weighted majority voting, a country could be outvoted by its partners.[33] To Thatcher, this constituted a means of centralising power in Brussels and, as such, was anathema to her. She made her views public in a speech in Bruges in September 1988. "We have not successfully rolled back the frontiers of the state in Britain," she declared, "only to see them reimposed at a European level, with a European super-state exercising a new dominance from Brussels."[34] The speech served as a battle cry to the Euro-sceptics, who thereupon organised themselves into the Bruges Group. Thatcher and her supporters were saying, in effect, "so far and no further."

Chancellor Nigel Lawson and Foreign Secretary Sir Geoffrey Howe wanted to go further. Stage 1 of the 1988 Delors Report on economic and monetary union envisaged full realisation of a single market and membership by all member states of the exchange rate mechanism (ERM) of the European monetary system.[35] Thatcher not only opposed vehemently the later stages envisaged by the report (a central banking system and monetary union) but also membership in the ERM. Lawson and Howe believed that membership was necessary to combat inflation. Thatcher said that Britain would join when "the time was right." At the European summit in Madrid in June 1989, Lawson and Howe forced her—apparently by threatening to resign—to stipulate the terms under which Britain would join. It was this action that apparently motivated Howe's removal from the Foreign Office in the following month.

The effect of all this was to split the Conservative party and at an inopportune time. The party entered the campaign for the European Parliament elections in June 1989—shortly before the Madrid summit—in disarray. The party was defending forty-five of the UK's eighty-one seats in the Parliament, against Labour's thirty-two. In the election, the Labour party reversed the figures. It won thirteen seats, taking its representation to forty-five. The Conservatives were reduced to thirty-two seats. The first election in which Margaret Thatcher had led her party to defeat added to the discord within Conservative ranks. Many backbenchers —not just the Euro-fanatics but increasingly the Euro-agnostics—began to see at the heart of the problem the prime minister's unbending approach: it was not just what she said but how she said it. There was no attempt to smooth over differences; she still assailed her fellow heads of governments at European summits and was still left in a minority of one. A growing number of Conservative MPs began to question what benefits this approach was bringing for Britain and the party.

THE POLL TAX

As a "conviction politician," Margaret Thatcher knew what she was for —and what she was against. She was against further centralisation of power in Europe. She was also against Britain's rating system.

When the Conservatives went into opposition in 1974, Margaret Thatcher became, for a short time, the party's shadow environment minister. During her tenure, she made a commitment to abolish the domestic rating system, a commitment included in the party's manifesto in the October election of that year.

Domestic rates were based on the rentable value of property. The charge attached to a particular property regardless of the number of people who lived there and regardless of the income of the occupant or occupants. This system provided one of the three principal sources of income for local government (the others were central government grant and income from services) and had the attraction of being relatively simple to collect. Nevertheless, it was widely unpopular and was viewed increasingly as inequitable: a pensioner living alone paid the same rates as the total paid by several income-earning members of a family that lived next door.

A commitment to abolish domestic rates did not figure in the party's 1979 manifesto but was nonetheless resurrected by Margaret Thatcher once in Downing Street. It gained added force by virtue of the prime minister's antipathy to local government. Local government was a heavy-spending impediment to the realisation of the government's economic goals. It was therefore a prime candidate for "handbagging." In the first ten years of the Thatcher government, fifty bills were passed by Parliament that reformed or impinged significantly on local government.

Attempts to restrain local government spending initially took the form of restricting the levying of supplementary rates and "capping" the level at which rates could be levied. These measures occupied the first two Parliaments of the Thatcher premiership. Events north of the border were to precipitate more radical action in the third, and final, Thatcher Parliament. In 1985 there was a complete revaluation of property in Scotland, producing significant rises in ratable values. Conservative areas were particularly badly hit. A revaluation was also due in England. Fear of the consequences of this fueled attempts to find an immediate alternative to the rates. In the 1987 manifesto, the party in effect repeated its 1974 commitment to replace the rates with a "fairer community charge." The result was a charge popularly, and immediately, dubbed "the poll tax." Margaret Thatcher committed herself to it. The commitment was to prove politically fatal.

The poll tax was levied on each individual occupier of a property, rather than on the property itself. This, it was argued, was not only more equitable but also a means of strengthening local democracy. As everyone—with certain limited exceptions, such as the mentally ill—would pay, there would be greater awareness of the costs and benefits of local services. Local government would be more accountable. For most payers of the poll tax, however, the cost was more important than a claimed increase in accountability.

The tax was introduced in England and Wales under the provisions of the 1988 Local Government Finance Act. (An earlier measure had brought it in for Scotland.) Passage of the bill divided the Conservative party in both houses. Seventeen Conservatives voted against the bill's second reading, and thirty-five voted for an amendment moved by a Conservative backbencher, Michael Mates, to introduce different poll-tax bands.[36] A similar amendment in the House of Lords was crushed by the government's rare use of a three-line whip. The debates were acrimonious, and the tax was unpopular even before it took effect. A Gallup poll taken in 1987 found that 47 percent of respondents considered the tax "not as fair" as the rates, with only 27 percent considering it "fairer"; just over a year previously, these figures had been reversed.[37] The argument over equity was also now reversed: a millionaire in a castle paid the same as a poor pensioner living in a small cottage. The 1974 manifesto had committed the party to a tax related to the ability to pay. The new tax did not fulfill this commitment. It was this that motivated the Mates amendment and the principal opposition to the tax in the country.

The first poll-tax demands were delivered in the spring of 1990. They were accompanied by hostile demonstrations in different cities and towns. In March London witnessed its worst riot in modern history. An NOP survey found that the tax eclipsed all others in the minds of voters: 50 percent said it was the most important issue influencing their choice of party; 72 percent disapproved of it replacing the rates.[38] A *Sunday Times* survey of one hundred Conservative MPs found that half of them did not agree with the poll tax in its present form; ten said it should be scrapped, and forty said it should be amended.[39] One observed, prophetically, "Poll tax is to Thatcher what Suez was to Eden." Just over a quarter of those questioned wanted the prime minister to step down before the next election.

The tax remained a central political issue. There was a significant increase in nonpayment compared with the rates. Local authorities had difficulty maintaining track of residents. A significant proportion failed to register. Nonpayment resulted in councils having to increase the rate of tax for the following year, thus increasing its unpopularity among those who did pay it. It remained one of the most important issues in electors' perceptions. Throughout 1990, it competed with other issues that were also electoral negatives for the Conservatives: the health service, unemployment, inflation, and Europe.[40] Conservative unpopularity peaked when the poll tax demands were delivered. In April 1990, the party trailed Labour by well over twenty points.[41]

For Margaret Thatcher, the poll tax constituted her "flagship" policy. She was committed to it. She had pushed it through the cabinet. She was not willing to see it amended during its passage through Parliament. She was convinced that it was right and that in time it would be accepted. Her name was indelibly attached to the tax. Conservative MPs knew only too well that as long as she remained leader, the poll tax was going to stay. Either both stayed or both went. When Michael Heseltine challenged her for the leadership, scrapping the poll tax was a central plank in his manifesto.

THE ECONOMY

Compounding the unpopularity of the poll tax was a worsening of the economic situation. Inflation, having fallen to below 4 percent at the beginning of 1988, began to rise: it reached almost 7 percent by the close of the year and peaked at 11 percent at the end of 1990. Interest rates increased, rising from 7.5 percent to a high of 15 percent in October 1990. As interest rates went up, so, consequently, did mortgages. For homeowners, it was becoming a struggle to maintain mortgage payments *and* pay the poll tax. Unemployment, having peaked in 1986 and then fallen in every succeeding month for three years, began an upwards climb in 1990. The threat of layoffs reached into the middle classes. New homeowners were threatened by repossession. Small businesses increasingly found it difficult to survive. The party's natural constituency—those whom Margaret Thatcher liked to call "our people"—were feeling the pinch.

The worsening economic situation had tangible consequences for homeowners as well as affecting attitudes. There was a significant increase in the "feel bad" factor. When the Conservatives were returned to power in 1987, more people thought the economy would improve over the next twelve months than thought it would get worse. In the two succeeding years, those who felt conditions would get worse outnumbered those who felt things would get better. In late 1989 an absolute majority of respondents felt conditions would get worse: 51 percent to 18 percent. The gap widened in the spring of the following year and became even more pronounced in August and September. In September 1990, 60 percent felt conditions would get worse. Only 14 percent thought they would improve.[42]

Though the government was able to draw attention to the worsening international economic situation, many critics—including some within the ranks of the Conservative party—placed the blame for Britain's poor performance on the government's own policy. Nigel Lawson's expansionary 1988 budget was variously blamed for fueling inflationary pressures; one leading backbencher, the former cabinet minister John Biffen, had voted against the budget precisely because he foresaw inflation as a consequence of the chancellor's proposals. Confidence in the government's handling of the economy was also undermined by an increasingly public split between the prime minister and her chancellor on economic policy. Lawson wanted the pound to shadow the German mark; Thatcher did not. He wanted Britain to join the ERM; she did not. He wanted to be responsible for Britain's economic policy; she continued to listen to her economic adviser, Sir Alan Walters. When she refused to sack Walters, Lawson resigned. The prime minister lost not only her chancellor but also her economic adviser; given the furore, Walters also decided to go. It left her politically exposed.[43] The speed and nature of the chancellor's resignation upset backbenchers and, as the *Daily Telegraph* noted, "also raised questions about Mrs. Thatcher's style of gov-

ernment, which Ministers and MPs have complained is increasingly autocratic."[44] The prime minister's case was not helped by a highly defensive
interview she gave on a Sunday television programme nor by Lawson's
resignation speech in the House of Commons. The *Daily Telegraph,* in
its leader, had demanded a return to cabinet government. Lawson demanded the same.[45]

Lawson was replaced as chancellor by a rising but relatively unknown politician, John Major. Rather than adopt a Thatcher-like stance
on the Delors plan—resisting it without offering any alternatives—Major
proposed a common European currency (the "hard ecu") as an alternative to Delors's proposal for a single currency.[46] He lobbied his European
counterparts and made some running in the debate. He also scored a major success in 1990, persuading the prime minister finally to accept British membership of the exchange rate mechanism. The announcement of
Britain's membership was made just before the party's autumn conference. It was allied with a one-point cut in interest rates.

Thatcher, however, could not resist explaining that membership of
the ERM meant no reduction in the government's hostility to monetary
union—"not in any way at all. They know full well that we are totally
against the single currency."[47] Whatever the decision taken, the sentiments remained the same. Any doubts on this score were scotched on 30
October when she reported to the House of Commons on a European
summit in Rome. She made clear her hostility to European integration.
She also expressed the view that the "hard ecu" would not become
widely used throughout the Community. This single off-the-cuff remark
pulled the rug from under her chancellor's feet. "At that moment," as
one sketch writer put it, "Chancellor John Major ... looked as if he had
swallowed a toad."[48] In the event, as we later see, he was not the only
minister to be dismayed by the prime minister's comments that day.

POLITICAL MANAGEMENT

The difficulties that Thatcher encountered over policy were to be compounded by a degree of political mismanagement. Indeed, this mismanagement finally destroyed her leadership. The policy clashes provided the
necessary but not sufficient conditions for her fall. Her mishandling of
her own MPs was to prove the sufficient condition.

As we have seen, the prime minister was not good at handling her
relationships with senior cabinet ministers. She compounded her difficulties by not paying much attention to her supporters outside the cabinet.
As one of her closest supporters was later to complain, she never got
enough of those "who were both able and agreed with her aims into the
places in Government where it mattered."[49] For appointments to junior

office, she relied heavily on the advice of the whips. Reshuffles were always discussed with the chief whip. Some backbenchers were pushed by the chief whip for junior office, and some appointments were effectively vetoed by him. One new Thatcherite MP, for example, was earmarked for quick promotion after the 1987 election; the chief whip is reported to have delayed the MP's elevation for two years ("not ready yet"). In the latter half of the 1980s, the deputy chief whip, Tristan Garel-Jones, enjoyed particular influence. Backbenchers, according to one Thatcherite MP, only got promoted if they had their "MOT" certificate—meaning "Mate of Tristan's."[50] Garel-Jones was a noted "damp" and during the Parliament the "damps" were well represented in ministerial ranks. Indeed, in 1989, almost half of the forty MPs who fell into the damp category held office.

For a conviction politician, Thatcher's neglect of her political power base in government was both remarkable and damaging. The extent of her failure to grasp its significance was revealed after she left office. At a social gathering, she approached one of the most loyal Thatcherite backbenchers and asked, "Why was it that you were never given ministerial office?" The somewhat stunned reply was, "I was rather hoping, Margaret, that you could tell me."

This failure to promote her own supporters amounted to mismanagement. It was to be compounded by specific failures. In 1989 and again in 1990 she was challenged for the party leadership. Her reluctance to heed the message sent by MPs in the first ballot undermined her position and created conditions that made the second challenge possible. In the second, she was abroad when the ballot took place. She took her support and the competence of her campaigners for granted. As we later see, she miscalculated and her campaign managers mismanaged. The combination proved fatal.

The First Challenge

On Tuesday, 5 December 1989, Conservative MPs trooped into committee room 14 in the palace of Westminster to do something they had not done since 1975: vote in a contested election for party leader.

In precipitating the contest, the issue of Europe proved crucial. The prime minister's stance on European union was anathema to the EC's strong supporters. The most ardent of them—the Euro-fanatics—were concentrated in the wets and the damps, the "critics" in the parliamentary party. For sixty-nine-year-old former diplomat Sir Anthony Meyer, MP for Clwyd North-West and an established wet, the prime minister's stance went too far. "It is her distaste for everything that emanates from the EC," he wrote in *The Times*, "that has pushed me from hesitation into a conviction that I should provoke a leadership election if no one else will. And that is why such an election is necessary now, when crucial decisions about Europe are about to be made."[51] When no other challenger stepped forward (Meyer himself hoped that Michael Heseltine would be a candidate), he obtained a proposer and seconder and triggered an election.

Margaret Thatcher appointed a former defence secretary, George Younger, as her campaign manager. (As it was an internal party, not a government, matter, the whips decided not to be involved.) Meyer did not need a campaign manager. Although he undertook a string of media interviews, he did not lobby MPs for support. The initial stance of some Thatcher supporters—ridiculing Meyer as a "stalking donkey"—generated unwanted and unfavourable publicity; the more strident her supporters' criticism, the more Meyer's dignified attitude attracted favourable comment. Thatcher's campaign managers then shifted to a more low-key approach. A call by one minister for local parties to extract loyalty oaths from their MPs was, in effect, disowned.

Some Meyer supporters initially predicted that as many as seventy to a hundred MPs might withhold their support from the prime minister. As the brief contest got under way, however, these figures were scaled down. It was generally accepted that Meyer could not muster enough supporters to deny Thatcher a majority. Under the rules, to win on the first ballot Thatcher required a majority that was both absolute and, as a separate condition, constituted 15 percent of all eligible voters. This meant that she not only had to get more votes than Meyer (with only two candidates, that would ensure complying with the first condition) but that her lead over him had to be at least fifty-six votes (15 percent of the parliamentary party, thus fulfilling the second requirement). Even on the most optimistic of the Meyer camp's initial predictions, the challenger was nowhere near the figure necessary to deny her mustering that majority. Given that this was so, many Conservative MPs were worried about the prospect of wounding the prime minister and generating further uncertainty. The higher the dissenting vote, the more serious the wound would be. To many waverers, the harm to the party would outweigh any good that might come from it. Against this, some critics feared that a derisory vote for Meyer could lead Thatcher to draw the conclusion that her position was unassailable and that there was no serious criticism of her leadership. As many MPs were determined to keep their own counsel (most local parties were loyal to Thatcher), there was a massive exercise of second guessing by Conservative MPs about how their colleagues would vote. The day before the vote, the position was one of considerable uncertainty.[52]

As MPs began to cast their ballots, it became known that a number of members were voting for Thatcher but sending messages to her campaign manager to the effect that "we are supporting you this time, but, ..." This action suggested that the actual vote for Meyer would be small, possibly disastrously so. Voting finished at six o'clock; thirty minutes later, the results were announced: Margaret Thatcher 314, Sir Anthony Meyer 33, spoilt ballots 24, absent 3.

Margaret Thatcher was reelected, but sixty MPs, 16 percent of the parliamentary party, had withheld their support by voting against her or abstaining. The result was one that sent a message to the prime minister without humiliating her. The large number of "yes, but" letters—most, apparently, on the issue of Europe and the prime minister's style and numbering, according to one source, as many as sixty[53]—ensured that the message was clear. After the result was announced, George Younger signaled—publicly so, from the steps of 10 Downing Street—that the message had been understood. The moderated tones of the prime minister at the European summit in Strasbourg at the end of that week suggested she had heard it and heeded it.

As it turned out, however, recognition of the signal sent by the MPs proved short lived. George Younger, though remaining an MP, went off to take up a directorship at the Royal Bank of Scotland. Thatcher reverted to type. The following July she appointed as her parliamentary party secretary Peter Morrison, the very MP who had suggested that local parties should require loyalty oaths of their MPs. He was not one for telling his leader unpalatable truths.

ANALYSIS OF THE VOTING

The ballot was a secret one. Under the rules as they then stood, even the names of Meyer's proposer and seconder were not announced. Nonetheless, it is possible to provide some indication of the sources of Meyer's support. The core of his support was expected to come from, and may safely be assumed to have come from, the wets and the damps in the party. Of the sixty-seven MPs in these two categories, twenty-one were ministers and are believed to have stayed loyal to the prime minister. That leaves forty-five backbench critics. A number of these fell into the category of "yes, but" letter writers. It is thus probable that the number of Meyer voters and abstainers drawn from the critics was up to, but certainly no more than, forty. This leaves *at least* twenty votes and abstentions unaccounted for. Apart from one Thatcherite who voted against the prime minister, the additional rebels must have been drawn from the populists and the party faithful. As the number exceeds the total number of populists, and some populists are known to have voted for Thatcher, Meyer's support of necessity included some MPs—at least five, possibly fifteen—drawn from the party faithful. More significantly, a majority of those writing letters were also drawn from the same category. (If the figure of sixty letters is correct, there was no other category they could have come from.) This should have constituted an important warning signal to the prime minister. The opposition of wets and damps could be swept aside as the action of known, and expected, critics. Opposition from normally loyal backbenchers could not.

The Second Challenge

Just under a year after she saw off the challenge from Sir Anthony Meyer, Margaret Thatcher was out of office. A second challenge to her leadership had proved successful.

An analysis in *The Economist* subsequently identified three principal figures in Thatcher's fall: Michael Heseltine, Nigel Lawson, and Sir Geoffrey Howe.[54] Though Lawson's resignation in 1989 contributed to the prime minister's vulnerability, it was not central to the events of November 1990. The three principal figures were actually Howe, Heseltine—and Margaret Thatcher. Howe created the conditions that allowed Heseltine to mount a challenge for the leadership. Thatcher was responsible for the events that precipitated Howe's action. She was later responsible for the inaction that denied her the few crucial votes that would have secured her victory.

Though the first half of 1990 was bad for the Conservative party and the prime minister, it was by no means certain that a challenge for the leadership would be mounted in the autumn. On the one hand, there was no point in another challenge by a "stalking horse." On the other, few potential contenders could mount a serious challenge. No member of the cabinet would stand against the prime minister. And the most serious contender on the back benches, Michael Heseltine, had repeatedly said he could foresee no circumstances in which he would contest the leadership against Margaret Thatcher. Though he had devoted his time since leaving the cabinet in 1986 to raising support in the constituencies and among backbenchers, the assumption was that he was waiting until after the next election before seeking the leadership. He knew that if he precipitated a challenge before then, he might deny Thatcher a majority in the first ballot but then fall prey to an anti-Heseltine backlash in the second. He had no wish to play Brutus to someone else's Mark Antony.

Furthermore, the Conservatives' unpopularity in the spring of 1990 had receded somewhat by the autumn. The threat of a war in the Persian Gulf reduced the likelihood of MPs wanting to replace the prime minister, especially one with Margaret Thatcher's record in foreign affairs. The party conference in Bournemouth at the beginning of October produced no upsets, and MPs and party delegates left believing that there would not be a contested election. Then, on 1 November, came the event that changed the situation completely: the resignation as Leader of the House of Commons of Sir Geoffrey Howe.

Howe was one of the government's most senior figures. He had been chancellor of the exchequer from 1979 to 1983 and had shown great loyalty to Thatcher in pursuing a rigorous neoliberal economic policy. In 1983, he was appointed foreign secretary, a position he relished. He was mentioned as a possible leader of the party should the current leader fall under the proverbial bus. But he had been an unhappy member of the cabinet since his enforced departure from the Foreign Office in July 1989. He had been made Leader of the House, a post in which he was visibly uncomfortable. He had also been given the courtesy title of deputy prime minister, but that (as the prime minister's press secretary had been keen to explain to reporters at the time it was conferred) entailed no substantive powers. He was no longer at the heart of policy making on Europe, and he was alarmed by the prime minister's continuing animosity towards European integration. He found it increasingly difficult to defend his leader's position publicly. The final straw was Thatcher's appearance at the despatch box on 30 October, when she reported on the European summit that had just ended in Rome. The summit meetings had not gone well for her. The Italians had forced a vote on the timetable for the implementation of Stage 2 of the Delors Report. Thatcher had been outvoted by eleven votes to one. In the House, she read out a statement that had been agreed with the Foreign Office. "Sir Geoffrey, who now regarded himself as a kind of supernumerary Foreign Secretary, was not wholly displeased with what he heard."[55] When the prime minister started answering questions, however, he was far from pleased. She departed from the line embodied in the statement. She made her negative comments about the hard ecu that dismayed her chancellor, John Major, and she attacked Jacques Delors, the president of the European Commission. He wanted the European Parliament, she declared, to be the democratic body of the Community. "He wanted the Commission to be the Executive and he wanted the Council of Ministers to be the Senate. No. No. No."[56] Those three negatives brought Howe to the end of his personal road.

Within forty-eight hours of Thatcher's combative performance at the despatch box, Howe had decided to resign. At the cabinet meeting on the Thursday morning, he was berated by the prime minister for inadequate preparation of the legislative programme for the session. He gave no inkling of what was in store. At six o'clock that evening he had a private meeting with Thatcher and resigned. "He told Mrs. Thatcher he could no longer support her hostile opposition to European integration. He wanted the freedom to express his views from the back benches."[57] By seven o'clock the news was public.

Though many commentators had expected Howe to leave the government, the timing took the political world by surprise. It had the same impact that Lawson's resignation had had exactly a year before. Howe, in his resignation letter, criticised Thatcher's stance on Europe. Michael Heseltine promptly wrote to his constituency party regretting Howe's departure—"not just a sadness and a loss; it is potentially a crisis"—and reiterating the need to "reach for the world of tomorrow ... with our partners in Europe."[58] He just stopped short of announcing his candidacy for the leadership.

Even in the wake of Howe's resignation, a challenge to Thatcher's leadership was far from certain. Some MPs thought such a challenge "inevitable,"[59] but that was not a view that was universally held. What made the difference was Howe's resignation speech in the House of Commons. Delivered on 13 November, it proved devastating. Angered by attempts to play down his resignation as having been over a matter of style rather than substance, he laid into the prime minister's views on Europe. Britain, he declared, had to be centrally involved in the debate on economic and monetary union. The prime minister's stance undermined her own ministers and risked minimising the country's influence. "We have paid heavily in the past for late starts and squandered opportunities in Europe.... We dare not let that happen again."[60] He ended his eighteen-minute speech—broadcast live on television—with words that left some Conservative MPs audibly gasping. It was no longer possible, he said, for him to resolve the conflict between loyalty to the prime minister and loyalty to what he perceived as the true interests of the nation from within the government. "That is why I have resigned. In doing so I have done what I believe to be right for my party and my country. The time has come for others to consider their response to the tragic conflict of loyalty with which I have myself wrestled for perhaps too long."[61]

The impact of Howe's speech, declared one former minister, "cannot be overstated. In twenty-one years in the House, I cannot remember a speech like it. I do not speak with admiration. It was an attempt at assassination and that is perhaps the greatest tragedy of all."[62] According to the political editor of the *Guardian,* it was "the most damning indictment of a prime minister by a senior colleague in living memory. Many Tories now believe she cannot recover from it—even if the party can."[63]

Margaret Thatcher and the chairman of the parliamentary party (known, for historical reasons, as the 1922 committee), Cranley Onslow, had previously agreed that if there was to be a contested election, the first ballot would be held on Tuesday, 20 November. Nominations had to be handed in five days prior to that—the preceding Thursday. The effect of this, apart from the implications of Thatcher's being in Paris on 20 November, was to add to the pressure on Michael Heseltine. Howe's speech created a new situation. If Heseltine was to mount a challenge for the leadership, he had to decide within forty-eight hours. In the event, he decided within twenty-four hours. The day after Howe's speech, Heseltine declared his candidacy.

The ensuing contest fell essentially into three stages: (1) the first ballot, (2) the entry of "the men in grey suits," and (3) the second ballot. It was at the end of the second stage that Margaret Thatcher decided to resign the premiership.

THE FIRST BALLOT

The contest initially was a straight one between Thatcher and Heseltine. Heseltine was proposed and seconded by two backbench knights, Sir Neil Macfarlane and Sir Peter Tapsell. His campaign was run effectively by his two closest parliamentary supporters, Michael Mates and Dr. Keith Hampson, from his offices in Victoria Street, close to the palace of Westminster. The candidate lost no time in soliciting support. Waverers were identified and targeted. Campaigning was undertaken by twenty MPs.[64] As the weekend of 17–18 November progressed, the number of Heseltine supporters was put at between 130 and 140, up from the initial starting point of about 100. Heseltine looked in sight of having enough votes to force a second ballot. His case was boosted considerably by weekend opinion polls suggesting that under his leadership the party could win the next election.

Thatcher, for her part, was proposed and seconded by Douglas Hurd, the foreign secretary, and John Major, the chancellor. Their support was important, and obtaining their signatures was an astute move by those in the Thatcher camp. It was probably the only astute move they made. George Younger was persuaded to head her campaign team. He was heavily involved in his new job at the Royal Bank of Scotland and was not able to give the campaign his undivided attention. The rest of the "team" announced to the press was anything but a team. One member, Michael Jopling, only knew he was part of it when his name appeared in the press, and he played no active role. Another, John

Moore, was abroad at the time of the announcement. Most of the active campaigning was undertaken by less senior backbenchers, and their activities were neither comprehensive nor sensitive. Not all MPs were contacted. Some who offered their help were turned away.[65] The prime minister made no attempt to rally support before she flew to Paris. Her PPS, Peter Morrison, exuded confidence, so much so that some MPs, fearing a Thatcher landslide, may have voted against her in order to prevent one.

The ballot boxes closed at six o'clock on 20 November, and the result was announced just over half an hour later, amid some confusion. (Conservative MPs crowded into the room into which the ballot had been held; the chairman of the 1922 committee was meanwhile announcing the result to the press in another room.) The results were: Margaret Thatcher 204, Michael Heseltine 152, abstentions 16. To be elected in the first ballot, a candidate had to achieve an absolute majority and one that constituted 15 percent of those eligible to vote. The latter requirement, as we saw in the 1989 contest, entailed achieving a fifty-six-vote majority. Thatcher obviously fulfilled the first requirement. She was four votes short of fulfilling the second. The rules necessitated a second ballot.

THE MEN IN GREY SUITS

When the results were telephoned to her in Paris, Thatcher immediately announced her intention to contest the second ballot. When she returned to London the following day, she appointed Energy Secretary John Wakeham to be her new campaign manager. During the day she received reports of soundings taken among the cabinet and backbenchers. She then saw members of her cabinet individually. It was as a consequence of what she heard in these meetings that she decided not to contest the second ballot.

It is part of popular mythology, purveyed by the popular press and believed by many politicians, that the traditional way of getting rid of a Conservative leader, prior to the introduction of the new rules for election, was by a delegation of party worthies—"men in grey suits"—telling the leader privately that it was time to go. This process, according to Nicholas Ridley, "left the leader free to leave with dignity."[66] It may have done so had the situation ever arisen. In practise, there had previously been no instances of Conservative prime ministers going as a result of such a delegation. Ironically, the closest it ever came to happening was on 21 November 1990.

Few members of the cabinet offered Thatcher an optimistic assessment of her chances. Two, the education secretary, Kenneth Clarke, and the environment secretary, Chris Patten, were prepared to resign if she did not stand down. A number of others declared their support but offered a pessimistic assessment of her chances of survival. "Only a small minority urged her to fight, said she could win, and pledged their support."[67] Thatcher realised she no longer had the support of her cabinet. The chief whip, Tim Renton, also offered a gloomy assessment. But the meeting that finally broke her spirit was one that took place with one of her junior ministers. Alan Clark, a defence minister, was one of her most stalwart supporters. He urged her to stay on and fight. If she did so, he said, she would lose, but she must fight.[68] Thatcher decided not to. Instead, she resolved that evening to resign and the following morning informed the cabinet of her decision.

Various Thatcher supporters soon saw in the events of 21 November a cabinet conspiracy. Indeed, so convinced were some Thatcherite backbenchers that there had been a cabinet coup that they refused to support any cabinet member who stood in the second ballot. A number of events fueled the conspiracy theory. On Tuesday evening there had been an ad hoc meeting of ministers at the home of Foreign Office Minister (and former deputy chief whip) Tristan Garel-Jones. At that meeting, several ministers came to the conclusion that the prime minister was unlikely to win on the second ballot. Most of those present later emerged in the second ballot as supporters of Douglas Hurd. Some observers also saw the role of John Wakeham as suspicious, first taking on the role of campaign manager and then advising Thatcher to see ministers individually.[69] Similar suspicions were voiced about the chief whip's role. He had been appointed on the prompting of Sir Geoffrey Howe. The hands-off stance taken by the whips was regarded by some Thatcher supporters, including the prime minister herself, as a form of disloyalty.

Yet there is little to sustain this theory. There is no evidence of deliberate collusion by ministers. The initial sounding of the cabinet was undertaken by the Leader of the House, John MacGregor, who had no particular axe to grind. Most members said they would support Thatcher, even though most felt she would not win the second ballot.[70] The advice to see cabinet ministers individually, according to Thatcher loyalist Nicholas Ridley, came from within the Thatcher camp. "On Peter Morrison's advice, she resolved to see each one separately. Her advisers believed that if she could ask members of the cabinet to come out in her support publicly, the Party would rally behind her."[71] Wakeham is also reported to have believed that she might still be able to turn things round.[72] The chief whip expressed the view that defectors could still be won back and that the election was too close to call.[73]

Though the most detailed accounts come from those who played partisan roles in the contest, the evidence would suggest that Margaret

Thatcher's demise was not so much the product of a conspiracy as a cock-up. The problem was the first ballot, not its aftermath. The prime minister was badly advised. Her campaigners were overconfident and ill prepared. Once she failed to win outright on the first ballot, the question became one of when, not if, she went. Even if she had won the second ballot, she was too wounded politically to lead the party into the next election. Ultimately, responsibility for her downfall lay not with the cabinet but with Margaret Thatcher herself: her policies, her style, her poor man management, her poor choice of advisers all coalesced and did so at a vitally inopportune time. For more than a decade, she had enjoyed more than her fair share of *fortuna*. In 1990 it deserted her.

THE SECOND BALLOT

Once Thatcher had decided to resign, she was adamant, and last-minute appeals by ardent Thatcherites urging her to contest the second ballot fell on deaf ears. Her announcement left the door open for cabinet ministers, who would not have contested a ballot against her, to step forward. (Under the election rules, nominations from the first ballot fall, and new nominations are sought.) Heseltine was nominated. So too, as had been generally expected, was Douglas Hurd. John Major, not so expectedly, was also nominated. Major was recovering at home from a dental operation and had not been centrally involved in the events of Wednesday. His nomination papers arrived just in time. As long as Thatcher intended to contest the ballot, both Hurd's and Major's hands were tied; they had committed themselves to supporting her. Now that she was out of the race, they were free to stand.

Their decision to stand was a blow to Heseltine. He believed that in a straight fight he could win. (Under the election rules, an absolute majority alone is required on the second ballot.) A third candidate, however, reduced his chances of achieving an absolute majority. He also had to fight against a strong Thatcherite backlash (the "Brutus factor"). Constituency parties stayed loyal to the fallen leader, in marked contrast to 1975, and put pressure on pro-Heseltine MPs. By comparison with the new candidates, he now appeared rather shopworn. Nonetheless, he had the kudos of having toppled the leader, he remained an electoral plus according to the opinion polls, and he attracted the support of some former Thatcher supporters. A number refused to support any cabinet minister; others, quite simply, saw him as an election winner.

The Hurd campaign never really got off the ground. Reflecting the nature of the candidate, it was seen as too gentlemanly in composition and approach. It was overshadowed by the Major campaign. Within hours of Major's nomination, more than a hundred MPs pledged their support. A campaign team was organised, as much by luck as by design. Strategy was determined from 11 Downing Street by the chancellor himself, his campaign manager Norman Lamont, and by two junior Treasury ministers, Richard Ryder, in charge of media relations, and Francis Maude, responsible for campaign organisation. The actual campaigning was conducted from a house close to the Commons, lent by a friend of Lamont's PPS. A card file was created, covering every Conservative MP. More than fifty MPs were used to canvass their colleagues. About thirty MPs were added to the list of supporters over the weekend, and a momentum built up on Monday when MPs returned to Westminster. The general expectation was that a third ballot would be necessary, but on the eve of ballot it was clear that Major's support was growing. Some of his campaign managers believed he was close to victory.[74]

Shortly after 6:30 P.M. on 27 November, Cranley Onslow announced the results: John Major 185, Heseltine 131, Hurd 56. Major was just two votes short of securing an overall majority. Since it was obvious that he would have no difficulty in securing those votes in a third ballot, Heseltine and Hurd immediately conceded defeat. Though there was no formal provision for cancellation, the third ballot was immediately abandoned. John Major was declared the victor. The following morning, he went to Buckingham Palace. Britain had a new prime minister.

ANALYSIS OF THE VOTING

On the first ballot, Thatcher could expect the support of the Thatcherites and, given her stance on Europe, most of the populists. That provided a core support of eighty-nine MPs. Heseltine could expect only the partial support of the critics; sixteen damps held ministerial office and were presumed likely to remain loyal to the prime minister. Heseltine thus started from a much lower base of core support. And Thatcher, of course, was prime minister; Heseltine was not. The loyalty of most of the party faithful on the back benches was expected to flow, reluctantly but overwhelmingly, to the leader.

What happened? Thatcher lost the support of eight Thatcherites and at least a couple of the populists. Heseltine, in contrast, did better than expected among the critics, gaining the support of a number of ministers. He may have won the votes of as many as sixty critics. If this is an accurate analysis, it means that the party faithful split 118 for Thatcher and 98 for Heseltine. This division is crucial. A leader should have been able to carry these loyalists by a margin of at least two to one. I penned an analysis of the voting on the evening the results were announced. My concluding words were that, for the prime minister, "the writing is on the wall." Twenty-four hours later, the prime minister came to the same conclusion.

In the second ballot, there was an interesting flow of votes. In political terms, Heseltine and Hurd were basically competing for the same constituency: both were damps. Major, however, was drawn from the party faithful. He carried no significant, or rather no obvious, ideological baggage. He could thus appeal to all parts of the party. Thatcherites saw him as fiscally conservative. Thatcher herself supported him and lobbied on his behalf. Wets and damps were attracted by his reputation for being liberal on social issues and by his advocacy of membership of the ERM. There was also a social dimension: Heseltine was a self-made millionaire, Hurd a scion of a landed family. Major was neither. He had left school at sixteen and had experienced several jobs and a period of unemployment before becoming a banker at the Standard Chartered Bank. He had cut his political teeth as a local councillor in the London borough of Lambeth. He represented a growing breed of middle-class, self-made men (and a few women) in the parliamentary party. Such men, and women, voted for one of their own.

Major, the new young face in politics at the age of forty-eight, also had a public appeal. Opinion polls showed that he could match, if not better, Heseltine in attracting votes to secure a Conservative victory at the next election. He secured the support of most of those who had voted for Thatcher in the first ballot. The flow of votes from the first to second ballot appears to have been as follows:[75] Of Thatcher's 204 supporters in the first ballot, 147 probably went to Major, 38 to Hurd, and 19 to Heseltine. Of Heseltine's 152 first-round supporters, about 111 appear to have stayed loyal in the second round, 11 shifted their support to Hurd, and a more significant 30 switched to Major. Of the 16 abstainers first time round, 8 appear to have gone for Major, 7 for Hurd and 1 for Heseltine. The Thatcher votes alone would have put Major in the lead in the second ballot. It was the switchers from Heseltine who helped create the decisive lead.

A continuing Thatcher leadership or a Heseltine victory would have divided the party. Major drew his votes from the different groupings within the parliamentary party. He had the advantage of being the one best placed to heal the wounds following a bruising contest.

The Major Premiership

Margaret Thatcher generated Thatcherism. Her style was aggressive and confrontational. John Major differed from his predecessor in both substance and style. He was a member of the party faithful par excellence. He held decided views on a number of issues, but nothing that marked him out as having distinctive ideological leanings. Thatcher was later to assert that there was no such thing as "Majorism." It was not a view from which Major dissented. For him, there was no Majorism, only Conservatism.

BELIEFS

In terms of his specific beliefs, Major placed particular emphasis on achieving a classless society. For Thatcher, that was a meaningless goal because there was, in her view, no such thing as class. (In practise, though, the difference was more semantic than substantive; for Major, classlessness meant social mobility on the basis of ability.)[76] He was liberal in his views on race, capital punishment, and homosexuality. On the economy and Europe, he was closer to Thatcher. He shared her belief in financial prudence and her determination to combat inflation. "First and foremost," he declared, "I loathe inflation."[77] He was, if anything, more a Euro-sceptic than a Euro-agnostic. He also shared Thatcher's views on other constitutional issues: he was firm in his opposition to electoral reform, devolution, and a new bill of rights.

But where he differed most significantly from Thatcher was in his being a pragmatist. Like one of his political heroes, R.A. Butler, he believed in the art of the possible.[78] This explains both the continuity with past policies shown by his administration and the significant changes. He recognised that he was constrained both by the lack of economic resources (the country was in recession) and by political commitments from instituting a radical break with his predecessor. In any event, there was no need to; as we have seen, there was an empathy between Thatcher and Major on a range of issues. What immediate changes he did make, which had resource implications, were at the margins; for example, he agreed to a more generous settlement for haemophiliacs suffering from AIDS. Those changes that were significant were essentially those expected of him by the parliamentary party: an end to the poll tax and a different approach to Europe.

During the leadership contest, Major had made clear to potential supporters that if the poll tax had to go, it had to go. (Heseltine had made the same commitment publicly; Major, as a minister, made it privately.) Once in Downing Street, the process of getting rid of the poll tax was set in train. A tax to replace it, based on property value but with reductions for single occupants, was agreed upon and subsequently embodied in a new Local Government Finance Act. Sceptical about further European integration, Major began coalition building as a way of limiting the ambitions of Jacques Delors and the more ambitious integration-ists among other heads of government. He traveled to other European capitals, currying support for various UK positions at the European summit at Maastricht in December 1991. He was successful, more so than had been anticipated, in achieving his goals.[79] He achieved a rapport with his fellow premiers, notably Helmut Kohl of Germany, that was singularly lacking in Thatcher's relations with them.

As the Major premiership progressed, there were other digressions from the policies of the Thatcher era as well as new emphases, both the product of pragmatism—as with a public sector borrowing requirement (PSBR) of £13.8 billion for 1991–92 and an estimated £28 billion for 1992–93—and Major's personal views. The latter led most notably to a Citizen's Charter, stipulating the standards that citizens could expect the public services to meet and to a greater stress on openness in government. He also departed from his predecessor in signaling a willingness to accept parliamentary reform and a new attitude on homosexual rights: he held a highly publicised meeting at Number 10 with a leading gay rights activist, the actor Sir Ian McKellen. He also showed a greater willingness to listen to bodies that had previously been kept at arm's length by Thatcher.

STYLE

A willingness to listen was symptomatic of John Major's style. Whereas Thatcher hectored and challenged, Major listened and questioned. His greatest political asset was his skill at personal relations. When Nigel Lawson was chancellor, Major was the Treasury whip. Lawson admired him for spotting and handling political problems. "The Treasury would have problems with the back benches and his rapport with them was exceptional."[80] Major was not a great orator; he lacked Thatcher's grand conference style. Though his budget speech in 1990 was well delivered, he was often not good at delivering set text speeches. His strength lay in small-group discussions and face-to-face meetings. He palpably liked such personal contact. (When Major was chancellor, this writer quizzed a senior Treasury official about his views on economic policy. "We don't know what they are," came the reply. "All we know is that he likes meeting people.") His unpretentious and unflappable style—no one in government could ever remember him losing his temper—made him a popular parliamentary figure, not only in the ranks of his own party but also elsewhere in the House of Commons.

His personal and open style was reflected in his approach to the conduct of government. When it came to senior appointments, Thatcher was prone to inquire: is he (virtually never she) "one of us"? For Major, it was not a relevant question. His cabinet was more open in composition and in working arrangements than that of his predecessor. In ministerial appointments, he not only rewarded his supporters (Norman Lamont, for example, became chancellor, Richard Ryder became chief whip) but he also brought in Michael Heseltine as environment secretary, kept Douglas Hurd as foreign secretary, and brought a number of Hurd supporters into government. (Heseltine supporters, though, were not so rewarded.) The leading figure in Hurd's campaign, Chris Patten, was appointed party chairman.

In the cabinet, Major allowed ministers to speak without being told what was expected of them. He liked to weigh the arguments. Cabinet meetings became more relaxed than under Thatcher, and ministers were allowed to question one another. In the words of one minister, the cabinet now had far more of the air of a seminar about it.[81] Television cameras were allowed in to record ministers arriving and assembling for a cabinet meeting. There was less interference in the affairs of departments than there had been under Thatcher. Ministers were left to get on with their jobs, though approval for policy announcements still required Number 10's sanction.

The new style and approach were political pluses. They generated a more cohesive, less abrasive cabinet. The more open approach reduced the feeling of alienation harboured by many interest groups that had been largely ignored during the Thatcher era. Major's handling of the Gulf War also demonstrated a good instinct for handling crises. He maintained close and regular contact with President George Bush and other allies, eschewing the declamatory approach of his predecessor. He presided calmly over a small war cabinet. There were none of the tensions among ministers that existed during the Falklands crisis. He avoided any tendency to gloat over the allied victory or to engage in partisan comments. His handling of the coup in the Soviet Union in 1991 also demonstrated a consistency and calmness that was contrasted with the reaction of his U.S. counterpart. Whereas the initial U.S. response to the attempted coup appeared uncertain, Major immediately condemned what had happened and, when it looked as if the Russian Parliament might be attacked, telephoned Boris Yeltsin in the building to express his support. His handling of the European issue also showed a good grasp of what was politically acceptable as well as what was achievable. His response to an IRA mortar bomb attack on Downing Street early in 1991 ("Gentleman, I think we had better move to another room") confirmed his unflappability and—a quality he shared with Thatcher—physical courage.

THE PARTY

Major's style also stood him in good stead in trying to calm and rally a worried Conservative party. The leadership election had been divisive in many constituency parties. Many party workers resented the manner in which Thatcher had been turned out of office. There was considerable ill will towards Heseltine for triggering a contest.

The new leader utilised his emollient style to calm the party. He was considerably aided by the facts that he had enjoyed Thatcher's support in the second ballot and that his beliefs meant that different parts of the party could claim him as one of their own. He was also considerably aided by the fact that, as party leader, he controlled patronage over senior professional party appointments. Thatcher had not paid much attention to party organisation, and Major inherited a party that had not changed substantially either in nature or structure during Thatcher's leadership.[82] Thatcher had attracted strong support from many party activists, but that support appeared largely the product of her combative style rather than her particular ideology. As we have seen, Thatcher failed to create either a Thatcherite electorate or a Thatcherite parliamentary party. There is little evidence that she created a Thatcherite party outside Parliament.[83]

Immediately after his election, Major, in his first speech to party workers, appealed to local parties not to take action against MPs who had supported Heseltine. The party chairman also sent a similar message. Paradoxically, Major's own support among party workers increased as Thatcher started to make comments critical of his leadership. The more she criticised, the more party supporters began to rally to their leader. The deference that Thatcher had received when she led the party now began to transfer to the new leader. Thatcher was accused of "doing a Heath," emulating Edward Heath, who had bitterly and frequently criticised Thatcher after she ousted him in 1975. Major's handling of government was a further bonus. His handling of the Gulf War increased not only his own popularity but also that of the party. Party workers, conscious that an election could not be long delayed, came to recognise that in their new leader they had an electoral asset. Major's popularity in the polls exceeded that of his own party. His tenure of the leadership was also secure, at least until after the election. After November 1990, the parliamentary party had no stomach for a new contest.

PROBLEMS

Nonetheless, the new premiership was not trouble free. Major incurred adverse publicity for his failure to appoint a woman to the cabinet. He was overly sensitive to press criticism, and he sometimes seemed uncertain at the despatch box. There were occasional gaffes (he once referred in a Commons' statement to "Swindon" instead of "Sweden"), and he had difficulty shaking off claims that he lacked charisma. The pressures of the job appeared initially to tire him. "As the first one hundred days of his office passed, he demonstrated that he is not the polystyrene Premier. . . . His wife told journalists he had been overworking and should rest."[84] In terms of policy, the government faced a recession that lasted far longer than ministers, not least the chancellor, had anticipated. The 1991 March budget was generally assumed to be geared to an autumn election, with an economic upturn taking place in the run-up to that election. The expected upturn was supplanted by the reality of the recession deepening. Unemployment continued to rise, the housing market was stagnant, and economic growth was lower in 1991 than in 1990. Small businesses continued to struggle. In 1991, 44,000 of them went out of business. The recession hit particularly hard in the south of England, the heartland of Conservative support. Signs of growing economic optimism on the part of the electorate slumped.[85] The prime minister had to defend his chancellor against criticism of his policies and his claims that recovery was near.

Nor was he totally secure within the party. Thatcherites may have been in a minority, but they were a vocal and determined minority. Any straying by Major from the Thatcher path incurred their criticism. Thatcher remained a powerful figure able to command immediate media attention. Though personally popular among party workers, Major's low-key style raised worries about his capacity to rouse both the party faithful and the electorate. Though Major was secure in the leadership until the election, there were doubts as to his capacity to hold on to it after an election defeat. Heseltine and Education Secretary Kenneth Clarke were being touted as likely leadership challengers in the wake of a defeat. Everything thus hinged on the outcome of the next general election, and when it was held depended on John Major.

CHOOSING THE DATE

When Major was elected leader, it was known that an election could not be long delayed. By law, the latest an election could be held was the beginning of July 1992. Few Parliaments went before their fourth session, however. The first two Parliaments under the Thatcher government had each lasted four years.

The date of an election is chosen by the monarch on the advice of the prime minister, thus making the effective decision that of the prime minister. For Major, there was a strong desire to seek an electoral mandate as soon as possible. Until he achieved that mandate, he would be seen by many, especially Thatcherites, as having only a Thatcherite mandate bestowed by the 1987 election. He was known to be keen to achieve a mandate in his own right. Against that, there was a natural reluctance to call an election if it looked as if the Conservatives would lose it. Conservative support picked up in the polls in the wake of Major's accession to the premiership and during the Gulf War, but the economic situation militated against a sustained improvement. By May 1991, Labour had a five-point lead in the opinion polls. Major received conflicting advice from cabinet colleagues. Some, like Home Secretary Kenneth Baker, favoured an election in the autumn. Others counseled waiting until the spring of 1992. As spring gave way to summer in 1991 and the party continued to trail Labour in the opinion polls, the cautious counsel prevailed, and the prime minister let it be known that there would be no autumn election. Parliament was to run to five sessions.

Although Major may not have been the polystyrene premier, he nonetheless exhibited some of the characteristics of a "teflon" one. He was prime minister during a deep recession, but opinion polls suggested that electors blamed Thatcher for the country's economic problems, not her more emollient successor.[86] In the polls, as we have seen, Major, unlike his Labour opposite number, outstripped his party in popularity. He also gave the party something Thatcher no longer could: a sense of newness. Thatcher and the old guard had gone. Major and his cabinet were the antidote to staleness after almost twelve years of Conservative government.

Notes

1. The more unexpected the victory (as in 1970), the greater the authority flowing to the leader. On the electoral mandate as one of the several elements of the compound of prime ministerial power, see Bernard Donougue, *Prime Minister* (London: Cape, 1987), 4.

2. 10 Downing Street Press Notice, 22 November 1990.

3. Richard H.S. Crossman, "Introduction" to Walter Bagehot, *The English Constitution* (London: Fontana, 1963 ed.). See Philip Norton, *The Constitution in Flux* (Oxford: Basil Blackwell, 1982), chap. 1.

4. Lord Hailsham, *Elective Dictatorship* (London: BBC, 1976).

5. In the words of one critical backbencher, Thatcher could not see an institution "without hitting it with her handbag." Julian Critchley, *Westminster Blues* (London: Futura, 1986), 126.

6. Quoted in Trevor Russel, *The Tory Party* (Harmondsworth, Middlesex: Penguin, 1978), 21.

7. Andrew Gamble, *The Free Economy and the Strong State* (London: Macmillan, 1988).

8. One clash was on the issue of tax relief for mortgage payers. On a free market approach, there was no justification for such relief. On Thatcher's moral approach, hard-working couples deserved to be helped to own their own homes. The latter stance won, and the relief was maintained.

9. Ivor Crewe and Donald Searing, "Ideological Change in the British Conservative Party," *American Political Science Review* 82 (1988): 377.

10. Roger Jowell, Sharon Witherspoon, and Lindsay Brook, *British Social Attitudes, Fifth Report* (Aldershot: Gower, 1988).

11. On the importance of this in the context of statecraft, see especially James Bulpitt, "The Discipline of the New Democracy: Mrs. Thatcher's Domestic Statecraft," *Political Studies* 34 (1986): 19–39.

12. Factional divisions in the Labour party weakened the opposition, especially in the 1983 general election. See David Butler and Dennis Kavanagh, *The British General Election of 1983* (London: Macmillan, 1983).

13. See, generally, Philip Norton and Arthur Aughey, *Conservatives and Conservatism* (London: Temple Smith, 1981), chap. 2.

14. Philip Norton, " 'The Lady's Not for Turning': But What about the Rest? Margaret Thatcher and the Conservative Party 1979–89," *Parliamentary Affairs* 43 (1990): 41–58.

15. "Usually" because the category includes a number of members whose loyalty was to Mrs Thatcher personally rather than to the party (or Thatcherism). See ibid., 49.

16. Ibid., 56–57.

17. The 14th Earl of Home. He immediately renounced his title and, as Sir Alec Douglas-Home, entered the House of Commons at a by-election. On the events of his "emergence," see Robert Shepherd, *The Power Brokers* (London: Hutchinson, 1991), 149–59.

18. See Philip Norton, *Conservative Dissidents* (London: Temple Smith, 1978), especially chap. 9.

19. See Philip Norton, *Dissension in the House of Commons 1974–1979* (Oxford: Oxford University Press, 1980), 449–51.

20. In the first ballot, the voting figures were: Margaret Thatcher 130, Edward Heath 119, Hugh Fraser 16. Heath then withdrew from the contest. In the second ballot, in which new challengers were permitted to enter, Margaret Thatcher received an overall majority with seven votes to spare.

21. Max Hastings and Simon Jenkins, *The Battle for the Falklands* (London: Michael Joseph, 1983), 77–78.

22. See Magnus Linklater and David Leigh, *Not with Honour* (London: Sphere Books, 1986), 172.

23. James Prior, *A Balance of Power* (London: Hamish Hamilton, 1986).

24. One of the resigning ministers (Leon Brittan) was a close ally of the prime minister, and the new political situation strengthened the position of non-Thatcherite ministers such as the home secretary, Douglas Hurd.

25. James D. Barber, *The Presidential Character,* 3d ed. (Englewood Cliffs, N.J.: Prentice-Hall, 1985).

26. See Martin Burch, "Mrs. Thatcher's Approach to Leadership in Government," *Parliamentary Affairs* 36 (1983): 409; Martin Holmes, *The First Thatcher Government 1979–83* (Brighton: Wheatsheaf, 1985), 83; and Hugh Stephenson, *Mrs Thatcher's First Year* (London: Jill Norman, 1980), 94.

27. See Philip Norton, "Mrs. Thatcher and the Conservative Party: Another Institution 'Handbagged'?" in *Thatcherism: Personality and Politics,* ed. Kenneth Minogue and Michael Biddiss (London: Macmillan, 1987), 25.

28. See Philip Norton, "The House of Commons: Behavioural Changes" in *Parliament in the 1980s,* ed. Philip Norton (Oxford: Basil Blackwell, 1985), 33–36; and Francis Bown, "The Defeat of the Shops Bill, 1986," in *Parliament and Pressure Politics,* ed. Michael Rush (Oxford: Clarendon Press, 1990), 213–34.

29. Conservative backbencher to author.

30. Peter Hennessy, "How Much Room at the Top? Margaret Thatcher, the Cabinet and Power-Sharing," in *New Directions in British Politics?* ed. Philip Norton (Aldershot: Edward Elgar, 1991), 27.

31. See Uwe Kitzinger, *Diplomacy and Persuasion* (London: Thames & Hudson, 1973); Philip Norton, *Dissension in the House of Commons 1945–74* (London: Macmillan, 1974), 395–98; and Norton, *Conservative Dissidents,* 64–82.

32. See Anthony King, *Britain Says Yes: The 1975 Referendum on the Common Market* (Washington, D.C.: American Enterprise Institute, 1977); and David Butler and Uwe Kitzinger, *The 1975 Referendum* (London: Macmillan, 1976). Voting was: 17,378,581 yes, 8,470,073 no.

33. Under weighted majority voting, each country has a number of votes (the larger countries—the United Kingdom, Germany, France, and Italy—each having ten and the others fewer, with Luxembourg having only one), with 54 votes needed for a proposal to be carried. It is thus possible for a measure to be adopted and applied within the United Kingdom despite the opposition of the U.K. government.

34. Margaret Thatcher, *Britain and Europe* (London: Conservative Political Centre, 1988), 4.

35. Under the ERM, participating members took the action necessary to keep their exchange rates within an agreed banded range. The Delors report on economic and monetary union had been commissioned by the European council in 1988. Jacques Delors was president of the commission and the principal figure in the move towards European union.

36. There were a total of twelve divisions during the passage of the bill in which Conservative MPs cross-voted. See *Conservative Dissent* (Biggleswade: Campaign Inc., 1989), 29–30.

37. *Sunday Telegraph,* 27 July 1987, cited in Alan Watkins, *A Conservative Coup* (London: Duckworth, 1991), 66.

38. *Independent,* 17 March 1990.

39. *The Sunday Times,* 11 March 1990.

40. MORI, *British Public Opinion* 13, no. 11 (December 1990): 2.

41. Ibid.

42. Ibid.

43. See Hennessy, "How Much Room at the Top?" 25–28; and leader, "A Case of Duplicity," *Guardian*, 6 December 1989.

44. *Daily Telegraph*, 27 October 1989.

45. *House of Commons Debates* 159, c. 208–10. Lawson delivered the speech during a debate on economic policy rather than as a separate and distinct formal resignation statement.

46. A common currency—dubbed a "hard ecu" after the existing European currency unit—would exist alongside national currencies. Under the single currency plan, the national currencies would disappear.

47. *Independent*, 9 October 1990.

48. Bruce Anderson, *John Major: The Making of a Prime Minister* (London: Fourth Estate, 1991), 96.

49. Nicholas Ridley, *My Style of Government* (London: Fontana, 1991), 258.

50. In the United Kingdom, cars that are three or more years old must have a Ministry of Transport (MOT) certificate. The "Mate of Tristan's" quip is attributed to Nicholas Bennett. See "Profile: Tristan Garel-Jones," *Sunday Telegraph*, 28 June 1992.

51. Sir Anthony Meyer, "Why I Am Challenging Thatcher," *The Times*, 30 November 1989.

52. This paragraph and the subsequent analysis derives from Philip Norton, "Choosing a Leader: Margaret Thatcher and the Parliamentary Conservative Party 1989–1990," *Parliamentary Affairs* 43 (1990): 250–56.

53. Edward Pearce, *The Quiet Rise of John Major* (London: Weidenfeld & Nicolson, 1991), 137. The figure includes some who expressed their views by word of mouth rather than by letter.

54. "The Fall of Thatcher," *The Economist*, 9 March 1991, 21.

55. Watkins, *Conservative Coup*, 145.

56. 178, c. 873.

57. *Financial Times*, 2 November 1990.

58. Open letter to the chairman of the Henley constituency association, published in abridged form in *The Sunday Times*, 4 November 1990.

59. "Out Come the Knives," *The Sunday Times*, 4 November 1990.

60. *House of Commons Debates*, 80, c. 465. The speech occupies columns 461–65.

61. *House of Commons Debates*, 180, c. 465.

62. Norman Fowler, *Ministers Decide* (London: Chapmans, 1991), 347. Howe himself did not regard his speech as an attempt at assassination but as an invitation to other cabinet ministers to consider resigning.

63. Michael White, "Howe Assault Puts PM on Battle Alert," *Guardian*, 14 November 1990.

64. More wanted to campaign for Heseltine, but numbers were kept down in order to ensure proper coordination. It was a decision that the Heseltine camp apparently later regretted. Shepherd, *The Power Brokers*, 19.

65. Anderson, *John Major*, 107–8.

66. Ridley, *My Style of Government*, 251.

67. Ibid, 248.

68. Private information. According to Shepherd, *The Power Brokers*, 35, the conversation took place by telephone early that morning.

69. This view is expressed most notably in Watkins, *A Conservative Coup,* chap. 1. See also Anderson, *John Major,* 120–21.
70. See Anderson, *John Major,* 119.
71. Ridley, *My Style of Government,* 248. However, see Anderson, *John Major,* 121–24, and Watkins, *Conservative Coup,* 14–15.
72. Anderson, *John Major,* 120.
73. Ibid., 122–23.
74. This paragraph is based on the author's interviews with those involved in the campaign. A fuller insider's view is presented by Anderson, *John Major.*
75. This analysis derives from private information provided from within one of the campaign teams.
76. See Shepherd, *The Power Brokers,* 207.
77. Speech in December 1990, cited in Anderson, *John Major,* 294.
78. His two political heroes in the 1950s and 1960s were Butler and Iain Macleod. Nesta Wyn Ellis, *John Major: A Personal Biography* (London: Futura, 1991), 206. Butler titled his autobiography *The Art of the Possible* (London: Hamish Hamilton, 1971).
79. Among other things, Major achieved an "opt-out" clause (or, rather, in his view, an opt-in clause) for the United Kingdom on a single European currency, the omission of reference to a "federal" Europe, and a reaffirmation of the primacy of NATO for European defence.
80. Pearce, *The Quiet Rise of John Major,* 109.
81. Cabinet minister to author, October 1991.
82. Norton, "Mrs. Thatcher and the Conservative Party," 21–37.
83. Ibid., 32.
84. Ellis, *John Major,* 178–79.
85. *Independent,* 23 August 1991, reporting the findings of an NOP poll.
86. See David Smith, "Why Nobody Is Relying on the Feelgood Factor," *The Sunday Times,* 15 March 1992.

3

Labour: The Great Transformation

Patrick Seyd

I t may appear a truism to suggest that parties need to adapt to changing economic, political, and social circumstances if they are to survive in a liberal democracy. There are numerous examples of party
decay and failure as a consequence of the inability to perform satisfactorily the linkage function between citizens and the state,[1] and if ever
there appeared to be a party destined for such decline and decay it was
the Labour party in 1983.

In a plurality electoral system, a party needs to appeal to as broad a
constituency of voters as possible. Traditionally, the Labour party had
drawn the bulk of its support from manual-worker trade unionists and
their families, but it had always cast its net wider in order to maximise
its support. Its major electoral successes in 1945 and 1966 were partly
achieved because it mobilised a large proportion of middle-class voters.[2]
By the 1970s, however, the class alliance that Labour had welded was
threatened by the breakup of traditional Labour-supporting communities. As Ivor Crewe has shown in chapter 1, there was a decline in the
manufacturing sector and growth in the service sector of the economy;
decline in male, manual, full-time employment and growth in female,
part-time employment; decline in the manual-worker trade unions and
growth in white-collar unions or nonunionism; decline in the percentage
of households renting accommodation and growth in owner occupation;
and decline of population in urban areas and the growth of small towns.
These socioeconomic changes undermined Labour's traditional political
base.

Even where traditional communities remained, however, the Labour
party was no longer the automatic feature of the locality that it had been
in the interwar and immediate postwar years.[3] Generational change and
membership decline minimised the party's continuing identification with
these communities. In addition, some moribund inner-city parties had become dominated by Trotskyist infiltrators.[4]

Another factor contributing towards Labour's decline was that its traditional supporters were no longer so confident that their party would maintain and improve their standards of living. Labour governments of the 1960s and 1970s produced only limited economic successes; for many workers, the combination of wage policies, high inflation, and regressive taxation meant a relative decline in their living standards. By 1979, the Conservative party appeared better able to meet some of their needs as far as personal income, taxation, welfare, and safety were concerned. Nothing the Labour party did in the early 1980s was likely to win back these previous supporters, and an emphasis in its 1983 election manifesto on nuclear disarmament, nationalisation, and protection of trade unionists' rights further antagonised many traditional supporters.[5] On instrumental grounds, Labour's traditional voters were deserting it. A spiral of decline threatened, in which the party would finish up as a small, peripheral group representing fringe communities excluded from the mainstream of economic change. Labour seemed to be on the same track to electoral oblivion as the French Communist party. So in 1983 the Labour party faced the electoral abyss, after winning just over one-quarter of the vote in that year's general election, its lowest share since 1918. Just as the Liberals had become a fringe party after 1931, both geographically and politically, so the Labour party seemed destined to suffer a similar fate.

Parties have the ability to survive, however. One essential requirement is a leadership with the skill to shift the party in such a way as to relate it to voters' demands. After the 1983 electoral debacle, the Labour party elected a new leadership. It was dubbed the "dream team," as both Neil Kinnock and Roy Hattersley were relatively young, and they were drawn from both the left-wing and right-wing tendencies within the party. This alliance of left and right was of considerable symbolic importance, both within and outside the party, because between 1979 and 1983 Labour had been racked by a bitter factional division that cost it a large number of votes. Intense intraparty factional division reached its height in 1981 when Denis Healey and Tony Benn fought an election for the relatively innocuous post of party deputy leader. The election was marked by bitter personal attacks on the candidates from the rival camps. It marked the point, however, when the left began to divide into Benn supporters and opponents, from which emerged the subsequent division between "hard" and "soft" left factions.

Neil Kinnock was one of the most prominent of the left-wingers who refused to support Benn in the election. Kinnock had developed a radical reputation in the late 1970s as a young Welsh MP, with brilliant powers of oratory. He was closely identified with the Tribune group of

Labour MPs and with the *Tribune* newspaper, around both of which left-wingers congregated, and with the Campaign for Nuclear Disarmament (CND). During the 1974–79 Labour government he was one of the cabinet's most persistent critics. But his refusal to vote for Benn marked his first prominent stand against the direction in which some left-wingers wanted to take the party.

Roy Hattersley, in contrast to Kinnock, had strong roots on the party right and close links with the main right-wing faction, Labour Solidarity. Many of his factional allies had left the party to join the newly formed Social Democratic party (SDP) in the early 1980s, but he remained a key figure organising and advancing the views of this important strand in Labour politics.

So the result of the 1983 leadership election, which produced this alliance of two men with hitherto opposing close factional connections, reflected the fact that parliamentarians, trade unionists, and party members overwhelmingly desired party unity and a fresh political initiative.[6]

Notwithstanding this desire for a new start, the leadership's scope for initiatives to renew the party was limited. Structural constraints have always made Labour an extremely difficult party to lead. One of these constraints has been that, as a consequence of its formal institutional links with the trade unions, the party has operated within certain political parameters. For example, it has been taken as given that collective, legal, trade union immunities are sacrosanct.[7] Another has been the party's divided power structure, with no single source of legitimate authority. As one past leader, Michael Foot, has complained, the Labour party is saddled with an "anomalous, theoretically impractical, constitutional arrangement" in which its leader and its National Executive Committee (NEC) are both vested with sovereign powers.[8] Lewis Minkin writes of "the hydra-headed character of Labour's national power structure."[9] In addition, the party leadership has been constrained by a cultural ethos that has placed great stress on the democratic role of party members. The membership has had powers that could not be ignored. Yet these members have lacked ideological and social cohesion.[10] Moreover, many have joined for expressive reasons and therefore have been more committed to principles and less interested than the leadership in concessions to electoral opinion in order to gain office. Finally, the party activists, who may have been most dedicated to principles, gained significant powers in the late 1970s. So even though the party elected a new leadership in 1983, apparently with widespread internal support, their task of re-creating a winning electoral coalition was by no means an easy one. Internal party constraints on the leadership's scope for action had to be confronted if the task was to succeed.

Attempts to remodel the party began soon after the new leadership had been elected. For example, Kinnock was personally very closely identified with an attempt at the 1984 party conference (unsuccessful as it turned out) to reduce activists' powers in parliamentary selection and reselection contests by shifting the decision from delegates to individual members. It seemed too early in his leadership to attempt to reduce the relative power of activists. It was to take another four years before the principle of individual membership participation in party decision making was accepted.

Kinnock did succeed in initiating an administrative reorganisation of the party's Walworth Road headquarters, which resulted in both new structures and new staff appointments. In 1985 the party's administrative tasks were concentrated in three directorates—policy, organisation, and campaigns and communication—and a new general secretary, Larry Whitty, and a director of communication, Peter Mandelson, were appointed by the NEC.

Policy shifts were more difficult to introduce over a short period of time. By the time of the 1987 election, the party had modified some of the manifesto commitments that had cost it votes in 1983; for example, it had tempered its outright antagonism to the European Community, it had toned down its public ownership commitments, and it had abandoned its opposition to local authority sale of council houses. Throughout the period between 1983 and 1987, however, the party remained very much on the defensive and for much of the time was responding to events, such as the 1984–85 miners' strike and local authorities' conflicts with central government on the question of rate capping, over which it had only limited control and in which the Conservative government was able to force it on to the defensive.

Labour's long march back to power commenced in 1983, but it was a two-step process. First, the party had to secure its position as the major non-Conservative electoral alternative by eliminating the threat of replacement by the Liberal–Social Democratic Alliance. This was partly achieved in June 1987 as a consequence of the well-executed general election campaign fought by Kinnock and his team. Nevertheless, 1987 was Labour's third consecutive electoral defeat; fewer than one-third of voters had been convinced enough by the party's policies actually to vote for it. The party's share of the total vote was still, with the exception of 1983, its lowest since the 1931 disaster; it had failed to reestablish itself as the major non-Conservative alternative in the South of England; and there remained an 11 percent difference between the Conservative and Labour votes. The party had failed to reestablish its electoral credentials in such a manner as not only to eliminate the Liberal–Social Democrat Alliance but also to pose a significant challenge to the Conservative's electoral hegemony. That task required more than a public relations success during the four-week election campaign; it needed a complete political overhaul involving both policies and organisation. It required a combination of determined leadership from Kinnock, a desire by leading trade unionists that Conservative governments were not to be permanent, and a widespread recognition by the majority of party members that fundamental changes were necessary.

The shock of electoral defeat in 1987 was thus the stimulus for the party's transformation. There were no obvious excuses this time, as there had been in 1979 and 1983. In 1979 defeat could be explained by the unpopularity of some Labour government policies and by trade unionists' militancy in the winter of 1978–79; in 1983 by factional divisions, the limitations as Labour leader of Michael Foot, and the Conservatives' successful defence of the Falkland Islands from Argentinian invasion. In 1987 no such excuses existed; instead, it was apparent to most Labour MPs and union leaders that voters did not like the party's policies. Their immediate dilemma, however, appeared to be that if they abandoned many of these policies, they would provoke considerable internecine party warfare as the grassroots activists stoutly defended their principled points of view. But a majority of these grassroots were also desperately keen to win the next general election and therefore either willingly acquiesced in the changes that occurred or else remained loyally silent. At all levels within the party, most were heartily sick of opposition politics. What Kinnock provided was the drive, determination, and direction of the move away from this unsuccessful past; and in so doing, he initiated reforms that went beyond what others originally envisaged, so that by 1991 Labour had been moulded very much in his image.

Two party conference speeches capture the mood for change that first emerged in 1983 and became unstoppable in 1987. The first was Neil Kinnock's speech immediately after his election as party leader in 1983, when he reminded delegates of their feelings "on that dreadful morning of 10 June [i.e., the day following the general election]. Just remember how you felt then, and think to yourself: 'June the Ninth 1983; never again will we experience that.' "[11] And the second was that of John Edmonds, the general secretary of the General and Municipal Workers Union (GMB), at the conference after Labour's 1987 election defeat, when he told delegates:

> It is time to be frank after such an election defeat. A Labour party that always comes second is no good to the GMB, it is no good to GMB mem-

bers. We put money, we put effort, we put time, we put commitment into that election campaign. No union, but no union, did more.... But be in no doubt. We shall not waste our members' money. We are not going to throw it away on the sort of time consuming nonsense that we put up with in the past—self-indulgent position papers with no conclusions, policy statements with no timetable for action, reorganisation plans that just decorate pigeonholes.[12]

The major reforms in the party were thus not initiated until after Labour's third successive defeat at the polls in 1987. Between then and 1991 reforms were introduced from which emerged the "new model" Labour party; by 1990 the party's director of communication, Peter Mandelson, could claim:

We have now effectively completed the building of the new model party.... The product is better, the unity is real, our democracy is healthier, our grassroots more representative and the whole outlook now geared to the realities of government rather than the illusions of opposition.[13]

Transformation 1: Policies

In its 1987 election manifesto the party had already begun to shift away from some of the unpopular commitments of 1983. Public ownership was now reserved only for the specific public utilities of gas, water, and telecommunication. Workers' individual rights were now emphasised rather more than collective trade union legal immunities; and there were no proposals to repeal the trade union reforms initiated by the Conservative government. The manifesto still, however, reflected the trade unions' boundary restraints, and one central task after 1987 was to "loosen or remove these boundaries."[14] In addition, the party replaced its anti-EC stance with a commitment to work constructively with the EC countries. Nevertheless, it promised to stand up for British interests and to reject EC interference in policies designed to stimulate economic recovery. What had not been modified was its nonnuclear commitment. In other words, policy shifts had been made by 1987, but following the election defeat, Labour embarked on a fundamental reappraisal of its entire political strategy.

After the 1987 election, various interpretations of the party's defeat were presented to the NEC, and eventually from these emerged the commitment to a wide-ranging "Policy Review."[15] The 1987 party conference approved a resolution, moved by John Edmonds, calling for "a review of the Party's policies to ensure that Labour's programme for government is attractive, imaginative, responsive to the concerns of working people and relevant to the needs of Britain in the 1990s while emphasising Labour's traditional values and collective approach."[16] Thus was initiated the most comprehensive attempt to reconsider the nature of the party's political commitments since the writing of the party's original constitution in 1918.

Although the NEC approved the proposal to initiate the review, and two years later approved the final review document, its participation and involvement in the review process was in fact marginal. Part of Kinnock's revitalisation strategy was to downgrade the NEC's role in party affairs and to replace it by the Parliamentary Labour party (PLP), in particular the shadow cabinet, and his own private office. The party leader chose the seven review group convenors[17] and, in consultation with the convenors, chose the review group members in such a manner as to ensure "a political mix which ... would bring about the results he wanted, while ensuring that dissident views were fairly reflected."[18] The coordinating work of the seven review groups was not given to the NEC, as might have been expected, but to a campaign management team made up of senior party headquarters officials, members of the party leader's office, and the PLP's campaign coordinator. Lastly, the drafting and final editing of the report was again the work of the party leader and his staff.[19] Much of the review process confirmed a significant shift of power away from the extraparliamentary to the parliamentary party, and to the party leader in particular.

The intricacies of the debate and the personal manoeuverings within the various review groups have been well covered elsewhere.[20] Here, I propose to concentrate on the contents of the Policy Review document, *Meet the Challenge, Make the Change* (1989), because of its trail-blazing importance. There were two subsequent policy documents, *Looking to the Future* (1990) and *Opportunity Britain: Labour's Better Way for the 1990s* (1991), but all the significant features of the party's renewal strategy were contained in the first.

Overall, two major themes emerged from *Meet the Challenge, Make the Change*. First, intraparty political debate over the extent of public and private ownership was outdated; and, second, the quality of public services should be improved by putting the needs of the user before those of the producer.

On the public/private ownership debate, the report came down in favour of private ownership and affirmed that a Labour government's task would be to stimulate a successful market economy and that it would intervene only where that stimulation was not coming from market forces. Throughout the report, there was a stress on the essential role of market forces. For example, the group reporting on the economy asserted that "the market and competition are essential in meeting the demands of consumers, promoting efficiency and stimulating innovation, and often the best means of securing all the myriad, incremental changes which are needed to take the economy forward."[21] In similar vein, the group considering consumers and the community argued that "markets are the most appropriate means of efficiently distributing many goods and services. Competition is one way of securing consumer choice."[22]

This wholehearted embrace of the market was new. In the past, the party had never wanted to eliminate private enterprise, but it had stressed its unpleasant characteristics. Party rhetoric had equated private enterprise with profit and public enterprise with service and had made clear its preference for the latter. Labour now adopted the "responsible social market model" in which government would intervene only when provision was necessary but the market was not providing, such as in the areas of labour training or environmental protection or to establish agencies to control exploitation of market power. Labour wanted an active, "developmental state," intervening to generate growth and efficiency. For example, there were proposals to create British Technology Enterprise—an institution investing in new technologies—and a British Investment Bank, plus regional investment banks, in order to help establish new industries.

The document made clear that public ownership was not a fundamental priority. Some forms of common ownership were appropriate for the public utilities, particularly British Telecom and water, but what would be returned to public ownership would depend on the situation when the party was returned to office. What was stressed was the need for the major utilities to be more sensitive to consumers. This was where market forces were flawed, and so the utilities should be answerable to regulatory commissions that would be responsible for pricing, investment, and service standards.

Regarding the second theme, the quality of public services, the review group on consumers and the community emphasised the need to improve public services from the consumer's, not the producer's, point of view. This was an attempt to shift the party away from its close identification with the public-sector trade unions and to flag its awareness of public criticisms of the welfare state for benefiting the producer rather than the user. The report proposed that the party should adopt "a consumer centred approach to the provision of goods and services."[23] Local authorities would be required to agree service agreements with their customers, and if the agreed service levels were not achieved, then financial sanctions would result.

If the commitments to market forces and user-friendly public services were the two most important themes running through *Meet the Challenge, Make the Change,* the two most significant specific changes it contained were the redefinition of the party's nonnuclear and industrial relations policies.

The review group examining the party's defence policies tried to steer a middle course between two distinct strands of opinion among members and supporters. The first wanted Britain to be adequately defended by all means, nuclear and nonnuclear, while the second was concerned at the dangers of a world reliant on nuclear weapons. The group insisted that the party was not "soft" on defence in an attempt to undermine traditional Conservative criticisms. It stated that the "defence of our country is an essential component of foreign policy and clearly a prime responsibility of any government,"[24] and went on to assert that the party was "determined that in the 1990s and beyond, Britain shall be properly defended. Our armed forces must be efficiently and effectively trained and equipped. We must maintain our vital contribution to NATO."[25] The party's recent objections to nuclear weaponry were reflected in the commitment to cancel the fourth Trident submarine, to adopt a policy of no-first-use of nuclear weapons, to seek to place Britain's nuclear weaponry into international disarmament negotiations, and to end the testing of all British nuclear devices. But the report contained no proposals to end Britain's nuclear capability or remove American nuclear bases.

The People at Work group tackled the difficult issue of the party's policies on the unions. Discussions were conducted against the background of a Trades Union Congress (TUC) that was reticent about becoming formally involved in the Policy Review because its leaders feared their involvement would harm the party among the voters. Informal contacts were maintained between party and TUC leaders, however, partly by means of a Contact Group, composed of leading shadow cabinet and TUC General Council members, and party and TUC officials.[26] There were divisions in the party between those demanding a complete repeal of the Conservatives' trade union legislation and those, including the leadership, who believed that statutory limitations on trade unions' actions were popular with the public—trade unionists and nonunionists alike—and should not be repealed.

The report made clear that "trade unions have a central role to play in a successful economy,"[27] but its emphasis was not on any commitment to restore and maintain collective rights for trade unions. Instead, it shifted towards guaranteeing basic legal rights for individual workers, including their negotiation of decent wages and working conditions, their protection from discrimination for union activities and from unfair dismissal, their ability to take time off work for family care, and their entitlement to union representation. The report made no commitment to repeal the law on the closed shop or on picketing. The only repeals of Conservative legislation proposed were those allowing workers to be sacked after a strike ballot decision, enabling employers to split companies in such a way as legally to avoid primary dispute action, and, finally, enabling employers to use ex-parte injunctions to curb industrial action. Conservative legislation requiring ballots of union members prior to strike action and for the election of union executives would be retained. The report claimed its proposals set a "new constructive framework of industrial relations law."[28]

This section of the review introduced a shift of major proportion in the party's commitments. Labour's nonnuclear stance between 1983 and 1987 had been a temporary aberration from its previous orthodox defence record, and therefore the proposal to retain Britain's nuclear forces was no more than a return to the political mainstream. In contrast, its previous industrial relations commitments had always concentrated on the maintenance of unions' legal immunities, and therefore the shift in policy from protecting collective union immunities to asserting individual rights at work was "a profound break with past definitions of one of the central values of the [party/union] relationship—trade union freedom."[29]

What the Policy Review managed to do most effectively was to loosen the party's commitment to such specific, electorally unattractive policies as nationalisation, unilateral nuclear disarmament, and the trade unions' legal immunities. What was not so clear from the whole exercise was the nature of the party's proposals to replace these electoral deadweights. There are four areas, however, in which the policy review did suggest something specific.

First, *Meet the Challenge, Make the Change* stressed the supply side of economic management. There was no repetition of the party's alternative economic strategy of the early 1980s, which had been based on a national, protectionist strategy for economic regeneration. Now the proposal was to make Britain competitive in the world economy by introducing a medium-term industrial strategy that would strengthen the Department of Trade and Industry, raise the rate of Britain's investment, encourage a national science programme, stimulate regional growth, and expand training.

Second, Labour's hostility to the European Community in 1983 had been consistent with its nationalist approach to economic issues. Its new attachment to the world economy made a pro-EC stance logical. The

Policy Review stressed the party's commitment to a socialist European Community in which environmental, women's, and social and consumer rights would be protected. Only as Margaret Thatcher's antagonism towards a European currency and monetary policy emerged during 1990 and 1991 did Labour's pro-EC economic commitments begin to develop and attract attention.

Third, *Meet the Challenge, Make the Change* affirmed a commitment to redistribution, albeit a very tentative one. For example, the document included no proposal for a specific wealth tax but instead argued that the most effective means of redistribution was to tax transfers of wealth occurring through gifts and inheritance. What was innovative, after years of opposition from many trade unions, was the proposal to introduce a statutory minimum wage to be fixed at 50 percent of male median earnings. There was no mention of incomes policy, but there was a commitment to establish a Fair Wages Commission to promote and encourage fair wages. Very few proposals for social welfare expenditures or taxation were included because of the desire not to be portrayed as the high-spending, high-taxing party. But three specific proposals were included. First was the proposed abolition of the flat-rate National Insurance contribution for all income earners above £16,900 per year. The report claimed that National Insurance was a disguised form of regressive income tax, hitting the average income earner and benefiting the rich.

Second, the report claimed that the real value of the universal child benefit had been cut by the Conservatives and proposed instead a "generous" increase during the lifetime of a Parliament. Third, the report proposed "an immediate and substantial increase"[30] in old-age pensions of not less than £5 and £8 per week for both single and married persons. These specific commitments were to have considerable consequences during the election campaign.

Finally, the Policy Review devoted more space to extending democratic rights for British citizens than would have been the case in the past. Historically, Labour had been wedded to the maintenance of Britain's state institutions.[31] Pressures for institutional reform, however, had come both from within the party[32] and from newly emerging extraparty organisations such as Charter 88. There was a distinct unease about the manner in which the Thatcher government had used parliamentary majorities to drive through controversial and sometimes unpopular policies. Whereas in the 1980s Labour's sole constitutional reform proposal had been the abolition of the House of Lords, now the Policy Review proposed a reformed second chamber, which would reflect regional, Scottish, and Welsh interests in the United Kingdom and would also be given a delaying power to protect fundamental human rights. These rights would not be incorporated into a bill of rights; this was rejected on the grounds that the most vulnerable would not be adequately protected by the courts. Instead, Labour would legislate piecemeal to protect individuals' rights to privacy, equal opportunity, citizenship, assembly, and freedom of information.[33] Labour's move away from its centralist past was apparent in the proposals for a directly elected Scottish Assembly with separate legislative and taxing powers and for elected regional authorities in England. Labour, however, maintained its traditional commitment to the simple plurality electoral system.

The Policy Review had expunged unpopular policies, it had restricted the number of commitments that might cause electoral embarrassment, and it had made some specific proposals to move the party in new directions. What was missing was any clear sense of an underlying value system that would both offer an alternative to Thatcherism and guide the party beyond the next election. It was clear that the party found it difficult to articulate any clear and distinctive socialist values. In 1988 the NEC had endorsed *Democratic Socialist Aims and Values,* a document that emphasised equality, justice, and freedom, but this never became the central guiding feature of later policy proposals. The party seemed unable to clarify the nature of democratic socialism enough for it to become the driving force of its commitments.

How was the Policy Review received by the party? On the hard left were those who regarded the whole exercise with suspicion as an elaborate means of abandoning key socialist principles. They believed in public ownership, close links with the unions, active party support for trade unionists involved in industrial disputes, and reaffirmation of the party's links with its working-class supporters. Neither Tony Benn nor Dennis Skinner, both members of the NEC, participated in any of the review groups so that they would not be compromised or constrained in criticising the final document. Eric Heffer described the Policy Review as "a retreat away from our basic socialist policies."[34] All three were prominent figures on the left. After ministerial experience in the Harold Wilson and James Callaghan governments, Benn had moved away from the majority of his cabinet colleagues and developed a powerful critique of their policies. By 1981, he had become the left figurehead in challenging party orthodoxy, and he came within 1 percent of winning the election for deputy leader. Between 1974 and 1984, he topped the poll each year for election as one of the constituency party representatives on the NEC. One of Kinnock's first tasks as leader was to reduce Benn's influence within the party. Skinner was another MP who was very popular among constituency party activists for his aggressive, highly principled, class-based approach to politics. Benn and Skinner consistently opposed Kinnock's strategy and were often a minority of two in the NEC. By the time the Policy Review report was discussed by the NEC, Heffer was no longer a member. Heffer's loss of place in 1986 was one sign that Kinnock was beginning to shift the party in a direction of his own choosing. Heffer had been first elected to the NEC in 1975 and by the late 1970s was prominent in expanding the powers of the grassroots activists. After his unsuccessful attempt to be elected as party leader in 1983, Heffer became an outspoken critic of the new party leadership. In 1988 he was part of the hard-left ticket, with Benn, to challenge Kinnock and Hattersley.

These critics were marginalised within the party, and their formal challenge to the direction in which the party was going—by forcing a leadership ballot in 1988—was crushed.[35] Nevertheless, we see later that the party's members remained committed to some distinct socialist principles that ran counter to the general tenor of the Policy Review. The ideas and proposals contained within the Policy Review came from the top. Kinnock claimed in his introduction to *Meet the Challenge, Make the Change* that local parties, branches, and trade unions had discussed the issues during the two years since the review was established, but in fact there had been very little attempt to gauge opinion at the grassroots. A "Labour Listens" exercise, intended to create a dialogue with the party's target voters and its members, was more of a public relations exercise than a serious attempt to sound out opinions.[36]

Apart from a procedural argument over amendments to *Meet the Challenge, Make the Change,* there were only three topics—public ownership, trade union rights, and defence—on which any significant opposition was expressed by delegates at the 1989 party conference. Critics of the social market idea argued that capitalism would not act in a socially responsible manner and therefore demanded that the party maintain its commitment to public ownership. But the case for public ownership mustered less than half a million votes in a total ballot of 6 million and was overwhelmingly rejected. Opponents of the trade union proposals demanded the repeal of all the Conservative governments' trade union legislation, but they too were defeated, albeit by a smaller majority than in the case of public ownership. The sharpest debate and the closest vote came over the party's defence policies. Critics of the Policy Review demanded a continuing commitment to unilateral nuclear disarmament and a sharp reduction in Britain's defence expenditures. The unilateralist position was defeated, but the party voted, against the leadership's wishes, to reduce defence expenditures to the average of other European countries.

The fact that Kinnock had succeeded in convincing the party's main deliberative body to affirm enormous changes in policy on nationalisation, trade union laws, and unilateralism was extraordinary. Most people in the party faced up to the dilemma of reconciling deeply held beliefs and the need to win power by opting for the latter. This dilemma was succinctly expressed by a constituency delegate from Surrey, the southern heartland of Conservatism:

> I have over thirty years of active membership in this party and for most of that time I have been a committed unilateralist.... We know the hardships that the majority of people have suffered under Thatcher. We have witnessed the dismantling and the destruction of the public and social services and know the importance and the desperate need for a Labour government next time. I have given a lot of thought and consideration to this matter and have decided that support for Composite 46 [on general disarmament] is the only way forward because I am not prepared to put the election of a Labour government at risk by clinging on to a unilateralist policy and I make no apologies for considering electoral chances at this time ... because, like it or not, those of us who were on the doorsteps during the last election, especially in the south, know that it was one of the reasons why we did not win.[37]

It was sentiments like these that sustained the party's transformation.

INTERPRETATIONS OF THE POLICY REVIEW

Did the Policy Review signify a fundamental change of direction for Labour? Did it represent a transformation equivalent in historical importance to that which its sister party, the German Social Democratic party (SPD), carried out in 1959 at its conference in Bad Godesberg? Had the party finally, unambiguously, adopted social democracy, or had it adopted Thatcherite values?

In the German case, the SPD had formally jettisoned its old ideological baggage. It had abandoned Marxism and accepted the principle of private ownership, and it had decided to improve and reform, rather than abolish, the competitive market.[38] In the British case, the Labour party made clear its explicit acceptance of the market economy as both efficient and effective. Whether a service would be provided by private or public enterprise would be decided pragmatically rather than on principle. Nevertheless, one of the constitutional objectives of the party, as defined in clause 4, remained to "secure for the workers by hand or by brain the full fruits of their industry and the most equitable distribution thereof that may be possible upon the basis of the *common ownership* of the means of production, distribution and exchange," and the failure to remove this clause limits the extent to which the two can be treated as similar. Nevertheless, the Labour party's past commitment to public ownership should not be exaggerated. Ever since 1918 there had always been an ambiguity over clause 4, and it had meant different things to different people. Notwithstanding Hugh Gaitskell's failed attempt to remove clause 4 in 1959, the party leadership had since then only proposed a very limited number of industries for nationalisation. In the early 1970s the Labour left had "rediscovered" the relevance of public intervention and control,[39] but even so, its proposal for a state holding company to invest in parts of the British economy was very much within the dominant social democratic traditions of the party.[40] It seems, therefore, that the new model Labour party of 1989 had done little more than return to its social democratic traditions of the 1960s.

Some, however, claimed that the party had gone further than this and had adopted the programme of the breakaway Social Democratic party (SDP) (see chapter 4). Back in 1981, the SDP had been established in protest at Labour's leftward leanings, in particular at its commitments to nationalisation, unilateral nuclear disarmament, close attachments to the trade unions, and withdrawal from the European Economic Community. Eric Heffer had articulated his fears that the Labour party was becoming too closely identified with the SDP as early as 1986.[41] By the time the Policy Review had been completed, some of those who led the original breakaway from the Labour party were claiming a close proximity between the SDP and Labour. For example, Bill Rodgers wrote that "over a wide spectrum the Labour Party has been remade in the image of the SDP."[42] When the split took place in 1981, a common assumption in some Labour circles had been that the new SDP would prove to be yet another historical example of a minor party destined for electoral oblivion.[43] It may be true that the SDP did not succeed in transforming the British party system, but it did contribute to Labour's rethinking after 1987. Labour could not ignore the SDP's electoral successes, either as part of the Alliance in 1983 and 1987 or in its individual, stunning by-election victories in constituencies like Crosby (1981), Glasgow Hillhead (1982), Portsmouth South (1984), and Greenwich (1987). The impact of this electoral success is seen in the fact that Labour's new programme and the SDP's programme were in fact strikingly similar. One commentator noted that "on almost every issue there is not a tissue paper's worth of difference between Labour policy now and SDP policy in 1981."[44]

An alternative, more extreme claim was that the Labour party had adopted Thatcherite values. For example, Ian Aitken in the *Guardian* commented that the new policy document represented "the final acceptance by Labour of the intellectual victory of market economics, as preached by Mrs. Thatcher."[45] There is no doubt that the parameters of political debate had shifted in the 1980s, and some of the old social democratic traditions of the 1950s, particularly the emphasis on public services and public provision, had lost their political appeal. The tenor of much political discussion regarding markets, economic intervention and planning, industrial relations, quality of public services, consumer rights, and discipline and testing in schools had certainly shifted in a Conservative direction.[46] There is no doubt the Labour party was reacting to this shift, but at the same time it was also asserting, very strongly, that markets were unable to meet all economic and social needs. There was still a place for collective, cooperative, and community action. In addition, the Thatcherites regarded the market as morally right, whereas the Policy Review took a pragmatic view: The market was efficient and fair, but there would still be many occasions when intervention would be required. The claim that the Labour party had adopted Thatcherism is at least questionable.

The Labour party had thus responded to negative electoral feedback on specific policy commitments, for example, unilateral nuclear disarmament; on structural relationships, for example, the close collaboration between the trade unions and the party; and on values, for example, the lack of priority for users' needs in public service provision. But what was missing from its response, as I have said, was any sense of the party's creating an identity around positive feedback. Opinion surveys revealed that competitive individualism was by no means entirely dominant and that voters retained a commitment to community provision;[47] but the party made little attempt to capitalise on public support for redistribution of wealth, income, and profits and to weld support for these into a distinct progressive identity.[48]

The policy changes contained within the Policy Review were, in part, a restoration of the party's past social democratic traditions and in part a radical shift towards a future that involved an embrace of the market and a rejection of traditional trade union legal immunities. The second feature of the party's restructuring exercise, namely organisational change, represented an even sharper break with its past and a move away from previous traditions of delegatory democracy and trade union power.

Transformation 2: Structures and Organisation

The party leadership had conflicting motives in its strategy for organisational reform. First, it wanted to reduce MPs' dependence on constituency party delegates (i.e., persons nominated by local party and trade union branches to attend meetings of the constituency general management committee), and so it wanted to reduce the likelihood of reselection contests occurring and to ensure that individual members, rather than the delegates, would cast the votes. Second, it wished to reduce, but not eliminate entirely, the trade unions' role within the party. It felt unable, however, to go so far as to create a party entirely based on individual, direct membership because the affiliated, indirect membership provided considerable political and financial resources for the party leadership. Finally, it wished to strengthen the administrative powers at the centre of the party to determine parliamentary candidates, to remove elected party representatives causing political embarrassment, and to expel individuals regarded as infiltrators. On the one hand, the leadership's aim was to increase the power of the individual member; on the other hand, its aim was to increase its own power. The conflict between these two aims was never resolved, and by 1991 the legacy of this conflict, as we later see, was a "de-energised" party. What above all motivated the leadership was its desire to ensure that the party's image was as favourable as possible among voters, and this necessitated greater central control of both the message and the messengers.

The "forward march of the Labour Left" in the late 1970s[49] had secured a powerful position for party activists, defined here as those who regularly attended local party meetings. The MPs' previous dominance of the party no longer prevailed.[50] The party leadership was elected by an electoral college in which MPs cast a minority of the vote and all Labour MPs faced reselection—by those local activists who attended party meetings—during the lifetime of each Parliament. This shift in power towards the activists had been a key factor in prompting the party split in 1981; the Social Democratic party's leaders opposed the decline in the MPs' powers. The immediate impact of candidate reselection was much exaggerated by opponents of this particular reform; only eight Labour MPs were deselected before the 1983 general election and six before the 1987 general election. Others, however, retired rather than face the prospect of reselection. Labour MPs now had to stick much more closely to the views of their local activists if they were to survive. Thus the parliamentary party's political outlook was being shaped more by these local activists than had ever been the case in the past.

Since it was an activist party that had adopted policies so unpopular with the voters, Kinnock's first task was to reduce the activists' powers. He could not afford to ignore them because of their significant constitutional powers. It was also both electorally and politically inexpedient for the leadership to be seen to rely too closely on the trade union bloc vote at the party conference because the unions were generally unpopular, even among their own members, and because some union leaders were unreliable in delivering their votes in the way the leader might wish. Therefore, a strategy of empowering ordinary party members was developed on the assumption that they held more moderate opinions.

As already pointed out, Kinnock's first attempt in 1984 to limit activists' powers by introducing the one-member, one-vote principle for the selection and reselection of parliamentary candidates was defeated at the party conference. Opponents of the reform argued successfully that it would certainly reduce the role of the affiliated members (principally trade unions), would allow the less active members to be influenced by the outside media, and would weaken the accountability of MPs to their local parties. Kinnock refused to let the matter rest. An NEC working party was established to consider reform and, after the party's election defeat in 1987, returned to the party conference with two proposals: either the party should adopt a procedure of one member, one vote or, if unwilling to abolish trade union participation in local parties entirely, then the party should agree on a modified version in which local constituency party electoral colleges would be created. In these electoral colleges trade unions would be restricted to a maximum of 40 percent of the vote, while 60 percent or more would be allocated to individual members, all of whom would be entitled to participate in a ballot. The conference opted for the second proposal, with the result that trade unions would now find it more difficult to dominate candidate selection conferences as they had done for so long in individual constituencies in the past. One example of such dominance had been the National Union of Mineworkers' ability to determine the choice of candidate in many mining constituencies. Now, for the first time, the individual member had a right to participate in the choice of the party's parliamentary representative without respect to whether he or she attended local party branch meetings or was a delegate to the general committee of the local constituency Labour party. The individual party member had at last been enfranchised.

The fact that this second, rather messy, proposal was approved, rather than the simpler individual ballot procedure, reflected the unions' unwillingness to lose all their powers at local level. But one conference delegate accurately predicted during the debate that the scheme adopted would soon be abandoned as too complicated and unsatisfactory. Ever since his election as party leader, Kinnock's long-term objective had been a large individual membership at local level with only a very limited role for either branch delegates or trade union affiliates. In 1990 the NEC again returned to the question and proposed that the selection and rese-lection of parliamentary candidates should be based solely on a ballot of individual members; the only role for affiliated unions would be in nomi-nating and shortlisting candidates. The conference agreed that this should be the principle that would operate after the next election. The question of what role the unions would play in the selection procedures was left open for further negotiation, but the days of the activist delegate casting votes on behalf of a passive individual membership had passed. The principle of decision making by the individual member rather than the delegate had been adopted.

In addition to giving individual party members the power to choose their parliamentary candidates, the practice was then extended to in-clude, first, the election of the party leadership and, then, the choice of the seven constituency representatives on the NEC. In 1988, when part of the Labour left challenged the direction the party was taking by nomi-nating Tony Benn and Eric Heffer, who were subsequently joined by John Prescott, to stand against the incumbent leadership, the NEC ad-vised all local parties to consult their individual members by means of a ballot before deciding how their delegate would cast the constituency vote in the electoral college. A survey revealed that 53 percent of constit-uency Labour parties (CLPs) that participated in the leadership elections conducted some form of ballot among their members.[51] The procedure that CLPs had been recommended to use in the 1988 leadership elections was then adopted as mandatory at the 1988 party conference. One year later, the principle of one person, one vote was extended to cover the election of the seven constituency representatives on the NEC.

Part of the leadership's strategy to empower individual members was based on the assumption that they were more representative of Labour's actual and potential voters than were party delegates. In fact, little was known at the time about the membership, and therefore the strategy was something of a leap in the dark. What evidence there was revealed a steady decline in membership from 1984 onward; by 1988, it had dropped by 60,000 to 266,000. In the past, the party had rarely given much priority to the recruitment of individual members,[52] but now from the top of the party hierarchy came a determination to expand numbers. Local parties were not regarded as necessarily the most efficient recruit-ing agents, and therefore the radical move of shifting the point of recruit-ment from locality to party headquarters in London was initiated in 1988 and came to fruition in 1991. The loss of members was halted, and a steady growth was achieved after 1988. What was missing from this new recruitment strategy was a commitment to members as communica-tors, which would have required a much greater encouragement of their political involvement in party affairs. But this did not fit in with other aspects of the leadership's strategy.

Kinnock's determination to empower individual members was at the expense of both local party branches and union delegates. At the national level, his intention was more to reduce union influence than to eliminate it altogether. Trade union affiliated members (6.3 million in 1988) have played a key role in party affairs,[53] but they have been essentially paper members, helping to determine the level of trade union affiliation fees paid to the party and the number of votes cast at party conferences. Kinnock was confronted with a variety of complex and conflicting pressures in his reconsideration of the trade union/party relationship. First, he needed the union affiliation fees to sustain party expenditures; second, he wanted the guarantee of some significant blocs of votes at the party conference to sustain his strategy; third, he was aware of an electoral cost of reliance on the unions; and, fourth, he recognised the disincentives to greater individual membership participation if the policy process was dominated by the unions. Many trade union leaders were aware of the hostility party members felt at the overwhelming dominance of the bloc vote and were willing to consider ways of reducing their relative voting strength at conference,[54] but most union leaders were hostile to the elimination of their indirect role in local party decision making. On this issue an impasse had been reached by 1991, which would be resolved only after the election.

The leadership's objective of a more participative membership and a reduced role for the trade unions took up much of the time it devoted to structural reorganisation after 1987. But a third major reform, concerning the party's policy-making process, was also discussed. Pressure for reform of the annual party conference procedures had emerged, in part, from dissatisfaction in many parts of the party with the way in which the Policy Review had been conducted. Comparisons were made with the longer, more deliberative procedures of many European socialist parties. In 1989 a resolution, moved again by John Edmonds, recommended the creation of a new policy commission to discuss detailed policy. In response, the NEC issued a report in 1990, which the party conference approved for detailed implementation after the general election. The report was critical of the existing policy process because it failed to represent all elements in the party, especially women, ethnic minorities, and community groups, and it gave no formal role to local councillors, MPs, or Euro-MPs. The report argued that there was "a complete lack of general membership involvement" in the policy-making process leading up to the party conference, and stated that the outcome was often "muddled, sometimes even self-contradictory, of unclear status and arguable author-

ity."[55] It proposed a new structure, which would retain the NEC and annual party conference but would create a "policy forum" made up of
around 200 people, of whom the majority would be representatives of
the nine English regions into which the party is divided. Its work would
be distributed between seven standing commissions, where details of the
party programme would be discussed. Rather than policy making being
concentrated in one week in the year, the policy forum would work on a
two-year rolling programme.

What was unclear were the motives for this proposal. Was the leadership acting because the existing policy-making procedure was unsatisfactory and there was a need to involve a wider range of people, or was
it intending to weaken leadership accountability to the extraparliamentary party? The bulk of representatives in the new policy forum
would come from regional parties, yet Labour's structure has never af-
forded any importance to such bodies. If the policy forum was intended
to improve the party's policy-making procedures and maintain a tradition of leadership accountability, then the structures and powers of the
party regions would need careful reconsideration.

The fourth, and final, feature of structural reform covered the toler-
ance, or intolerance, of views and actions of party members. The Labour
party suffered in the early 1980s from its open divisions, dissent, and intense factional fighting and at the same time from hostile media coverage
of particular Labour-controlled local authorities and their leaders
("looney left" councils), of particular parliamentary candidates, and of
particular Labour MPs. The leadership took the view that Labour
needed to be united if it was to be judged fit to govern by British voters,
and it therefore pursued a policy of restraining intraparty dissent and
criticism.

Labour had been bedeviled by the problem of Trotskyist infiltration
from the mid-1970s onward. The left's advance in the 1970s had led to
the abolition of the proscribed list of organisations ineligible for affiliation to the party, which had previously been used to keep objectionable
individuals out of the party.[56] Its abolition had been meant as a symbolic
gesture registering the existence of an open, democratic party after the
authoritarian intolerance of the 1950s.[57] The Militant Tendency's success
in controlling particular constituency parties and local authorities forced
a reluctant NEC to expel individuals prominently associated with Militant in 1983. At the 1985 party conference Kinnock launched an aggressive attack on Militant's influence in Liverpool, and an NEC enquiry into
the Liverpool Labour party was established. By 1987, a long and tortuous process, often involving the courts, had resulted in only fourteen individuals associated with Militant being expelled. The party's procedures

for dealing with the problem were therefore overhauled, and between 1987 and 1991 over 200 were expelled for belonging to an organisation ineligible for affiliation, culminating in the expulsion from the party in September 1991 of two Labour MPs identified with Militant, Dave Nellist and Terry Fields. Whereas the party had prevaricated in the early 1980s over who could and could not belong to the party, the leadership had in the latter part of the decade become determined to rid Labour of the Trotskyist blight.

The boundaries of membership were now defined in such a way as to exclude not only known Trotskyists but also anyone deemed to be involved in conduct "prejudicial to the party."[58] This new rule gave the NEC wide enough powers to control any activities it pleased. In 1991, for example, it suspended twenty-seven Labour councillors in Lambeth, including the council leader, whose activities and attitudes it disapproved of.

The leadership was particularly concerned to ensure that Labour's most prominent standard-bearers, the parliamentary candidates, should fit the new realist mould, especially in by-elections where concentration of the national media on candidates was at its most intense. After minimal debate at the very end of the 1988 party conference, the NEC was given the power to intervene directly in the candidate selection process. The short list of candidates for each by-election was determined by the NEC, and it used its new power to exclude particular locally nominated persons from the short lists of candidates in the Vauxhall, Eastbourne, Bradford North, and Hemsworth by-elections. The NEC's powers were further extended in 1990 when it was given the right to remove the already-selected candidate if the candidate "would have difficulty in withstanding the particular rigours of a by-election."[59] Not only did the NEC intervene to determine the choice of candidate in by-elections, but it intervened to protect certain Labour MPs from deselection. For example, the Birkenhead constituency party was ordered to rerun its selection procedures after it had rejected its MP, Frank Field; only in a second ballot, after a number of local members had been suspended, did Frank Field win the nomination.

This strict management of the party was extended to the shadow cabinet and the party's front-bench spokesmen and women, of whom Kinnock demanded unity and loyalty. Individuals unwilling to accept this code of conduct and, in particular, the party leader's direction were demoted and sidelined or dismissed. For example, Bryan Gould, Michael Meacher, John Prescott, and Clare Short suffered because of their independence.

By 1991, the party was run in a very determined and ruthlessly pro-

fessional manner. The goal of political office was paramount, and the
party leader stipulated a party of unity and political uniformity. A divided party was regarded as a defeated party. Critics suggested that an
increasingly autocratic and unaccountable leadership was imposing its
policies, persons, and practices on the party. It was claimed that, by reducing the importance of the party conference, by limiting the role of the
affiliated trade unions, and by curbing the powers of the activists, the
leadership was intent on creating a party on the American model, where
leaders dominate and individuals provide money and other means of support and legitimacy but lack the power to play a significant part in policy
making. Ken Livingstone described the methods used to achieve the new
model party as "completely Stalinist."[60] Tony Benn and Dennis Skinner
were consistent but isolated critics of the NEC. For most MPs, however,
the prize for political loyalty to the leadership would be office in a Labour government. The patronage powers of a future Labour prime minister were an inducement also to some senior trade unionists on the
NEC, who in the early 1980s had been closely identified with the Labour
left, to stick very closely to the party leadership's reorganisation strategy.
But at every annual party conference from 1987 onward many delegates
would complain that the structural reforms were undermining the powers of the members and were weakening the party's traditional forms of
political accountability. Few among the rank and file would benefit from
a Labour leader's patronage powers. How representative of the 300,000
individual members were these and the other critics?

Transformation 3: The Views of Members

The strategy of empowering the party members was earlier described as
a leap in the dark. The party leadership had little clear idea who the
party's members were or what opinions they held because no systematic
research on the party membership had been conducted. In 1990 the first
ever national survey[61] of Labour party members revealed a clear commitment among them to four socialist "touchstones": public ownership,
trade union legitimacy, nonnuclear defence, and high public expenditures. Members were attached to a number of distinct principles, which
appeared to be at odds with the new model party. But it was also clear
from the survey that members recognised the need to ensure that policies
were electorally attractive, and a majority believed the party "should adjust its policies to capture the middle ground of politics." Members appeared to hold a principled political position but also to adopt a practical view of policies (see tables 3.1, 3.2, and 3.3).

TABLE 3.1

LABOUR PARTY MEMBERS' ATTITUDES TO
ELECTORAL STRATEGY, THE FREE
MARKET, AND TRADE UNIONS

	(1)	(2)	(3)	(4)	(5)	(6)
Agree	57%	60%	81%	24%	13%	72%
Disagree	33	28	8	59	73	17
Neither	10	12	11	17	14	11
Total	100	100	100	100	100	100

NOTE: Party members were asked to respond on a five-point scale ("strongly agree"/ "agree"/ "neither"/ "disagree"/ "strongly disagree") to the following propositions:

1. "The Labour party should adjust its policies to capture the middle ground of politics."

2. "The Labour party should always stand by its principles even if this should lose an election."

3. "The public enterprises privatized by the Conservative government should be returned to the public sector."

4. "The production of goods and services is best left to a free market."

5. "It is better for Britain when trade unions have little power."

6. "Workers should be prepared to strike in support of other workers, even if they don't work in the same place."

In addition, members were asked questions on their attitudes towards party reform. They strongly supported the principle of one member, one vote, were critical of the trade union bloc vote, believed that party activists held extreme views, and did not believe that Kinnock was too powerful in the party. On four propositions—that "the trade union movement has too much power over the Party," that "constituency Labour parties should have the exclusive right to select their own parliamentary candidates," that "Neil Kinnock will stick to his principles even if this means losing a general election," and that "the party leadership doesn't pay a lot of attention to the view of the ordinary party members"—members were more evenly divided (see table 3.4).

Party members' responses on a range of these Likert-scale items were structured in such a manner as to distinguish "modernisers," in favour of the party leadership's electoral strategy and its structural changes, from "traditionalists," who opposed the strategy and changes. One in three of the members were modernisers, and only one in five were traditionalists.[62] The answer to our original question is that more members supported the structural reforms than were opposed. Opponents of the modernisation strategy were a small minority of the membership closely associated with the party's hard left.

TABLE 3.2
LABOUR PARTY MEMBERS' ATTITUDES TO NATIONALISATION/
PRIVATISATION, NUCLEAR WEAPONS,
AND TAXES VS. SERVICES

Issue	Response
Nationalisation/privatisation	
More nationalisation	71%
More privatisation	2
Leave as now	27
Total	100
Nuclear weapons	
Britain: maintain independent nuclear weapons	5
Britain: maintain nuclear weapons in western defence system	21
Britain: no nuclear weapons	68
No opinion	6
Total	100
Taxes vs. services	
Reduce taxes/spend less on services	2
Tax and spend the same as now	6
Increase taxes/spend more on services	92
Total	100

TABLE 3.3
LABOUR PARTY MEMBERS' ATTITUDES TO TRADE
UNION LAW, DEFENCE SPENDING, AND
GOVERNMENT SPENDING GENERALLY

	(1)	(2)	(3)
Should	12%	86%	21%
Should not	78	11	73
Doesn't matter	10	3	6
Total	100	100	100

NOTE: Party members were asked to respond on a five-point scale ("definitely should"/"probably should"/"doesn't matter"/"probably should not"/"definitely should not") to the statements that the government should/should not do each of the following:
1. "Introduce stricter laws to regulate trade unions."
2. "Spend less on defence."
3. "Reduce government spending generally."
In all cases, the "definitely should"/"probably should" and the "probably should not"/"definitely should not" have been summed.

TABLE 3.4
DISTRIBUTION OF OPINIONS ON THE PARTY
REFORM INDICATORS

	Strongly agree	Agree	Neither	Dis-agree	Strongly disagree
Labour leader too powerful	6%	9%	15%	54%	17%
Conference bloc vote disreputable	23	49	12	13	4
One person, one vote for leadership	37	44	7	9	3
Leader ignores party members' views	10	29	17	39	5
Party activists are extremists	18	57	10	13	2
Trade unions have too much power in party	9	34	15	32	10
Right of CLPs to select candidates	26	7	11	22	4
Kinnock will stick to his principles	12	26	16	33	1

Conclusions

After 1987, the Labour party jettisoned most of its electorally unpopular policies. It reaffirmed its traditional social democratic credentials by asserting its ability to achieve its goals within a mixed economy. It restrained its radical, redistributory enthusiasms by stipulating that improvements in public services and benefits would come only as a consequence of economic growth, rather than higher taxation. It placed greater emphasis on achieving economic growth through supply-side measures for reestablishing Britain's world competitiveness, rather than on demand management. It abandoned its labourist commitments to trade union immunities and to close structural links with the unions.

Who deserves the credit for remodeling Labour's political appeal? First, Margaret Thatcher's influence cannot be underestimated. By winning three consecutive elections, she established an electoral dominance that Labour had to respond to if it was to survive. This is not to say that Thatcherism dominated either political values in general or Labour's Policy Review in particular. The fact that the Conservative party found it impossible to increase its share of the vote beyond 42 percent between 1983 and 1987 diminished its claims to have established an ideological hegemony. Nevertheless, the Conservative reforms of trade unions and local government had a considerable impact on Labour's political agenda. A Labour government would not have introduced these trade union reforms, and neither would it repeal them. A Labour government would not have dared do what the Conservatives did, and yet Labour must be grateful to the Conservatives for resolving the tricky issue of labour relations law. The trade unions were more dependent than ever on a Labour electoral victory, but their economic and political weaknesses left them with no alternative but to maintain a low profile.

Second, the Social Democratic party deserves credit for Labour's changes. Its initial by-election victories and its large vote in the 1983 and 1987 general elections confirmed that this new party was not the shooting star that some had predicted. A divided anti-Conservative vote has always reinforced the Conservative party's electoral dominance. In a noncoalition party system, Labour's only chance of regaining office was to woo Alliance voters, and this required a movement towards the policies of those who supported the SDP breakaway in 1981.

Third, Kinnock deserves considerable credit for Labour's changes. Surrounded by a small group of personal supporters in his private political office, the party headquarters, the shadow cabinet, and the NEC, he displayed a clear and consistent drive towards office. He capitalised on the mood within the party to reverse its decline and to become again a governing party. There were institutional, structural, cultural, and personal obstacles to his renewal project. For example, he had constantly to mobilise majorities in the extraparliamentary party; he had to calculate the trade union response to his reforms; he faced opposition from many party activists; and he was criticised by those claiming to have retained their socialist principles. One of his closest confidantes has written that the Labour party leadership is "the most thankless job in British politics."[63] The party has never been an easy one to lead, but the problems and difficulties Kinnock experienced when he was first elected were considerable, and yet by 1991 he had developed into the most powerful leader of the party since Clement Attlee. His goal was office, and the bulk of the party was willing to follow in his tracks. The party revealed a lust for power more often associated with the Conservatives. Many Conservatives must have been envious of Labour's new organisational strength, such as its ability to fight by-elections with a candidate chosen by the national party and a well-managed election campaign team. In some senses a reversal of political roles occurred in the late 1980s, with the Conservatives engaged in public factional fighting and arguments over ideology, and possessing an inefficient party machine.

But there was a price to be paid for Labour's lust for power. Earlier the point was made that a segment of the party had become totally detached from this renewal strategy. Maybe there was no way these members could have been incorporated into the party mainstream. But what was more worrying for the party was that its members had become "de-energised." Survey evidence reveals that 43 percent of the members were less active in the party, and only 20 percent more active, than five years previously.[64] Evidence from party headquarters itself confirmed greater difficulty in mobilising members into the traditional forms of party activity. A sense of disengagement prevailed, in which many members acknowledged the price needed to gain an election victory but displayed little enthusiasm for the process and the resulting policies. The Labour party needs its members and its activists; they are needed because an active membership wins votes for the Labour party. Recent research suggests that if Labour had recruited an additional 100 active members in its local constituency parties throughout Britain, it would have increased its total share of the national vote by 5 percent.[65] This was not, however, a view shared by Peter Mandelson and his shadow Communication Agency.

Finally, it was questionable whether the party had established a distinctive electoral appeal by 1991. It benefited from a growing anti-Thatcher sentiment as the impact of the poll tax began to be felt. But the changes in its defence and European policies appeared to have made little impact on the voters. In response to the question of which party would handle the problems of defence and Europe best, the voters preference for the Conservatives was *greater* in early 1992 than before the Policy Review recommendations had been approved. This was also true of industrial relations, the third area in which the party had abandoned electorally unpopular policies (see table 3.5).

TABLE 3.5
VOTERS' ASSESSMENTS OF PARTIES'
GOVERNING ABILITIES

	Defence		Europe		Industrial relations[a]	
	Cons.	Lab.	Cons.	Lab.	Cons.	Lab.
April 1989	51%	22%	39%	21%	45%	34%
February 1992	57	20	53	23	49	32

SOURCE: *Gallup Political Index.*
a. The industrial relations question was first asked in May 1991 as "Which political party you personally think would handle the problem best?"

Labour's support among the voters at the beginning of the 1990s seemed to be the product initially of the unpopularity of Mrs. Thatcher and her community charge and then of the recession into which the country was quickly plunged. There was always the danger for Labour that if, for any reason, the Conservative party managed to reassert itself, Labour would find itself left without a distinct—and persuasive—social democratic appeal.

Notes

1. Kay Lawson and Peter Merkl, *When Parties Fail* (Princeton: Princeton University Press, 1988).
2. Richard Rose, "Voting Behaviour in Britain, 1945–1974," in *Studies in British Politics,* ed. R. Rose (London: Macmillan, 1976), 204–15.
3. Sue Goss, *Local Labour and Local Government* (Edinburgh: Edinburgh University Press, 1988).
4. Michael Crick, *The March of Militant* (London: Faber, 1986).
5. Ivor Crewe, "Why Labour Lost the British Elections," *Public Opinion,* 1983, 7–9, 56–60. Also David Butler and Dennis Kavanagh, *The British General Election of 1983* (London: Macmillan, 1984).
6. Kinnock received 71 percent and Hattersley 67 percent of the votes cast in the electoral college.
7. Lewis Minkin, *The Contentious Alliance: Trade Unions and The Labour Party* (Edinburgh: Edinburgh University Press, 1992).
8. Michael Foot, *Another Heart and Other Pulses* (London: Collins, 1984), 160–61.
9. Minkin, *Contentious Alliance,* 597.
10. Jean Blondel, *Voters, Parties and Leaders* (Harmondsworth, Middlesex: Penguin Books, 1963).
11. Labour Party, *Conference Report* (London: Labour Party, 1983), 30.
12. Labour Party, *Conference Report* (London: Labour Party, 1987), 7.
13. *Guardian,* 16 February 1990.
14. Minkin, *Contentious Alliance,* 623.
15. Colin Hughes and Patrick Wintour, *Labour Rebuilt* (London: Fourth Estate, 1990), chap. 3.
16. Labour Party, *Conference Report,* 1987, 7.
17. The review groups were organised in such a way as to discuss the following: A Productive and Competitive Economy, People at Work, Economic Equality, Consumers and the Community, Democracy for the Individual and the Community, the Physical and Social Environment, and Britain in the World.
18. Hughes and Wintour, *Labour Rebuilt,* 102.
19. Ibid.; Minkin, *Contentious Alliance,* 465–67.
20. Hughes and Wintour, *Labour Rebuilt.*

21. Labour Party, *Meet the Challenge, Make the Change* (London: Labour Party, 1989), 10.
22. Ibid., 41.
23. Ibid., 54.
24. Ibid., 84.
25. Ibid., 85.
26. Minkin, *Contentious Alliance*, 468.
27. Labour Party, *Meet The Challenge*, 21.
28. Ibid., 25.
29. Minkin, *Contentious Alliance*, 623.
30. Labour Party, *Meet The Challenge*, 35.
31. Barry Jones and Michael Keating, *Labour and the British State* (Oxford: Clarendon Press, 1985).
32. Tony Benn, *Arguments for Democracy* (London: Cape, 1981).
33. Labour Party, *The Charter of Rights* (London: Labour Party, 1990).
34. Labour Party, *Conference Report* (London: Labour Party, 1989), 20.
35. Kinnock won 89 percent and Hattersley 67 percent of the electoral college votes.
36. Hughes and Wintour, *Labour Rebuilt*, 100.
37. Labour Party, *Conference Report*, 1989, 33.
38. William Paterson, "The German Social Democratic Party," in *Social Democratic Parties in Western Europe*, ed. W. Paterson and A. Thomas (London: Croom Helm, 1977), 176–212.
39. Stuart Holland, *The Socialist Challenge* (London: Quartet, 1975).
40. Noel Tracy, *The Origins of the Social Democratic Party* (London: Croom Helm, 1983).
41. Eric Heffer, *Labour's Future: Socialist or SDP Mark 2?* (London: Verso, 1986).
42. Bill Rodgers, *London Review of Books*, 7 February 1991.
43. Ben Pimlott, "When the Party's Over," *New Socialist* 1 (September/October 1981): 63–65.
44. Ivor Crewe, "The Policy Agenda," *Contemporary Record* 3 (February 1990): 2–7.
45. *Guardian*, 21 May 1990.
46. The extent to which Thatcherite values had been adopted within the country should not be exaggerated. See Ivor Crewe, "The Labour Party and the Electorate," in *The Politics of the Labour Party*, ed. D. Kavanagh (London: Allen and Unwin, 1982), 9–49; Ivor Crewe, "Has the Electorate Become Thatcherite?" in *Thatcherism*, ed. R. Skidelsky (London: Chatto and Windus, 1988), 25–50.
47. Roger Jowell, S. Witherspoon, and L. Brook, *British Social Attitudes: The 7th Report* (London: Gower, 1990), 1–26.
48. Roger Jowell and C. Airey, *British Social Attitudes: The 1984 Report* (London: Gower, 1984), 63; Roger Jowell, S. Witherspoon, and L. Brook, *British Social Attitudes: The 1986 Report* (London: Gower, 1986), 22, 28.
49. Patrick Seyd, *The Rise and Fall of the Labour Left* (London: Macmillan, 1987).
50. Robert McKenzie, *British Political Parties* (London: Mercury Books, 1964);

Robert McKenzie, "Power in the Labour Party: The Issue of Intra-Party Democracy," in Kavanagh, *Politics of the Labour Party,* 191–201.

51. Hughes and Wintour, *Labour Rebuilt,* 92.

52. Patrick Seyd and Paul Whiteley, *Labour's Grass Roots* (Oxford: Clarendon Press, 1992), chap. 2.

53. Minkin, *Contentious Alliance.*

54. Ibid., chap. 12.

55. Labour Party, *Democracy and Policy Making for the 1990s* (London: Labour Party, 1990), 2.

56. Eric Shaw, *Discipline and Discord in the Labour Party* (Manchester: Manchester University Press, 1988).

57. Ian Mikardo, "The Fateful, Hateful Fifties," *New Socialist* 4 (March/April 1982): 45–47.

58. Labour Party, *Rule Book 1990–91,* (London: Labour Party, 1991), 6.

59. Labour Party, *NEC Report 1990* (London: Labour Party, 1990), 12.

60. *Guardian,* 24 March 1990.

61. Seyd and Whiteley, *Labour's Grass Roots.*

62. Ibid., 160–69.

63. Patricia Hewitt, *Guardian,* 14 April 1992.

64. Seyd and Whiteley, *Labour's Grass Roots,* 89.

65. Ibid., chap. 8. Further research on the 1992 general election confirms this thesis. See Paul Whiteley and Patrick Seyd, "Local Activism and the Labour Vote," *Parliamentary Affairs,* forthcoming.

4

The Centre

David Denver

In the 1987 general election every constituency in Britain had a candidate representing either the Liberal party or the Social Democratic party (SDP). For the second successive election, the two parties offered a joint programme and campaigned together as "the Alliance." Five years later, in the 1992 general election, almost all constituencies were contested by the Liberal Democratic party, but there were also some candidates calling themselves Liberals and a few who stood as Social Democrats. This chapter is concerned with explaining this transformation. In order to understand the events of the years 1987 to 1992 and put them in context, however, it is necessary to review briefly the prior postwar history of the centre in British politics.[1]

The formation of the SDP in March 1981 appeared to herald a new era in centre politics. Throughout the postwar period the standard of the centre had been carried, somewhat unsteadily and erratically, by the Liberal party. At their lowest point, in the 1951 general election, the Liberals were reduced to just 2.5 percent of the vote and six seats in the House of Commons. In 1957–58 and 1962, however, there were midterm Liberal "revivals." Spectacular by-election results were achieved, significant gains were made in local elections, and the opinion polls recorded sharp increases in Liberal support. But in both cases the revivals were short lived. Support evaporated as the next general election approached, and a pattern of third-party surge and decline between elections appeared well established.

Another Liberal surge occurred in 1972–73 with, as before, major advances in by-elections and local elections and a marked increase in popularity in the polls. This time, however, at least partly as a result of the unexpectedly early calling of a general election, support did not evaporate; the Liberals won 19.3 percent of the vote and fourteen seats in the

February 1974 election, easily their best postwar performance. They slipped back only slightly (to 18.3 percent and thirteen seats) in the second 1974 general election. Between 1974 and 1979, however, the Liberals suffered from unsavoury publicity attaching to their leader, Jeremy Thorpe, and under David Steel (who was elected leader in the summer of 1976) they declined to 13.8 percent of the vote and eleven seats in the 1979 general election. The Liberals, it appeared, were doomed to the status of a near-fringe party, occasionally showing signs of life in the midterms of governments as disappointed government supporters sought an electoral outlet to register their discontent, but never achieving a major electoral breakthrough.

The Alliance

These unpromising prospects for the centre were transformed by the emergence of the SDP. Essentially the SDP was a product of the struggle between the left and the right in the Labour party, which reached new heights of bitterness and intensity in the late 1970s. The left, it appeared, was steadily gaining influence within the party. Left-wing policies were adopted by the party conference, "moderate" MPs were said to be threatened with dismissal by left-wing activists, and Labour's National Executive Committee came under the control of left-wingers. In 1980, the party conference was dominated by the left, and delegates voted in favour of withdrawal from the European Community and unilateral nuclear disarmament, among a series of other left-wing policies. In addition, the conference passed resolutions giving activists in constituencies where there was an incumbent Labour MP the automatic right to select a new Labour candidate between general elections and widening the franchise for electing the party leader, which had formerly been the prerogative of Labour MPs alone. These were two constitutional changes of far-reaching importance because they implied a fundamental shift of power within the Labour party from the parliamentary party, which was largely "moderate," to left-wing constituency activists.

Initially the leaders of the Labour right—and in particular the "Gang of Three" (David Owen, William Rodgers, and Shirley Williams) —were hostile to the the idea of forming a breakaway party. During 1980, however, the Gang of Three linked up with Roy Jenkins, a former Labour home secretary and chancellor of the exchequer, who had called for a realignment in British politics in an influential televised lecture, and this "Gang of Four" moved in a series of steps to launch a new party. For many on the right the election of Michael Foot, a hero of the left, as

Labour leader in November 1980 was the last straw, proving beyond doubt that Labour was beyond redemption.

The Liberals were now joined in the centre by a party offering novelty, apparent dynamism, a number of MPs, and experienced and high-profile leaders. At the time of its formation the SDP had fourteen MPs (thirteen having defected from Labour and one from the Conservatives), making it the third largest party in the House of Commons, and this number inched upwards, as a result of further Labour defections and two by-election victories, to thirty by March 1982. Within eight weeks of the spectacular launch of the new party, it had 52,000 members, and this rose to a peak of 78,000 in 1982.[2]

Among voters the initial impact of the SDP was dramatic. Just before it was founded, a series of opinion polls reported that support for a new social democratic party was running at between 23 and 31 percent of the voters. In part, this initial popularity was a matter of good luck, since the founding of the SDP coincided with a period of extreme unpopularity for both the Conservative government (and Prime Minister Margaret Thatcher) and the Labour opposition (and Michael Foot). Nonetheless, it was also clear that there was even greater public support for an alliance between the Liberals and the SDP than for the two parties separately. They quickly entered into negotiations and in June 1981 issued a joint statement entitled "A Fresh Start for Britain." This marked the formation of the Alliance, as the two parties together quickly came to be called. It began by asserting that "our two parties stem from different traditions and have their own identities," but it nonetheless included a commitment to an alliance "to avoid fighting each other in elections."[3]

The Alliance had an immediate and sensational impact on British politics. As soon as it was formed it went to first place in the opinion polls and stayed in that position until May 1982, peaking in December 1981 with 51 percent of voting intentions. Three consecutive by-elections were won between October 1981 and March 1982. Thereafter, support declined somewhat (largely because of the recovery in government support at the time of the Falklands War), but just before the 1983 general election the Alliance bounced back to win a very safe Labour seat (Bermondsey) in a by-election.

At one point during the 1983 general election campaign it appeared possible that the Alliance would overtake Labour in popular support—four separate polls put the Alliance in second place—but in the event it came third with 25.4 percent of the vote, only two points behind Labour. Due to the operation of the electoral system, however, and the fact that support for the Alliance was geographically relatively evenly spread, its reward for this performance was a meagre twenty-three seats (seventeen Liberal and six SDP) in the House of Commons. While the share of votes obtained was well in excess of the Liberals' best postwar performance, the Alliance had signally failed to "break the mould" of British politics. Immediately following the election, Roy Jenkins resigned as SDP leader and was replaced by David Owen.

Owen was much less favourably inclined towards the Liberals than Jenkins, despising their ramshackle institutional structure and what he perceived as their penchant for frivolous "protest politics" and their "softness" on defence policy. In Roy Jenkins's words, Owen "essentially regarded the Liberal Party as a disorderly group of bearded vegetarian pacifists,"[4] and Owen himself records that he believed that joining the Liberals in 1980–81 would have been like "jumping out of the frying pan into the cotton wool."[5] Relations between the SDP and the Liberals were also not helped by Owen's rather dismissive view of David Steel. He later wrote: "I never underestimated David Steel's manipulative skills; if they had been matched by an interest in the policies best suited to our country, he would have been a formidable politician."[6] Owen was convinced that a separate, independent centre-left party that was firmly social democratic in orientation was essential for achieving a realignment of British politics, since such a party would attract former Labour supporters who would never vote Liberal. Throughout his leadership of the SDP he consistently and abrasively sought to maintain the separateness of the SDP in organisation, policy, and style (demanding separate representation at the Cenotaph on Remembrance Day, for example) and resolutely opposed any form of convergence between the two Alliance parties. He was suspicious of having joint spokesmen in Parliament and of moves towards joint policy making and the joint selection of candidates, viewing these as attempts to achieve "merger by stealth."

The lengths to which David Owen was prepared to go in pursuit of his objectives became clear only during the moves towards merger after 1987. In the meantime, despite internal strains, the years between 1983 and 1987 were successful ones for the Alliance as compared with the centre's performance in previous interelection periods. Four constituencies were gained in by-elections (Portsmouth South in June 1984, Brecon and Radnor in July 1985, Ryedale in May 1986, Greenwich in February 1987). In addition, Truro was held with an increased majority in March 1987 after the death of a prominent and popular Liberal MP, David Penhaligon. In terms of the total votes cast in the sixteen by-elections held from 1983 to 1987 the Alliance was easily the largest party. Opinion polls, too, were good for the Alliance. For eleven of the thirteen months between May 1985 and May 1986 Gallup reported that it had more than 30 percent of voting intentions. And there was little sign of the normal preelection dip in support. In the first five months of 1987 the Alliance averaged just over 28 percent of voting intentions in Gallup polls.

As in 1983, however, the general election of June 1987 proved a disappointment. The Alliance share of the vote declined to 22.6 percent, and they won only twenty-two seats (seventeen Liberal and five SDP). Whereas the Alliance had appeared to be a much greater threat to the dominance of the two major parties than the Liberals alone had been, in the end it found itself in the same position. Alliance midterm support was consistently at a significantly higher level than the Liberals ever achieved, but midterm promise was not fulfilled in general elections. Gaining more than 20 percent of the votes was all very well—but in the House of Commons two-party dominance was not threatened, and the centre remained an insignificant minority. In retrospect, David Steel's call to Liberal delegates at their 1981 assembly to "go back to your constituencies and prepare for government" rang hollow.

From Alliance to Liberal Democrats

Despite the assertion in "A Fresh Start for Britain" that "our two parties stem from different traditions," the question of a merger between the Liberals and the SDP was never far from the political agenda once the Alliance had been formed. Indeed David Owen suggests that the SDP was regarded from the outset by Jenkins and his supporters as merely a staging post on the way to the formation of an enlarged centre party and that they constantly undermined the SDP's separate existence.[7] Jenkins flatly denies these charges, arguing that the idea of merger evolved gradually with the experience of the Alliance.[8] As early as September 1982, however, Owen himself began to fear that the way the Alliance was organised made merger inevitable, although he was determined to resist the proponents of merger, who wanted, he claims, an "amorphous amalgam" that would be "a cross between the Salvation Army and the Fabian Society."[9]

Nonetheless, a variety of practical arguments favoured merger. At the grassroots, "organic merger" was already taking place, with local Liberal and SDP parties and party groups in local councils cooperating closely. Moreover, maintaining two separate organisations each with its own headquarters was expensive and time-consuming. Much time was wasted in exhausting negotiations between the parties over matters such as the allocation of constituencies between the parties and the selection of candidates. Arrangements for joint policy making were cumbersome and gave rise to much friction, as well as to "Alliance Splits" headlines in the press. In 1984, for example, the Alliance was in turmoil over defence, with David Owen suggesting that it would be reasonable for the two parties to fight an election together each with its own distinctive defence policy. Defence again caused problems in 1986 when the Liberal Assembly passed a "unilateralist" motion, much to the annoyance of Owen and the SDP (as well as of David Steel). The system of joint leadership of the Alliance also did not work well. On the one hand, it provided too many opportunities for the leaders to be caught out making conflicting statements and, on the other, when the two leaders were in agreement—as at "Ask the Alliance" rallies during the 1987 election campaign—they seemed, according to David Steel, like Tweedledum and Tweedledee and "were both bored silly by listening to each other."[10] It did not help that Owen and Steel were "not bosom pals," while Steel found Owen "not the easiest person in the world to work with."[11] *The Times* commented in a leader in 1986: "The two-headed party is a stranger in the British political bestiary, and the animal appears the odder when the heads are snapping at each other."[12]

The failure, yet again, to make a breakthrough in the 1987 election was highly frustrating for Alliance supporters, and many blamed the dual leadership system. The Nuffield study of the 1987 election reports that there was almost universal agreement among Alliance candidates that dual leadership was a disaster.[13] But in his postelection analysis of Gallup data Ivor Crewe argues that this was not the main cause of the relative failure of the Alliance. Instead, he suggests, the fact that many voters believed that a vote for the Alliance was "wasted" (because it was clear that the Alliance could not come near to winning the election) accounted for the disappointing Alliance performance.[14] Even so, the problems of joint leadership were given by 16 percent of voters who switched from the Alliance as their reason for doing so, and the perception among many candidates and members of the Alliance parties was that the "two-headed beast" could not make further progress.

In any event, David Steel did not wait for any postelection analyses. As he was watching the election results on television, Steel, who had always favoured closer cooperation between the Liberals and the SDP, became convinced that there was no option but to seek a merger of the two parties. To his annoyance, however, David Owen gave a press conference the next day in which, while conceding that merger was a legitimate question for discussion, he made his own opposition clear. But other Alliance leaders, including Roy Jenkins, were publicly calling for a merger, and Steel issued a memorandum on the Tuesday following the election, 16 June, advocating "democratic fusion" of the Alliance partners. This call split the SDP leadership. Three of the original Gang of Four (Jenkins, Williams, and Rodgers) supported the idea of a merger, as did Alex McGivan, the national organiser, who resigned his position early in July in order to run a "Yes to Unity" campaign, and most leading figures in the party outside Parliament. In contrast, David Owen and his supporters (including all but Charles Kennedy among the SDP's MPs) were intensely hostile to a merger, arguing that Steel had attempted to "bounce" the SDP into a merger by unilaterally and publicly raising the issue so quickly after the general election. Steel himself disavowed any intention to "bounce" anyone and later claimed that to some extent a mix-up over telephone messages during the weekend after the election led to a misunderstanding on Owen's part.[15] It seems likely, however, that even if there had been no mix-up, Owen's attitude and subsequent behaviour would not have been altered.

The SDP National Committee met on 29 June and, after a bitter debate, agreed to put the question of the future relationship between the SDP and the Liberals to a postal ballot of the membership. The latter were to be asked whether they wanted the SDP leadership to negotiate (1) "a closer constitutional framework" short of merger or (2) a full merger of the two parties. The National Committee voted by eighteen to thirteen to recommend the first option. In a statement issued two days before the National Committee meeting, David Owen, having already abandoned the system of joint Alliance spokesmen in the House of Commons, asserted that he had "no intention of being persuaded to become a member of a merged party," and advocated an "amicable divorce" with the assets of the party being split proportionally between those who wished to join with the Liberals and those who wished to continue in the SDP.[16]

Chris Cook describes the subsequent debate within the SDP over the merger question, which was carried out in the full glare of publicity, as "both unedifying and vindictive, characterised by personal attacks and little constructive argument."[17] More succinctly, David Steel refers to "this summer bloodbath,"[18] and David Owen records bleakly "Civil war broke out,"[19] with the "Yes to Unity" campaign opposed by a "Vote for the SDP" campaign. According to Roy Jenkins, "bitterness and poison ... quickly came to flow along the divide.... Rarely, even in the voluminous history of family feuds, can there have been such unrelenting argument over the details of a will while the whole of the inheritance was manifestly being allowed to slip down the drain."[20] The bitterness of the debate was such that it ensured that there could not be an "amicable divorce" at the end of it.

The ballot result was announced on 6 August, and it showed that there were 25,897 votes in favour of merger (57.4 percent) and 19,228 against (42.6 percent). This was certainly not an overwhelming vote for merger and perhaps not even the "decisive result" that David Steel claims,[21] but it was at least a result, and it cleared the way for the next moves towards merger. Before any moves could be made, however, on the day after the result was declared, David Owen resigned as SDP leader.

It was widely assumed that Charles Kennedy, the only MP who had come out publicly in favour of merger, was heir-apparent to the leadership of the SDP, but on 15 August Kennedy announced that he was standing aside in favour of Robert Maclennan, the rather colourless MP for Caithness and Sutherland. The latter was not an enthusiast for merger, but he accepted the decision of the membership on the question, was duly nominated, and became leader of the party on 29 August 1987, the eve of the SDP conference at Portsmouth. According to the *Sunday Telegraph,* in a clever play on the Alliance's election slogan, he was "the ideal leader for a party whose time has gone."[22]

On 31 August the SDP conference voted decisively to confirm the ballot result and to enter into negotiations "to create a new party incorporating the SDP and the Liberal Party." It authorised the National Committee to set up a negotiating team. The conference also agreed that whatever was decided would be the policy of the whole party. This meant that the minority that opposed merger would not have the right to continue as the SDP; all the assets of the party would be transferred to the new party. During the conference, Owen spoke at a well-attended fringe meeting organised by opponents of merger, the "Owenites," to launch the Campaign for Social Democracy (CSD), which was to provide an organisational framework for diehard antimergerites. At this stage, however, although Peter Jenkins, the respected political columnist of the *Guardian,* criticised him for embarking on "the politics of sectarian fantasy,"[23] Owen was still uncertain whether the CSD could form the basis of a continuing SDP.

The Liberal Assembly began at Harrogate on 14 September, and here the atmosphere was very different. Delegates were enthusiastic for merger, and on 17 September they voted overwhelmingly (998 to 21) to begin merger talks. The composition of the Liberal negotiating team was also determined. In addition to the leading party officers and Welsh and Scottish representatives, the team was to include eight members elected by the Assembly (who were duly elected after a good deal of politicking by groups and individuals on behalf of the thirty-eight candidates nominated for the eight available positions). Steel was not happy at the outcome. He suspected (correctly, as it turned out) that a negotiating team comprising a total of seventeen people was too large and unmanageable and that some of those elected by the Assembly "were incapable of sighting new party horizons, and arrived at our first meetings determined to preserve all that was Liberal, bad as well as good."[24]

MERGER NEGOTIATIONS

The first joint meeting of the two negotiating teams took place on 29 September 1987. A detailed account of the negotiations and of discussions among the Liberals has been provided by two members of the Liberal team, Rachael Pitchford and Tony Greaves.[25] Their account is frankly partisan—both were "grassroots" Liberal radicals who had a lengthy history of antagonism towards David Steel's leadership. Indeed both, one would guess, were precisely the sort of people Steel had in mind in the comment quoted in the previous paragraph. Nonetheless, Alan Beith, a frontbench Liberal spokesman and a negotiator, concedes that their version of events is "generally reliable" up to the point when the authors resigned from the team in the following January.[26]

The main reaction that Pitchford and Greaves's blow-by-blow account elicits from the reader is one of sympathy for David Steel's *cri de coeur*: "We got hopelessly bogged down in specific points of detail, hour after weary hour, week after dreary week."[27] Even Greaves and Pitchford recognise that the negotiations often proved difficult "over a myriad of obscure issues that no-one outside the parties would begin to understand. It all seemed bogged down in details, personalities and fatigue."[28] The participants were regularly in meetings from early morning till after midnight, often in hot, stuffy rooms. They had to attend not only joint negotiating meetings but meetings of their own teams, meetings in subgroups set up to discuss specific topics, and consultative meetings with party members around the country, as well as attending to the normal business of being an MP, councillor, husband, wife, father, or mother. Not unexpectedly, the whole process involved great strain on those involved. The meetings were often fractious and fraught, and on several occasions the negotiations appeared to be on the point of breaking down.

Many of the "obscure issues" that bogged down the discussions involved the new party's constitutional structure. These disputes reflected the different constitutional traditions of the two parties. On the one hand, the constitution of the SDP, which had been drafted by Robert Maclennan, was largely a product of the recent (in 1981) experience of the SDP leadership within the Labour party. In their view, power in the Labour party had passed to unrepresentative and "extremist" activists, and the SDP's constitution had been specifically designed to avoid this. SDP leaders regarded the Liberal constitution as chaotic, were wary of the "sovereignty" of the Assembly—remembering especially the 1986 "unilateralist" vote—and were determined to retain as many elements of their own constitution as possible. On the other hand, some Liberal negotiators regarded the SDP's structure as centralised, oligarchical, and authoritarian. They were keen to retain a decentralised structure, constrain the leadership, and keep a powerful Assembly. (This view, it may be noted, was not shared by David Steel, who frequently had a stormy relationship with Liberal activists.)

Among the constitutional issues that wore out the negotiators were whether the annual policy-making meeting of local party delegates should be called an "Assembly" or a "Conference," the size and role of the conference (as it was eventually called), federal arrangements involving Scotland and Wales, the use of membership ballots, special arrangements for women and youth sections, the role of full-time staff, the composition of party committees, whether there should be a deputy leader, and many others. There was even "an unbelievably lengthy discussion about the minimum allowable size for a local party."[29]

The second major area that caused problems was the preamble to the constitution. Both teams agreed that there should be a general statement of principles attaching to the constitution, and early in the negotiations four people were deputed to write it: Michael Meadowcroft and Richard Holme for the Liberals and John Grant and David Marquand for the SDP. The main question at issue was whether the preamble should contain a commitment to NATO. Such a commitment was contained in the SDP constitution, and given the perception that the Liberals were "soft" on defence, the SDP was determined that a similar statement should be included in the preamble to the new constitution. This offended some strands of Liberal opinion, however, and was thought by many to be a statement of current policy rather than of enduring principle, which therefore should not be enshrined in the constitution. At a meeting of the Liberal Council on 21 November the draft preamble was strongly criticised, but the group that had written it was unwilling to attempt a redraft. After much to-ing and fro-ing, a final version, including the NATO commitment, was agreed on between Tony Greaves and Shirley Williams and was accepted by the joint meeting of the two teams on 15 December.

Another contentious matter was the new party's name. This was clearly a very delicate and important matter, since the overwhelming majority of the electorate would know nothing of the party's constitutional arrangements but all would become well aware of its name. The problem was to devise a name that would be electorally appealing, would give some indication of what the party stood for, and would satisfy activists with strong attachments to their different traditions. The simple solution of calling the new party "the Alliance" was ruled out as not meeting the last two criteria, despite the fact that this name had previously served rather well and had been successfully embedded in the public's consciousness at the 1983 and 1987 general elections.

The Liberal team proposed that the merged party should be called "The Liberal and Social Democratic Party," while the SDP team favoured "The New Social and Liberal Democratic Party" with the short title "Democrats." For some time there was deadlock on this issue. The SDP pointed out that the Liberal proposal resulted in the unfortunate acronym LSD and would end up being shortened simply to "Liberals." For their part, the Liberals refused to countenance any short title that did not contain the word "Liberal." Numerous other combinations and alternatives were suggested—Maclennan is reported to have considered "Reformers," "Radicals," and "Liberators,"[30] but was surely joking—but agreement was elusive, and this was one of the issues that nearly resulted in the breakdown of the talks on 8 and 9 December. In the end, the 15 December meeting compromised on a hopelessly tortuous title for the new party: "The New Liberal and Social Democratic Party, which may be known as the Alliance."

On a final contentious issue, no agreement was reached before the draft constitution of the new party was published on 18 December. This was the question of a policy prospectus or declaration. The initiative for such a declaration came from the SDP, who argued that it was needed to emphasise the newness of the party, to give a fillip to its launch, and to reassure SDP members who had left the Labour party over policy disagreements that the new party would be true to the SDP's original ideals. Liberals were originally hesitant about issuing such a statement, arguing that it was not part of their brief to become involved in policy matters, but they gradually came around to the idea. There was interminable discussion, however, over how the policy statement should be drawn up, what its status would be, and what it should contain. At one point there was a lengthy argument over whether the document should "draw on" or "have regard to" previous statements of Alliance policy![31] Alan Beith and Robert Maclennan were left to sort matters out, but little progress was made before 18 December.

When the draft constitution was published, press reaction was generally favourable. The *Guardian,* for example, commented that it "represents a sizeable shift towards the sort of political realism which most voters seem to respect. . . . The Alliance's negotiators look to have done a solid, sensible job."[32] But the birth pangs of the Liberal Democrats were far from over. The new structures had still to be accepted by the membership of the Alliance parties, and the policy statement had still to appear.

FINAL NEGOTIATIONS AND THE "DEAD PARROT"

David Steel's problems began immediately. The Liberal Council, which had an advisory role within the party and about which Steel was always scathing, met in Northampton on 19 December. Delegates condemned the choice of name for the merged party (and held a series of straw votes on a variety of alternatives), voted for the deletion of the NATO reference from the preamble, and criticised various aspects of the organisational arrangements. A motion in favour of merger in principle was easily passed, but even so the meeting represented a rebuff for Steel; and opponents of merger claimed that its criticisms reflected grassroots opinion among Liberals. Steel characteristically dismissed the proceedings contemptuously, however, commenting later, "Needless to say, they passed some motion demanding changes in the negotiations."[33]

There had been divisions on the Liberal side throughout the merger negotiations, between promerger enthusiasts on the one hand and a minority of radicals on the other. Meadowcroft, Greaves, and Pitchford had minuted notes of dissent to the agreement reached on 15 December. In the last two negotiating meetings, however, there was an open split. These were held on 5 and 12 January 1988 and were extremely tense and emotional. Various amendments were made to the constitutional arrangements, the preamble was tidied up but the NATO commitment left intact (although obscure changes were made to the provisions for party membership to try to assuage Liberal sensibilities on this issue), and the party's name was altered to "The Social and Liberal Democrats" (with no short title). Meadowcroft resigned from the Liberal team on the NATO issue and Greaves, Pitchford, and Peter Knowlson on the question of the name. While all this was going on, attempts were being made to finalise the policy declaration.

According to Chris Cook, the events surrounding the launch of the SLD's policy proposals "came close to reducing the entire centre stage of British politics to a pantomime farce."[34] The *Guardian* commented that "fiasco is too mild a word," while Hugo Young in the same paper described the events as "an act of Kamikaze politics.... Neither [Steel or Maclennan] on this showing, is fit to run a whelk stall."[35] For David Steel, it was "a bizarre episode," which he put down largely to shortage of time and tiredness while accepting that the attempt to go beyond a statement of existing policies was a serious error.[36]

The first discussions on the content of the policy statement had been held at David Steel's home on 22 December between Steel, Beith, Maclennan, and the latter's two assistants. According to Greaves, these assistants were sympathetic to radical right ideas. Apparently only general principles were considered, and immediately after the meeting Maclennan went off on a visit to the United States. By the time he returned, Steel was on a visit to Africa. A draft had been prepared, however, and this was left with Alan Beith. It was a second redraft of the document that had to be finalised for presentation to a press conference that had already been called for noon on Wednesday, 13 January.

At 3:00 P.M. on the day before the press conference, the document was seen by the Liberal negotiating team, and it produced astonishment and dismay. Among the policies proposed were an end to universal child benefit; the phasing out of mortgage tax relief; firm support for the Trident nuclear missile system; and the extension of VAT to food, children's clothing, domestic fuel, and newspapers. The members of the Liberal party's policy committee met at 6:00 P.M. and were likewise horrified by the contents of the document. Des Wilson, past president of the party, described them as "a gratuitous insult" and wrote an open letter to Steel describing the document as "barely literate" and "politically inept."[37]

Under a storm of criticism, Steel, Maclennan, and others worked through the night until 5:00 A.M. to try to improve the document, now entitled "Voices and Choices for All," but at 10:00 A.M. the Liberal chief whip informed Steel that MPs were in open rebellion over it. The Liberal party president urged him to call off the press conference and convened a special meeting of the party's national executive for that evening. After all the efforts of the negotiating teams, the merger seemed doomed. Steel considered resigning as party leader but agreed with Maclennan to go ahead with the launch of the policy prospectus provided it was postponed to 5:00 P.M., so that they could both meet with MPs at 2:00 P.M. To complicate matters, any opportunity to make significant last-minute amendments to the document was lost when copies were inadvertently distributed to members of the press who had gathered for the scheduled noon press conference.

The meeting between the two leaders and their MPs was tense and gloomy and the discussion anguished, according to Steel, with Maclennan at one point "sobbing uncontrollably," according to Greaves.[38] In the end, however, it was decided that there was nothing for it but to go ahead with the press conference, even if all that could be done was to stall for time. Backed by silent and grim-faced MPs, the two leaders simply announced at the press conference that there would be a pause in the negotiations to allow a few days for reflection. Later that evening, the Liberal National Executive voted to abandon the policy declaration but to continue negotiations. The final nail in the coffin of the policy document came when it was referred to in a television broadcast, in the terms of the famous Monty Python sketch, as a "dead parrot," although it is unclear whether David Steel or Des Wilson was first to use the phrase.

FINAL STEPS TO MERGER

The "dead parrot" having been buried, it was obvious that something had to be done to rescue the merger. And it had to be done quickly because a special Liberal Assembly had been arranged for 23 January to make a final decision on merger—just ten days after the disastrous press conference. On the day after, 14 January, a new six-man team was formed and given the task of producing an acceptable policy statement. The six were Des Wilson, Jim Wallace, and Alan Leaman from the Liberals and Edmund Dell, Tom McNally, and David Marquand from the SDP. By the following Sunday they had produced a document ("A Democracy of Conscience") that was a synthesis of existing Alliance policies. This was accepted with relief by the MPs on Monday, 18 January, and later that day by the joint negotiating meeting. There was a final twist in the tail, however. Having agreed on the final deal at about 10:00 P.M., Robert Maclennan made a highly publicised "dash to Limehouse" to see David Owen, apparently to ask the latter to join the new party. Owen thought that this was simply a cheap publicity stunt and sent Maclennan (and Kennedy, who accompanied him) packing after a five-minute dressing down.

Attention now turned to the Liberal Assembly to be held in Blackpool. From early January, promerger Liberals, in particular the chief whip Jim Wallace, had organised a "Merger Now" campaign that sought to mobilise support for the package among party members. This determined effort to avoid any humiliation of the leadership at the hands of the radicals paid off handsomely. Although there were last-minute attempts to organise the antimerger vote (through "I'm Staying Liberal" and "No to Merger, Yes to Liberalism" campaigns), the merger resolution was passed by a huge majority: 2009 votes to 385. This was a triumph for David Steel, and the size of the majority tends to vindicate his view that many of the problems of the merger negotiations were caused by an unrepresentative minority within the Liberal team.

A week later, the SDP's Council for Social Democracy met at Sheffield and after a bad-tempered debate passed the merger motion by 273 to 28. Owen had consistently refused to try to block the merger—on the sensible grounds that there was no point in trying to keep people in one political party when they wanted to belong to another—and did not speak in or even attend the debate. He recommended his supporters to abstain in the vote and in the subsequent membership ballot, and he claimed a moral victory when only 57 percent of the 480 people eligible to vote at the Council actually voted for merger. Whatever the moral situation, however, the fact was that the decision effectively ended the separate existence of the SDP.

The last act in the merger process came when the results of the membership ballots were announced on 2 March. They were as follows:[39]

	Liberals	*SDP*
Members	101,084	52,086
For merger	46,376 (87.9%)	18,722 (65.3%)
Against merger	6,365 (12.1%)	9,929 (34.7%)
Did not vote	48,217	23,178

NOTE: The differences between the number of members and the totals of the three categories shown reflects people who voted but spoiled their ballots.

The various protagonists made their own interpretations of these results. Steel was "very heartened," Shirley Williams declared them a "ringing confirmation" of merger, while Owen suggested that the "merger or bust" campaign had alienated about two-thirds of the SDP's members.

On 3 March 1988 the Social and Liberal Democratic party was officially launched, with David Steel and Robert Maclennan as interim joint leaders. They presented a new party logo and claimed nineteen MPs, 3500 local councillors, and 100,000 members. The road to merger had been a rocky one, however, and the acrimony surrounding the formation of the new party did not augur well for its immediate prospects. While the leadership of the SLD hoped that it would quickly come to be recognised as the sole vehicle for centre politics in Britain, they had first to contend with confusion among the electorate arising out of the continued existence of the "Owenite" SDP and a separate Liberal party.

The "Continuing SDP" and the Liberal Party

Although David Owen was determined to keep the SDP going as a parliamentary party (consisting of himself, John Cartwright, and Rosie Barnes), he was initially hesitant about whether it was viable as a genuine national party, describing himself as a "reluctant recruit" to the idea.[40] By early 1988, however, the Campaign for Social Democracy claimed 15,000 members and had set up a small national office. At the time of the ballot on merger, a membership of 30,000 was claimed, and on 8 March the "continuing SDP" was formally reestablished with the original SDP constitution. But the continuing SDP was short lived. Apart from the Richmond by-election in February 1989, when a very good second place was achieved (see table 4.2), the story was one of steady decline. In May 1989 it was discovered that membership claims had been exaggerated and that there were in fact only 11,000 members; the local election results that month confirmed that the SDP was virtually nonexistent on local councils. An emergency meeting of the National Committee agreed to cut down the SDP's operations, but although the party struggled on for another year and held the last-ever SDP conference at Scarborough in September 1989, the writing was now clearly on the wall. Membership declined further at the start of 1990, and the final humiliation came in the Bootle by-election towards the end of May. The SDP candidate obtained only 155 votes, coming sixth behind the Green Party, a Liberal, and the Monster Raving Loony candidate, David ("Screaming Lord") Sutch. This was the end of the road for the continuing SDP. The National Committee met on 3 June and voted to suspend the operation of the constitution, close the party headquarters, and place its affairs in the hands of trustees. A few enthusiasts kept the Campaign for Social Democracy in existence, but by the end of 1990 it had only about 1000 names on its mailing list.[41] Before the 1992 general election, David Owen announced his decision not to seek reelection, and in the election itself the two remaining Social Democrat MPs, Rosie Barnes and John Cartwright, were to lose their seats, despite the fact that the Liberal Democrats did not put up candidates against them.

The continuing Liberals were a little slower off the mark than the Owenites, but they have proven somewhat more resilient. A meeting of about 300 Liberals opposed to merger with the SDP was held at the Liberal Assembly in January 1988, but it was not until March 1989 that the Liberal party was relaunched at a meeting of dissidents organised by Michael Meadowcroft. In the following October there was a party Assembly at Buxton at which it was agreed to elect a national executive committee, establish a national office, and restart publication of *Liberal News*. Unfortunately for the Liberals, at the time of their meeting the national press was full of reports of the resignation of the chancellor of the exchequer, Nigel Lawson, and they received little publicity. In October 1990, however, a full-time secretary general was appointed, although *Liberal News* reported that there were no bookings for the day-care centre at the party Assembly, which was held in Torquay.[42]

During 1990, the continuing Liberals fielded candidates in five parliamentary by-elections, but their performance was uniformly disastrous (see table 4.2). At the 1991 local elections, 132 seats were contested and 18 were won (out of about 11,000). The resilience of the Liberals was demonstrated, however, by the fact that they put forward 73 candidates in the general election in 1992. The best performance was achieved by Michael Meadowcroft, who obtained 3980 votes (8.3 percent) in his old seat of Leeds West, but in total the Liberals gained only 64,724 votes.

There must be some doubt as to whether the separate Liberal party can remain viable following this debacle (all general election candidates except Meadowcroft lost their deposits). Indeed, exactly how the Liberals have been able to sustain an office, employ a full-time official, and publish *Liberal News* ten times a year since 1989 is itself something of a mystery. It seems likely that the party will fade away as its enthusiasts drift back to the Liberal Democrats or quit politics altogether.

The Liberal Democrats 1988–91

In March 1988 the SLD (as it still was called at that point) had a number of urgent tasks. Membership had to be built up, the organisational structure made to work, and various holdovers from the merger negotiations attended to—including the preamble to the constitution and the party's name, which were still controversial among party members. More important, the party had to establish itself as *the* party of the centre in British politics and, as part of that effort, to resolve the question of leadership.

The first leadership election was held in the summer of 1988. Both David Steel and Robert Maclennan decided not to run—wisely, in view of the "dead parrot" affair—and the contest was between Paddy Ashdown and Alan Beith. Ashdown had been elected to the House of Commons only in 1983 and was not a nationally known politician. Within the Liberal party, however, the Chinese-speaking former marine commando had impressed successive assemblies with his dash, dynamism, and flair. In the leadership contest, while Beith was widely regarded as a "safe" candidate representing traditional Liberalism, Ashdown was perceived as a forward-looking and adventurous politician who would be attractive to voters, and he won easily. The result, announced on 28 July, showed that Ashdown obtained 41,401 votes to Beith's 16,201. The fact that under 58,000 ballots were cast in this election is indicative of the low membership of the party and the poor state of morale among members.

As far as membership was concerned, early omens were discouraging. Only about 78,000 people joined the new party—a far smaller total than the previous joint total of the Liberals and the SDP. Greaves and Pitchford assert that half of the Liberal membership did not join,[43] while survey evidence suggests that only 38 percent of former SDP members transferred to the SLD (with 21 percent staying with the Owenites and 41 percent refusing to join either party). Among those who had voted for the merger, two-thirds subsequently joined the SLD, but among those who had voted against or abstained, only 7 percent did so.[44]

Recruitment continued to be sluggish. At the September 1989 conference a membership of 82,000 was reported (although some speakers claimed that it was actually as low as 51,000), and renewals of membership were said to have virtually dried up following the party's poor performance in the European elections in July.[45] As a result, the financial position was precarious, and there had to be cutbacks among area agents and headquarters staff. By the spring of 1990, however, membership had slightly increased to 85,000, and party officials suggested that the trend in renewals was encouraging. Membership continued to improve during 1991 as the Liberal Democrats' popularity among the electorate increased, and by the end of the year memberships stood at about 92,000. This was still smaller than what might have been hoped for at the time of the merger, but at least it was on an upward trend.

For a time, the party's inability to agree on its name gave rise to much adverse publicity, becoming a standing joke in the media and in everyday conversation. It had been launched as the Social and Liberal Democratic party, but the 1988 conference voted to encourage the use of the short title "Democrats" and to allow local associations to call themselves more or less what they wanted. The parliamentary party was to use the full title but, with eight MPs insisting on referring to themselves as Liberal Democrats, confusion continued to reign. To resolve the issue, a ballot of the membership was held in the autumn of 1989 and the name "Liberal Democrats" proved to be the most popular. According to Paddy Ashdown, this result "ended the days of 'alphabet soup' when nobody could tell the difference between the SLD, the SDP and the SNP."[46]

SUPPORT AMONG VOTERS

There are three main sources for charting the popularity of parties between general elections: the annual rounds of local elections, regular monthly opinion polls, and parliamentary by-elections. All three sources tell a similar tale about the trend in Liberal Democrat support after 1988. A long period of decline and stagnation followed the launch of the party, and this began to be reversed only in the first half of 1991.

Table 4.1 summarises the Liberal Democrats' local election performances in this period. From 1988 to 1990 they sustained considerable losses and had no alternative but to grit their teeth and hang on in the hope that things would improve. The improvement came in 1991, when all English and Welsh district councils had elections, and the scale of Liberal Democrat successes surprised many commentators and even the Liberal Democrats themselves. They ended up in control of nineteen councils and were the largest party in a further twenty-two—a much stronger position in local government than had ever been achieved by the old Liberal party. Paddy Ashdown described their performance as "a stunning achievement," while a *Guardian* headline—"Lib-Dems hit the jackpot" —summed up the reaction of the press.[47] There is no doubt that electoral success at the local level is immensely heartening for party activists and supporters, and coming as they did at the end of a long lean period, the 1991 local election results were doubly pleasurable for Liberal Democrats. In the past, however, centre parties have frequently been unable to convert strength in local government into votes in general elections, and despite the increased strength of the Liberal Democrats at local levels (they currently hold about 3600 council seats over the country as a whole), it seems unlikely that they will ever be able to break this pattern.

TABLE 4.1

GAINS AND LOSSES OF SEATS BY LIBERAL DEMOCRATS
IN LOCAL ELECTIONS, 1988–91

Year	Gains	Losses	Net
1988	96	169	−73
1989	86	192	−106
1990	152	193	−41
1991	762	233	+529

SOURCES: Ivor Crewe, Pippa Norris, David Denver, and David Broughton, *British Elections and Parties Yearbook 1991* (Hemel Hempstead: Harvester Wheatsheaf, 1992); and Ivor Crewe, Pippa Norris, David Denver, and David Broughton, *British Elections and Parties Yearbook 1992* (Hemel Hempstead: Harvester Wheatsheaf, 1992).

NOTE: Since the various local authorities have different election cycles, the numbers of seats won and lost are not directly comparable from year to year. Nonetheless, the overall performance of a party in local elections in any one year is widely interpreted as an indicator of its standing among the electorate.

Parliamentary by-elections are now major political events in the lifetime of a government—at least as far as the media and the parties themselves are concerned—and there is a long tradition of third (and fourth) parties achieving spectacular results in them. The various Liberal "revivals" referred to earlier were all sparked off in part by good by-election performances, and by-elections were also important in the early progress of the SDP. The media attention given to by-elections provides a major opportunity for smaller parties to gain publicity, and good results help sustain the morale of party members. After 1988, however, the Liberal Democrats had additional reasons for wanting to do well in by-elections. The damage done to their reputation by the merger battles had to be repaired, and they desperately needed to crush the continuing SDP and Liberal party in these contests in order to demonstrate that these were marginal fringe groups and to justify their claim to be the sole credible party of the centre. This latter objective was achieved within two years.

Table 4.2 shows the share of the vote obtained by the Liberal Democrats, the Liberals, and the SDP in by-elections from 1988 to 1991 as compared with the Alliance share in the 1987 general election. As can be seen, the Liberal Democrats outpolled the SDP in all the early by-elections with the exception of Richmond (where the SDP candidate was a popular local figure). The *coup de grace* was administered in Mid Staffordshire and Bootle. Thereafter, with the continuing Liberals receiving insignificant shares of the votes, the situation was much clearer, and the Liberal Democrats were firmly established as the vehicle for normal midterm centre support.

This was not achieved without cost, however. The Epping Forest and Richmond seats were there for the taking, as it were, and in normal times they would almost certainly have been gained by the Liberal Democrats. Perhaps the only comfort was that the by-election fights between the former Alliance partners occurred early in the Parliament and left plenty of time for the Liberal Democrats to consolidate their position. Even so, by-election results in 1990 and 1991 were patchy. Three seats were gained in the old style, but elsewhere there were few staggering advances. In part this was simply bad luck. Seats such as Paisley North and South, Bootle, Bradford North, and Hemsworth are simply not the kinds of seats in which the Liberal Democrats would hope to do well, while Monmouth and Langbaurgh were two-party marginals in which the Liberal Democrat vote was almost bound to be squeezed. While the last set of by-elections of the 1987–92 Parliament ended on a high note for the Liberal Democrats with victory in Kincardine and Deeside, the party's overall by-election performance did not compare well with the previous performance of the Alliance. In the thirteen by-elections after Bootle (in May 1990), the average change in the Liberal Democrat share of the vote as compared with the 1987 election was 4 percent. This was a much smaller advance than the average of 25.9 percent achieved by the Alli-

TABLE 4.2

SHARES OF VOTES OBTAINED BY LIBERAL DEMOCRATS, SDP,
AND THE LIBERAL PARTY IN PARLIAMENTARY
BY-ELECTIONS, 1988–91

Date	Constituency	Alliance 1987	By-election shares Lib. Dem.	SDP	Lib.
14 Jul 88	Kensington	17.2%	10.8%	5.0%	—%
10 Nov 88	Glasgow Govan	12.3	4.1	—	—
15 Dec 88	Epping Forest	19.4	26.0	12.2	—
23 Feb 89	Pontypridd	18.9	3.9	3.1	—
23 Feb 89	Richmond (Yorks)	27.0	22.0	32.2	.1
4 Apr 89	Vale of Glamorgan	16.7	4.2	2.3	—
15 Jun 89	Glasgow Central	10.5	1.5	1.0	—
15 Jun 89	Vauxhall	18.2	17.5	—	—
22 Mar 90	Mid Staffordshire	23.2	11.2	2.5	—
24 May 90	Bootle	13.0	9.0	.4	1.3
27 Sep 90	Knowsley South	13.9	8.5	—	3.0
18 Oct 90	Eastbourne	29.7	*50.8	—	1.1
8 Nov 90	Bootle	13.0	7.9	—	.0
15 Nov 90	Bradford North	17.7	25.3	—	.5
29 Nov 90	Paisley North	15.8	8.3	—	—
29 Nov 90	Paisley South	15.1	9.8	—	—
7 Mar 91	Ribble Valley	21.4	*48.5	—	.3
4 Apr 91	Neath	14.1	5.8	—	—
16 May 91	Monmouth	24.0	24.7	—	—
4 Jul 91	Liverpool Walton	21.2	36.0	—	—
7 Nov 91	Langbaurgh	19.9	16.1	—	—
7 Nov 91	Kincardine and Deeside	36.3	*49.0	—	—
7 Nov 91	Hemsworth	17.2	20.1	—	—

NOTE: * = seat gained.

ance in thirteen by-elections between 1981 and 1983 and of 12.2 percent in the sixteen by-elections of the 1983–87 Parliament.

Much the most reliable indicators of trends in party support in Britain, however, are the monthly opinion polls. The problem for the analyst is that there are now so many polls that, for the sake of clarity, some way of summarising their results has to be used. The end-of-month averages produced by the *Guardian* provide a convenient way of doing this; and, using these data, table 4.3 (p. 124) shows the monthly share of voting intentions obtained by the centre parties from July 1987 to December 1991.

The figures in the first part of the table indicate that support for the Alliance declined quickly after the 1987 election. This decline was quicker and steeper than that experienced by the Alliance after the 1983 election. Indeed, between October 1987 and February 1988, when merger negotiations were under way and Alliance support hovered between 13 and 15 percent, the Alliance's position in the polls was worse than in any month between the 1983 and 1987 general elections. The disputes over the merger demonstrated that internal divisions, personal animosities, and public mud-slinging were not confined to the major parties, and this was a grave disappointment to many who had voted for the Alliance in 1987 in the hope of something better. As a result, the popularity of the centre parties was seriously dented, and the launch of the SLD—unlike that of the SDP seven years previously—took place in circumstances in which its electoral prospects appeared bleak.

The second part of the table relates to the period when the Liberal Democrats had to contend with the continued existence of the SDP. Both parties suffered badly with the SDP, in particular, falling to derisory levels. In the middle of this period, in June 1989, the Liberal Democrats were humiliated in the elections to the European Parliament, obtaining only 6.4 percent of the vote, less than half that obtained by the Green party. This was the worst performance by the centre in a nationwide election since 1959, and it prompted Paddy Ashdown to write to his constituency parties insisting that they were on the right track and encouraging members to hold their nerve. A good deal of nerve was required, for this was an extremely low point in the short life of the party. By this time it might have been hoped that the electorate would have forgotten or forgiven the ructions over the merger, but the new party faced other problems in trying to increase its electoral appeal. Between 1983 and 1987, the personal popularity of David Steel and David Owen had attracted voters to the Alliance. This support was now lost, and Ashdown was having little impact on the electorate. In addition, some long-time Liberal voters found it difficult to transfer their affections to the SLD; those who had flocked to the SDP in the heady early days of its existence were thoroughly disillusioned; and the general public were simply bemused by the splits and name changes among the centre parties. During a gloomy conference in September 1989, a *Times* leader referred to "whispers of slow extinction in the wings" and reported that "it is not just the death of a political party that is being predicted but that of the ever-fluctuating 'third force' in British politics."[48]

The Liberal Democrats remained in the electoral doldrums for more than a year, but after the SDP departed from the political scene, things improved a little. From September to November 1991, their support in the polls reached double figures for the first time. This probably reflected the unpopularity of Margaret Thatcher and her government and the effect of a spectacular by-election success in Eastbourne (see table 4.2). But John Major replaced Thatcher as prime minister at the end of November, and support for the Liberal Democrats declined again. In March 1991, however, there was a sharp increase in support, to 16 percent of voting intentions, and the party remained at about this level for the rest of the year. The most likely reason for this sudden improvement is that Paddy Ashdown received a great deal of exposure on television in January and February during the Gulf War and was widely perceived as having been impressive. Even so, the Liberal Democrats appeared to be anchored at a level of support that was well below that achieved by the Alliance in previous interelection periods, and was significantly lower than the share of votes obtained in the 1987 election.

The suggestion that the sudden jump in the popularity of the Liberal Democrats early in 1991 was at least in part an effect of an increase in Ashdown's personal popularity is supported by the data in table 4.4. This table shows his personal ratings in the Gallup poll from August 1988 to December 1991. As can be seen, the electorate's perception of the party leader were initially broadly neutral, with large proportions having no opinion. During 1989 and most of 1990, with "don't know"s having declined to around a third of the electorate, his net ratings were substantially negative. In September 1990, however, he began to achieve net positive ratings and improved steadily in the public's estimation from +13 in December 1990 to +15 in January 1991, +21 in February, and +31 in March. For the rest of the year, with "don't know"s now running at around one-fifth of the electorate, Ashdown's personal rating only once fell below +30. These trends follow closely the trend in the Liberal Democrats' share of voting intentions. There is, in fact, a simple correlation of +.92 between the monthly percentage of voting intentions obtained by the Liberal Democrats and Ashdown's net monthly rating from August 1988 to December 1991 (41 observations).

There is, of course, a problem in distinguishing cause and effect here. It could be that Ashdown's personal popularity rose and fell because the more general popularity of his party was rising and falling. The more plausible interpretation of the data is that it was the personal popularity of Ashdown that affected the general standing of the party. While this reflects well on the party leader, the problem for the Liberal Democrats is that a leader's popularity is a shaky base on which to build support. Party leaders sometimes fall from grace, and all leaders retire eventually. To be electorally successful, parties require more than a popular leader.

TABLE 4.3
GUARDIAN END-OF-MONTH AVERAGES FOR ALLIANCE /
LIBERAL DEMOCRAT / SDP SHARE OF
VOTING INTENTIONS, 1987–91

Alliance		Liberal Democrats and SDP			Liberal Democrats	
			Lib. Dem.	SDP		
1987		1988			1990	
July	19%	March	9%	5%	July	9%
August	17	April	8	5	August	8
September	15	May	8	5	September	12
October	13	June	8	4	October	14
November	14	July	9	5	November	10
December	15	August	9	5	December	9
1988		September	9	4	1991	
January	15	October	9	5	January	9
February	13	November	9	5	February	9
		December	8	6	March	16
		1989			April	14
		January	9	4	May	16
		February	9	7	June	15
		March	7	6	July	14
		April	9	6	August	13
		May	7	3	September	15
		June	6	3	October	13
		July	5	3	November	15
		August	6	2	December	13
		September	6	3		
		October	6	2		
		November	6	3		
		December	6	3		
		1990				
		January	5	3		
		February	6	3		
		March	6	3		
		April	7	3		
		May	7	2		
		June	7	2		

SOURCE: *Guardian.*

Conclusion

The years 1987–92 were certainly eventful ones for the centre in British politics. The old Liberal party, with roots going back to the middle of the nineteenth century, disappeared from the political scene, as did the SDP,

TABLE 4.4
THE ELECTORATE'S EVALUATIONS OF MR. ASHDOWN

Question: "Do you think Mr. Ashdown is or is not proving a good leader of the Liberal Democratic party?"

	Posi-tive	Nega-tive	Don't know	Net		Posi-tive	Nega-tive	Don't know	Net
1988					**1990**				
August	22%	16%	63%	+6%	January	25%	41%	34%	−16%
September	19	23	57	−4	February	28	41	33	−13
October	24	22	54	+2	March	29	39	32	−10
November	24	24	53	0	April	30	39	31	−9
December	25	25	50	0	May	34	35	31	−1
					June	29	41	30	−12
1989					July	31	38	32	−7
January	25	26	48	−1	August	31	38	32	−7
February	27	27	46	0	September	35	34	31	+1
March	26	35	39	−9	October	40	31	29	+9
April	28	31	41	−3	November	44	29	27	+15
May	23	39	38	−16	December	44	31	25	+13
June	26	40	35	−14					
July	22	44	34	−22	**1991**				
August	21	43	36	−22	January	44	29	27	+15
September	24	44	32	−22	February	48	27	25	+21
October	23	45	31	−22	March	55	24	21	+31
November	26	42	33	−16	April	53	24	23	+29
December	28	40	32	−12	May	58	22	21	+36
					June	58	21	20	+37
					July	58	21	21	+37
					August	56	22	22	+34
					September	57	23	21	+34
					October	56	22	21	+34
					November	59	22	19	+37
					December	55	25	20	+30

SOURCE: *Gallup Political Index.*

which had made a sudden and significant impact in the early 1980s. A new party assumed the mantles of the Liberals and the SDP, and a new generation of leaders emerged while the Gang of Four and David Steel went their different ways.

It might be argued, however, that the Liberal Democratic party is simply the Liberal party with trimmings. David Owen, it might be sug-

gested, has been proved right, and the Liberals have simply swallowed
the SDP. The final name change removed any reference to "Social" Democracy, and the 1989 conference voted to delete the commitment to
NATO contained in the original preamble to the constitution. The membership of the party is no greater than the Liberals alone had before the
merger and to a great extent consists of former Liberals. Electoral support, despite the recovery which took place during 1991, was still far
short of the levels achieved by the Alliance, and the Liberal Democrats
entered the 1992 general election with expectations that were no greater
than the Liberals had had in the early 1970s. Finally, in what is surely a
deliberate ploy to irritate Liberal Democrats, Labour and Conservative
politicians now routinely refer to the party as simply "the Liberals," as
do political commentators from time to time.

But to regard the Liberal Democrats as simply a continuation of the
Liberal party is an oversimplification. The party does include a significant body of people from the social democratic tradition, typified by the
current president, Charles Kennedy; its constitution is radically different
from that of the Liberals, and its organisation is more professional. Almost all political commentators have noted that Liberal Democrat conferences are much more organised, realistic, and responsible and that delegates are more serious players in the political game than was true with
the Liberals. In addition, the strength of the Liberal Democrats in local
government is much greater than anything achieved by the Liberals in
modern times.

Nonetheless, like the Liberals before them, the Liberal Democrats
face serious problems in attempting to be a major force in British politics. First, unlike the two major parties, they have no institutional
sources of financial support and depend entirely on members' subscrip-
tions and donations. That is why the failure to recruit and retain a large
membership in 1988 and 1989 was so serious and could have threatened
the party's existence. Second, the adversarial nature of British politics
and the way business is organised in the House of Commons mean that
media attention tends to be very heavily focused on the two main parties,
thus denying the Liberal Democrats vital publicity. Third, electoral support for the Liberal Democrats is "soft." Their core support—electors
who can be relied on to vote for them in successive elections—is much
smaller than that of the other two parties, and they have to attract voters
anew at each election. In other words, people who vote for the party
tend to lack any sense of continuing psychological attachment to it.
While they may support the Liberal Democrats at one election, they are
just as likely to switch to other parties subsequently. In addition, in the
perceptions of voters the party appears to lack a distinctive policy space

on important issues such as the economy, and they tend to turn to it for largely negative reasons—not liking the other parties. When the main parties are performing well and are popular with the electorate, therefore, the Liberal Democrats are always going to be "squeezed." Finally, and most important, the fact that the Liberal Democrats' support is relatively evenly spread both socially and geographically means that it is severely punished by the first-past-the-post electoral system, as was to be demonstrated in the 1992 general election.

Nevertheless, the British electorate is no longer strongly aligned behind the Conservative and Labour parties, and as the political editor of *The Times* concluded about the Liberal Democrats during their conference in September 1990: "Their survival is assured. They are no longer an endangered species."[49] To do more than simply survive, however, the Liberal Democrats need a change in the British electoral system. Until that happens—and there are some grounds for optimism given that in the near future Labour could come out in favour of reform—the breakthrough that the centre has sought throughout the postwar period will remain elusive.

Notes

1. I am very conscious of the fact that many members and supporters of the parties discussed in this chapter would strenuously object to the use of the term "centre" to describe their political positions. It is, however, a convenient shorthand way of distinguishing the Liberals, SDP, and Liberal Democrats from the Conservatives and Labour.
2. David Denver, "The SDP–Liberal Alliance: The End of the Two-Party System?" in *Change in British Politics,* ed. H. Berrington (London: Frank Cass, 1984).
3. Ibid., 82.
4. Roy Jenkins, *A Life at the Centre* (London: Macmillan, 1991), 587.
5. David Owen, *Time to Declare* (London: Michael Joseph, 1991), 446.
6. Ibid., 507.
7. Ibid., 482–83.
8. Jenkins, *A Life at the Centre,* 535.
9. Owen, *Time to Declare,* 482.
10. David Steel, *Against Goliath* (London: Weidenfeld and Nicolson, 1989), 280.
11. Ibid., 266.
12. Quoted in Steel, *Against Goliath,* 267.
13. David Butler and Dennis Kavanagh, *The British General Election of 1987* (London: Macmillan, 1988), 232.
14. Ivor Crewe, "The 1987 General Election," in *Issues and Controversies in*

British Electoral Behaviour, ed. David Denver and Gordon Hands (London: Harvester Wheatsheaf, 1992).

15. Steel, *Against Goliath*, 283–84.

16. Owen, *Time to Declare*, 712ff.

17. Chris Cook, *A Short History of the Liberal Party 1900–88*, 3d ed. (London: Macmillan, 1989), 189.

18. Steel, *Against Goliath*, 286.

19. Owen, *Time to Declare*, 725.

20. Jenkins, *A Life at the Centre*, 597–98.

21. Steel, *Against Goliath*, 286.

22. Quoted in Cook, *Short History*, 191.

23. Quoted in Owen, *Time to Declare*, 732.

24. Steel, *Against Goliath*, 287.

25. Rachael Pitchford and Tony Greaves, *Merger: The Inside Story* (Colne: Liberal Renewal, 1989).

26. Book review by Alan Beith, *Parliamentary Affairs* 32, no.4 (1990): 507.

27. Steel, *Against Goliath*, 288.

28. Pitchford and Greaves, *Merger*, 76.

29. Ibid., 40.

30. Ibid., 95.

31. Ibid., 45.

32. Quoted in Cook, *Short History*, 194.

33. Steel, *Against Goliath*, 288.

34. Cook, *Short History*, 195.

35. Pitchford and Greaves, *Merger*, 118–19.

36. Steel, *Against Goliath*, 288.

37. Cook, *Short History*, 196.

38. Pitchford and Greaves, *Merger*, 131–32.

39. Cook, *Short History*, 200.

40. Owen, *Time to Declare*, 732.

41. Alan G. Hayman, "Dr. Owen's SDP: A Study in Failure," MA dissertation, Department of Government, University of Essex.

42. *Liberal News*, no. 11, October 1990.

43. Pitchford and Greaves, *Merger*, 145.

44. This survey of former members of the SDP was carried out by the author and Hugh Bochel of Humberside Polytechnic in late 1991. More than 2000 responses to a postal questionnaire were obtained. The project was financed by the Nuffield Foundation.

45. *The Times*, 11 September 1989.

46. *The Times*, 17 October 1989.

47. See the *Guardian*, 5 May 1991.

48. *The Times*, 10 September 1989.

49. *The Times*, 21 September 1990.

5

Caring and Competence: The Long, Long Campaign

Kenneth Newton

At the heart of the 1992 election campaign lies a puzzle: how could a government in power for thirteen years and staking its reputation almost entirely on economic success manage to win an election held in the depths of the longest and most severe economic depression in sixty years?

The puzzle has many layers. First, the Conservatives came to power in 1979 primarily because of the economic record of the previous Labour government. For that matter, Margaret Thatcher soon made it clear that, in her view, the previous Conservative government under Harold Macmillan and Edward Heath had also got economic policy fundamentally wrong. Second, Thatcher made economic success the ultimate standard by which she and her government were to be judged. Third, whenever the news of the economy was bad, the Conservative response was a variation on the theme that good medicine is nasty medicine and that a lot of nasty medicine would make the economy leaner, fitter, and eventually more prosperous. Many suffered in the 1980s, but the country would, the government claimed, reap the benefits in the end. Fourth, in the late 1980s the government stated loudly and often that its policy had worked so well that Britain was now a model of economic success. Fifth, at the end of 1990, when the economy started to slide into the second serious recession in thirteen years of Conservative rule, the government, now with John Major as prime minister, began by denying it all, then reluctantly conceding that there were indeed some problems but that these would soon get better, before finally admitting what everyone knew, that the nation was in serious economic trouble. Some months before polling day, it was clear that a recovery would not start until well after the election.

The puzzle of the Conservative victory becomes even more perplexing if one considers the common idea that modern governments are judged, even judged mainly, on their economic records.[1] Moreover, the 1992 campaign was dominated, as no other postwar election had been, by economic issues and by a long succession of bad to appalling economic news. Finally, if one adds to all this the simple fact that no party has won four successive elections in Britain since the Great Reform Act of 1832, the result of the 1992 election turns from a puzzle into a full-blown mystery. How on earth can a government in this position possibly have won? The Conservatives should have lost, and by a landslide.

This chapter does not chronicle the campaign's events (for this, see the Campaign Diary at the end of the chapter) but tries to unravel the mystery of the Conservative victory by examining the course and nature of the 1992 election campaign from its beginnings to the eve of polling day. To do so, we have to go back a little in time. It will then become evident that the basic course and outcome of the campaign were almost certainly established months before 9 April and were not resolved in the last few days, as many observers now claim. The opinion polls tell us that there was a last-minute swing to the Conservatives (see chapter 6), but if so, the conditions were established long before the last few frantic days of electioneering.

Competence and Caring in the Long Campaign

In Britain it is difficult to tell when the real campaign starts, as opposed to the short campaign that runs from the day the election date is announced until the election itself, a mere four weeks in 1992. When there is no fixed election date and when the opposition parties are therefore in doubt about how much time they have to mount their campaign, they are inclined to play safe and start early. For their part, governments will keep their powder dry and wait for the opportune moment to name election day. In the 1992 election it was a long time in coming, and even when it was finally called, pessimists in the Conservative party thought the time was still not ripe.

LABOUR LISTENS

For the Labour party, the long campaign may have started soon after the 1987 general election. Although it lost that election, it was widely thought to have won the campaign, when it put up an altogether more accomplished (and expensive) performance than its abysmal showing in

1983. In 1987 Labour tried to present an image that blended competence and social conscience. It tried to build on this image in 1992.

It did so with its "Labour Listens" exercise. This consisted of a series of open meetings all over the country in which Labour advertised its willingness to listen to the general public. The meetings were not particularly well attended, but this did not matter because the real purpose was to kill two birds with one stone. First, Labour was to turn its back on the factional disputes that had divided the party and made it seem both inward looking and backwards looking. "Labour Listens" made the point that the party was turning a deaf ear to factions in the party (often called the "loony left") and was reaching out to the general public. Second, the campaign was an attempt to exploit one of the most conspicuous weaknesses of the Conservatives under Thatcher, who had a reputation for not listening. "Labour Listens" was an attempt to identify as a Labour strength one of the Thatcher government's notable weaknesses, but Labour activists were to be taught to listen to the general public too.

The message was strongly reinforced by the expulsion of the left-wing Militant faction from the party, by the Policy Review of 1989, which was presented as a "modernisation" of policy, and by a concerted attempt to present the party as responsible, competent, and fit to hold office. This image-making mixture of words and action worked well up to a point. By October 1991, a Gallup poll showed that almost two out of three voters rejected the idea of Labour as "extreme" and accepted it as the main alternative to the Conservatives. Fewer than in 1987 saw the party as divided. As a result, the 1992 campaign was quite unlike the three previous ones, when many electors saw Labour as both extreme and divided.

Labour still had severe problems with its image, however. The difficulty was not so much to convince the voters that it cared, for the polls showed that many believed this already.[2] On most of the caring issues—health, housing, unemployment, welfare, and education—Labour easily outstripped the Tories (see table 5.1). Labour's main task was to persuade the voters that it was competent to run the country, mainly the economy, but also defence and foreign affairs, relations with Europe, and law and order. This proved to be exceedingly difficult.

The Labour governments in the 1960s and 1970s had acquired an unenviable reputation for economic and industrial mismanagement, based on a devaluation, a loan from the International Monetary Fund, and most of all the Winter of Discontent of 1979. The latter, consisting of a series of widely publicised strikes combined with rising inflation and unemployment, was largely responsible for Thatcher's first election victory. Thirteen years after 1979, the Winter of Discontent was still firmly

TABLE 5.1

THE BEST PARTY: LABOUR LEAD
ON CARING ISSUES

Issue	May 1991	Sept. 1991	Nov. 1991	Feb. 1992	Mar. 1992	Apr. 1992
National Health	41%	32%	34%	25%	27%	25%
Education	19	9	18	8	14	14
Homelessness	39	30	38	31	31	28
Environment	0	n.a.	6	−2	1	4
Transport	28	21	31	19	24	21
Pensions	20	15	27	19	18	18
Status of women	15	7	12	9	12	15

SOURCE: *Gallup Political Index.*

NOTE: The figures show those who say the Labour party will handle the issue best minus whose who say the Conservative party will. It should be noted that "don't know"s range from 10 to 25 percent.

lodged in the public mind as a symbol of Labour's incompetence. In fact, Labour's postwar economic performance in government had been little different from the Conservatives', but the folk memory of the Winter of Discontent preceding the 1979 election was still strong, and the Tories took every opportunity to refresh it.

Consequently, by October 1991, a large majority of voters felt that Labour's heart was in the right place—it was, after all, the architect and defender of the welfare state—but only a third believed it would make a good job of running the country.[3] More people believed the country as a whole would be worse off, not better off, under a Labour government (by 38 percent to 31 percent), and many more thought a Labour government would cause taxes and inflation to rise and strikes and other economic troubles to increase. Most important, half thought the economy would be in a worse state under a Labour government. Since the party knew it could not win an election in the face of such opinions, and the Conservatives knew them to be Labour's great weakness, these beliefs and Labour's efforts to establish an image of competence, mainly economic competence, became the main battleground of the 1992 campaign.

THE CONSERVATIVES CARE

For the Conservatives, the long campaign started much later than Labour's, in practice when John Major replaced Margaret Thatcher as Conservative leader on 28 November 1990. The Conservatives in 1990 opted not just for a new leader but for new policies and a new image. In place of Thatcher's reputation for harsh, even ruthless domination, the party felt the need to create a softer and more caring style. In fact, the word "caring" had long been an internal code word for criticism of Thatcher's government. It is said (with a little truth) that the Conservative party consists of two camps: the Christian Union and the Forty Thieves. The Christian Union wanted its power back.

The election of the moderate and reasonable John Major was the first step. Labour had moved to the right on many issues after 1987, and now it was the Conservatives' turn to move to a less purist belief in market economics, a greater concern for social conditions, and a greater awareness of the responsibilities of the state towards its citizens. This approach began to take shape the day Major became prime minister, and by polling day the Conservatives had done their best to obliterate most of Thatcher's image and some of her central policies.

Major's impact on the electorate was immediate. The November 1990 polls showed that almost 69 percent were dissatisfied with Thatcher as prime minister, and only 26 percent satisfied. A month later, almost half were satisfied with Major as prime minister, and only 28 percent dissatisfied. In September 1990, 72 percent thought the Conservatives too rigid and inflexible. A year later, the figure had fallen to 52 percent. In September 1990, 70 percent agreed with the statement that the Conservatives did not care what hardships their policies caused. A year later, this had fallen to 58 percent.[4]

One of Major's first acts was more than merely symbolic. Michael Heseltine, who had carefully distanced himself from the Thatcher government after resigning from the cabinet in 1986, was brought back. Of the "caring" or "wet" tendency on social issues, he was given the job of abolishing the Thatcherite flagship of uncaringness—the widely hated poll tax (see chapter 2). This local government tax, officially known as the community charge, was called "the world's worst idea" by Labour, and the great majority of the population agreed. On 12 October 1991 the government announced plans to replace the poll tax with the council tax, a set of tax bands based on the capital value of houses. The new local tax was, in some respects, a return to the old rating system, which was so widely resented that the Conservative government replaced it with the poll tax in the first place. But a partial return to the old system did not seem to matter to the electorate, and it was certainly of no concern to the government, which knew that the poll tax was a serious obstacle to reelection and wanted it replaced with something, almost anything, that was not the poll tax.

After being well behind in the polls under Thatcher, the Conservatives took a small lead under Major (see table 5.3, p. 138). Nevertheless,
the party had its problems, mainly on the economic front, where it had
to hold on to its reputation for economic competence in the face of substantial evidence to the contrary. Economic growth in the previous three
decades had been between 2 percent and 3.3 percent, but in the 1980s
under Thatcher it was 1.8 percent, compared with a 2.8 percent in all
OECD countries.[5] And this at the expense of very high unemployment.
In the twelve months before the election, GDP fell by 2.5 percent, the
largest and longest fall in output since 1930.[6]

This had the impact one would expect on public opinion. Although
half or more of the electorate expressed their satisfaction with Major as
prime minister throughout his time in office in 1991, well over half also
expressed their disapproval of the government's record.[7] In September
1990, substantial majorities agreed with the statement that the government had failed to solve Britain's most important problems (defined as
unemployment and inflation); 66 percent said they had not kept their
election promises; 76 percent that they looked after the interests of rich,
not ordinary people; and 85 percent that the Conservatives had cut back
too much on health, education, and other services. Moreover, substantial
majorities disapproved of the government's handling of education, housing, roads, the health services, pensions, taxation, and economic and financial affairs generally.[8]

With the economy in a depression and public opinion figures of this
sort, how was Major able to turn around a Labour opinion poll lead?
The answer is that while expressing strong criticism of the government's
economic record and disapproval of many of its policies, a large section
of the electorate believed that a Labour government would do even
worse. Almost twice as many thought the Conservatives would handle
Britain's economic difficulties better than Labour (see table 5.2). The
message of the polls was clear: Most voters did not like the government's
economic record, and dissatisfaction was growing; nevertheless, and it is
a crucial "nevertheless," many more trusted the Tories to handle economic problems than trusted Labour.

These poll results are central to an understanding of the election,
and although they may seem odd at first sight, the beliefs underlying
them are not difficult to explain. First, the Conservative party has always
been the party of business, and in the minds of the public this appears to
be much the same as economic competence. Second, as we have seen, Labour's economic reputation was poor. What mattered insofar as voting
intention was concerned was the *relative* reputation of the two parties on
the vital issue of the economy. Indeed, it may even be that the worse the

TABLE 5.2

THE BEST PARTY: CONSERVATIVE LEAD
ON COMPETENCE ISSUES

	May 1991	Sept. 1991	Nov. 1991	Feb. 1992	Mar. 1992	Apr. 1992
Economic issues						
Inflation	12%	14%	7%	15%	14%	15%
Unemployment	–30	–24	–32	–23	–24	–22
Strikes	16	12	4	17	13	18
Taxation	9	7	4	13	11	12
Noneconomic issues						
Defence	43	35	22	37	28	30
Law/order	21	25	11	19	15	12
International relations/Europe	29	32	15	30	22	20

SOURCE: *Gallup Political Index.*
NOTE: The figures show those who say the Conservative party will handle the issue best minus those who say the Labour party will. It should be noted that "don't know"s range from 10 percent to over 25 percent.

economy, the more the electorate was inclined to turn to the Conservatives, even though they were at least partially responsible for Britain's difficulties in the first place.

For the two main parties, caring and competence became the main battleground of the long campaign, with the competence battle being easily the more important. In the long run-up to election day—a period of seventeen months following Major's accession—the Conservatives had to protect their image of competence and build up their reputation for caring; Labour had to protect its image of caring and try to build up its reputation for competence.

But if the two main parties had everything to fight for, they also fought over rather little. There was not much disagreement between the parties, or for that matter among the electorate, about the central issues. In this sense the 1992 election was a "valence-issue," not a "position-issue" election. The latter involves parties putting different issues at the top of the agenda or applying different policy solutions to the same problems. In contrast, valence-issue elections involve general agreement about the urgent problems and the best policy solutions for them. The winning party is the one that manages to persuade voters that it can handle matters better than the other parties. Thus matters of style, image, competence, and symbolism are vital, and not ideology or basic political values.

As an almost pure valence-issue election, the 1992 campaign was largely about images of party competence, of party caring, and of trust in leadership.[9]

The Phoney Campaign

Within six weeks of Major becoming prime minister, Britain was at war. The Gulf War was a stroke of luck for Major, who, in spite of reducing the government's unpopularity by virtue of the fact that he was not Thatcher, was still faced with trouble on almost every front. The war gave him the chance to avoid the difficult issues of domestic politics and to play the role of a national and world leader. Major was relatively unknown when he was elected party leader—the joke was that when he became prime minister, no one in Britain had heard of him, and a week after, no one in the world had heard of him. By common consent, however, his conduct during the war was measured and steady, and he came out of the war with exceptionally high ratings. A Gallup poll of March 1991 showed that 60 percent were satisfied with him as PM, and only 20 percent dissatisfied. These were unusually high approval ratings for a British prime minister. By comparison, only 40 percent thought Kinnock was proving a good Labour leader, while 50 percent thought he was not. There is no evidence that the Gulf War had a direct effect on the 1992 election, but without the war Major would have been pitched into the deep end of the country's economic and social problems and might have had considerably more difficulty in establishing his personal standing as prime minister. Having acquitted himself with distinction during the war, however, Major was faced with many problems when it ended. One of the trickiest was the crucial one of when to call the election.

THE CHOICE OF DATES

The choice of election date may well be the most important single decision taken by a British prime minister. In some circumstances the decision is not at all difficult, but the choices for Major were hard, and he had a series of them. As soon as he had settled into Number 10, the opposition demanded an election. Labour knew its chances were good, and in any case a refusal might encourage the general idea that Major was afraid to face the country. He needed, or so it was said, to win a general election in order to have a popular mandate. The Gulf War put an abrupt end to all this, but as soon as domestic politics returned to normal in March 1991, Labour returned to the attack. Speculation grew —would Major call a snap election and try to capitalise on the Gulf War, his strong personal ratings, improving consumer confidence, and a Tory opinion poll lead? But Conservative Central Office let it be known that the prime minister did not want to "exploit the war for narrow, party political purposes." Later, when the party was behind in the polls, this seemed a serious mistake, but at the time the Conservatives feared a backlash against a Gulf War election and wanted to give Major more time to play himself in. Besides, the much-hated poll tax was still in place. Most important, the Conservatives probably believed their own claim, based on Treasury forecasts, that the recession would soon be over. For whatever reason, the Conservatives passed up the chance of a spring 1991 election, and the phoney campaign rumbled on.

But Labour and the Liberal Democrats would not leave the matter alone, saying that political uncertainty was contributing to economic problems and that Major should call an early election for the good of the country. June 1991 was a possibility, depending among other things on the results of the local elections to be held on 2 May. The results were good for the Conservatives, but at the same time their opinion poll lead was not substantial in the first four months of 1991 (see table 5.3) and there were still predictions of an imminent economic recovery. Once again, Major refused to call an election. Once again, the opposition accused him of being afraid and of dithering, and once again Major seems to have lost a little credibility. In the spring and summer of 1991 his popularity fell from a high in March to a considerably lower level in July (see table 5.3).

As the economy worsened in the second half of 1991 and as Labour gained a small, fluctuating lead in the polls, so the pressure on Major increased. Should he go in the autumn on the chance that the economy might worsen during the winter, or should he hold on in hopes of an economic recovery? The Conservatives still seemed to believe that the economy would improve by the spring of 1992, and the polls were not reassuring, so a November election was rejected. Some now thought that Major had made a mistake in not seizing his chance in spring 1991 and that by waiting he was beginning to limit his options.[10]

When the Commons reassembled after the Christmas 1991 recess, all the parties, as the Speaker remarked, were in campaign mode: 1992 had to be an election year, and the only question was whether it would be sooner (March or April), later (May), or at the last minute (June or July). Much depended on economic indicators and poll results, but neither left the prime minister much room for optimism. He and the Treasury now admitted that a recovery was not in sight, and there was little to choose between Labour and the Conservatives in the polls. Speculation about the likely election date became a game increasingly played by the

TABLE 5.3
WHICH PARTY WOULD YOU SUPPORT?

Question: "If there were a general election tomorrow, which party would you support?"

	Con.	Lab.	Lib. Dem.	Others
1990				
June	33.7%	49.5%	8.8%	5.9%
July	34.4	47.9	9.9	7.8
August	35.1	47.6	9.3	7.9
September	34.6	46.6	11.1	7.6
October	34.3	46.4	13.0	6.3
November	37.9	42.1	13.7	6.2
December	44.6	39.1	10.5	5.8
1991				
January	44.3	39.2	10.8	5.7
February	44.3	39.3	11.0	5.4
March	41.2	36.2	17.3	5.2
April	40.9	37.1	16.5	5.6
May	37.2	38.3	19.4	5.1
June	36.5	39.7	18.7	5.0
July	38.3	39.1	17.6	4.8
August	38.5	38.8	17.1	5.5
September	40.5	36.9	17.1	5.5
October	41.0	40.4	13.8	4.8
November	39.5	38.9	16.6	5.0
December	40.6	38.8	15.0	5.6
1992				
January	39.0	39.2	16.8	5.0
February	38.9	37.6	18.3	5.2

SOURCE: *Gallup Political Index.*
NOTE: Number of interviews varies from 6436 (December 1990) to 13,112 (March 1992).

media, with most of the pundits now betting on 9 April, with the announcement to be made shortly after the March budget.

The pundits were right, but nevertheless it seemed a dangerous decision at the time. Previous elections had suggested that a party needed a clear poll lead for at least three months before it could be reasonably confident of election victory.[11] On the day Major called the election, Labour had a small advantage, but neither party had managed a sustained lead for months, and in effect they were neck and neck. Yet there was no sign of an economic upturn before the last possible election date, and there seemed to be no compelling reason for delay. Moreover, expectation of an April election had grown inexorably in the press,[12] and Major may have felt he had little choice. If so, he had done quite a lot himself to create this situation by turning down previous chances and by appearing to dither, so speculation grew. Whatever the reasons for his choice of date, there were plenty in the Conservative party who believed it was wrong. After all, only two recent prime ministers had called an election when they were behind in the polls (Sir Alec Douglas-Home in 1964 and James Callaghan in 1979), but neither had much choice and both lost.

However, in dealing with the crucial matter of the choice of election date, we have run ahead of the story. Between the spring of 1991 and the start of the campaign proper in March 1992, a lot of water flowed under the bridge.

The Competence Campaign

Each week of the long campaign brought more news of business closures, falling industrial output, balance-of-trade deficits, business losses, increasing unemployment, mortgage defaults, and bankruptcies. The culmination was "Black Thursday," 13 February 1992, which combined news of rising unemployment, large business losses, another balance-of-trade deficit, and the largest drop in business investment for ten years.[13] The severity of the economic depression had three main impacts on electioneering. First, it tended to undermine the Conservatives' reputation for economic competence, their main electoral asset. Second, it put the party on the defensive for much of the time. Third, it severely restricted the government's options in the spring budget, which would be its last main chance before the election to do something about the economy and restore economic confidence. The budget would also be an important opportunity to win back voters.

The Conservatives ran through a series of three responses to the economic situation before settling on a fourth. At first they denied there was serious economic trouble. At the end of 1991, however, the chancellor, Norman Lamont, admitted that there was a depression and switched to the theme that things would soon get better. All the ingredients for recovery were in place, he said. When the recession persisted, and it was evident that recovery would be delayed, it was argued that things were just as bad in other countries. There was some truth in this, but nevertheless the economies of France, Germany, Italy, and Japan grew in

1991, and a 1 percent decline in the United States was better than Britain's 2.5 percent decline. Besides, the idea that foreign economies are suffering does not do much to satisfy voters at home, and so, finally, the argument was switched to the claim that things would be worse under Labour.

The last tack was the most promising because it shifted ground from the known to the speculative, and it played on popular feelings about Labour's economic incompetence. The theme had been used by John Major in a speech designed to upstage the last day of the Labour party conference in October 1991, but it was not deployed as the government's main argument until it became clear that the economy would not recover in time for the election. From late 1991 onwards, however, cabinet ministers hammered out the claim that Labour would bungle and blunder and that its policies would fuel inflation, raise unemployment, increase interest rates, make mortgages expensive and difficult to get, cause financial chaos, reduce competitiveness, and bring back the Winter of Discontent. Like all good political messages, this one was short, simple, and clear: no matter how bad the economy might be, it would be much worse under Labour. It turned out to be the Conservatives' main argument for the rest of the campaign. Almost every Labour criticism of Conservative economic policy brought forth not a defence of the policy, but an attack on Labour's economic competence. For example, in reply to Kinnock's claim that "this government caused the recession, they continue the recession, and now they haven't got a clue how to get out of it," Major claimed that Kinnock was "an economic illiterate" whose policies "would mean perpetual recession for this country."[14]

Labour and the Liberal Democrats, for their part, concentrated on two themes. First, it became clear that the Conservatives seemed to be doing reasonably well in the polls because the depression was blamed on either the world situation or the legacy of the Thatcher government. Consequently, both main opposition parties set out to pin the blame on Major. They repeated the message that Major, first as chancellor between October 1989 and November 1990, and then as prime minister, was personally responsible. In Parliament, Kinnock greeted the official figure of a 2.5 percent economic decline in 1991 with the claim that Major was "not only the prime minister of recession but the prime cause of recession."[15] Labour produced a poster showing Major and Lamont cowering behind sandbags labeled "Tory Defence Policy" and the slogan "It's not our recession." There is no evidence that any of this had any impact on public opinion. At no point in the run-up to the election did more than one in ten voters blame Major or his government for what had gone wrong.

Second, both the opposition parties stressed the need for a new economic policy that would emphasize investment for recovery and growth; but they did so in a manner designed to create an image of caution and responsibility. In particular, the Labour shadow chancellor, John Smith, spent many hours lunching and dining with bankers and businessmen establishing his credibility as the future chancellor and establishing an image of economic rectitude and responsibility. This was a central part of Labour's competence campaign and as such was derided as the "prawn cocktail circuit" by Michael Heseltine in a Commons debate: "All those prawn cocktails for nothing. Never have so many crustaceans died in vain. Let me say to the shadow chancellor with all the authority of office as Secretary of State for the Environment—Save the prawns!"[16]

Against the backdrop of bad economic news, the first two months of 1992 were given largely to economic claims, counterclaims, and counter-counterclaims between the parties. In early February the polls showed that consumer confidence was low and continuing to fall and that unemployment was expected to increase. Sixty-two percent felt the government was not handling the economy well, and most felt that inflation was bound to continue.[17] Labour went on the attack with a concerted criticism of government economic incompetence and complacency and presented its alternative of modest tax increases to fund better services and invest for growth. "The British people," declared Kinnock, "do not want a Tory 'Save our Skins' budget, they want a 'Save our Country' budget."[18]

The Conservatives defended themselves with a poster campaign attacking Labour's tax policy. They produced on 6 January 1992 a large poster showing a World War II bomb, huge and black, labeled "Labour's Tax Bombshell" and the slogan "You'd pay £1000 more tax a year under Labour." The amount was later raised to £1250. The "tax bomb" poster was followed by another showing two boxing gloves looming out of the poster to hit the reader in the face with the words "Labour's Double Whammy. 1. More Taxes. 2. Higher Prices." But "Double Whammy" is an American term, and few in Britain understood it. A third poster portrayed Labour as a huge locust gobbling up all before it.

Approval of the government's economic record was low, but trust in Labour's ability to handle the economy remained still lower (see table 5.4). In February 1992, 44 percent said the Conservatives would handle Britain's economic difficulties best. Only 30 percent believed Labour would be better. Compared with the 37 percent who believed they would be worse off under Labour, only 29 percent believed they would be better off. Many voters believed Labour would introduce large tax increases; over half believed that income tax would rise by 10p. Mean-

TABLE 5.4
CONSERVATIVE AND LABOUR ECONOMIC COMPETENCE

Question: "With Britain in economic difficulties, which party do you think could handle the problem best? The Conservatives under Mr. Major or Labour under Mr. Kinnock?"

	Conservative	*Labour*	*Neither*	*Don't know*
1991				
March	53%	29%	9%	8%
June	42	38	13	7
September	45	29	17	10
December	45	31	15	9
1992				
January	44	29	17	9
February	44	30	17	9
March	43	31	17	9
7–8 April	45	38	10	6
10–11 April	52	31	11	6

SOURCE: *Gallup Political Index.*
NOTE: Figures based on between 4923 and 12,670 interviews.

while, the rancorous argument between the two main parties about economic policy and economic competence was fueled with speculation about the March budget.

THE BUDGETS

The government really needed two budgets: The economy required fiscal stringency and prudent investment for economic recovery; the election needed an interest rate cut and tax cuts. Whichever course was chosen, room for manœuvre was strictly limited. The government desperately needed to cut interest rates in order to stimulate the economy and relieve mortgage holders; but for its own reasons, it had joined the European exchange rate mechanism (ERM) in October 1990 at what many regarded as too high a rate. The pound had drifted to the bottom of its rate, and an interest rate cut might well provoke a sterling crisis.

Since this would severely damage the Tory campaign, attention turned to tax cuts. Here again, options were limited. The depression had reduced the government's tax revenues and in spite of massive privatisation receipts in previous years, the government's cupboard was now bare. In addition, Labour had limited the government's options by forcing it to state that it would not increase the Value Added Tax (VAT). Income tax cuts would, therefore, mean government borrowing—something contrary to Thatcherite principles of good household management and not recommended in the depths of a depression by many economists. Notwithstanding all this, the Tories were still lagging slightly behind in the opinion polls and had to pin their hopes on budget largesse. Tax cuts would also highlight differences between them and Labour. The polls also showed that many voters believed that tax cuts were as good a way as any of "kick-starting" the economy, even though some economists said they would do further damage by giving people more money to spend on imported goods.

In the event, budget day on 10 March produced something of a surprise, one that initially wrong-footed the opposition parties. Instead of taking a penny off the standard rate of tax, as had been widely expected, the chancellor lowered the lowest rate tax band to 20*p*, thus helping 4 million people on low earnings. Various other measures were designed to appeal to the motor trade, farmers, small businesses, and pensioners. The chancellor announced that the package meant that government borrowing would double from £14 to £28 billion.[19]

Business and public reaction to the budget was important to the government, faced with a choice of election dates; the stock market wobbled and lost points, the pound fell slightly, and business leaders were generally lukewarm. Margaret Thatcher's former economic adviser, Sir Alan Walters, called borrowing for tax cuts "a fraud" and "a sleight of hand." On Channel 4 News, he said, "It is certainly not a budget for recovery. The country needs tax cuts like an anaemic needs leeching."[20] Predictably the opposition parties savaged the whole package, but Kinnock's claim that the budget tried to bribe the voters with borrowed money had a ring of truth. The Gallup poll of March 1992 reported that 57 percent thought the budget had been generous for election purposes and only 31 percent thought it a serious attempt to handle the economic situation. As many thought it fair (45 percent) as unfair (44 percent), but, perhaps most important, 70 percent approved of the new 20*p* tax band. The day after the budget, the prime minister announced that 9 April would be election day.

The government seems to have misread the likely impact of the budget. During Lamont's budget speech, Major could scarcely suppress his glee, smiling and pointing derisively at the Labour front bench, as if he had pulled off a marvelous coup. The public turned out to be unenthusiastic. In the March Gallup poll 16 percent said the budget had made them more favourably inclined towards the government, 38 percent less favourably inclined, while 42 percent said it made no difference.

For the first time in British history, the opposition did not rest content with its criticism of the budget but produced its own full-dress affair and presented it with a photo opportunity of John Smith and his colleagues standing on the Treasury steps trying to look as much like the real Treasury team as possible. The alternative budget was designed partly to distract attention from the government's tax cuts and partly to show Labour as prudent and responsible. Since Labour's tax plans were a central campaign issue, it is worth summarising them briefly. On the one hand, the Labour "budget" reversed the new 20*p* lower tax rate but raised the threshold below which no tax or National Insurance contributions were to be paid. At the other end of the income scale, it introduced a 50*p* rate for those earning £40,000 or more and abolished the National Insurance ceiling of £21,000. An important part of the package, but one often overlooked in the discussion of tax, was that Child Benefit and pensions were to be increased.

Because it was generally recognised that the economic situation provided little room for manœuvre, John Smith's budget differed mainly in detail from Norman Lamont's. Nevertheless, there were differences of principle. The Conservatives opted for tax cuts, even borrowing to achieve them, whereas Labour planned for a some redistribution of income, some tax increases to pay for better health and education services, and for investment financed by borrowing. Labour had announced its general plans for a tax increase months before, in order to avoid last-minute shocks, and although the proposed tax increases applied only to high earners, the party was still gambling on the apparent preference of the electorate for higher taxes and better services.

Survey evidence over many years showed that the majority of voters were willing to pay higher taxes provided they were spent on the right things—notably health, education, and some social services—and provided the extra money produced better services. For example, a survey in early January found that seven out of ten voters thought the country would gain more from public spending increases than from income tax cuts.[21]

But whatever people tell opinion polls, they may still vote for tax cuts in the privacy of the polling booth. It has been suggested that a "shame-factor" (a reluctance to state a Conservative voting intention to pollsters) may have accounted for the fact that the polls underestimated the Conservative vote in 1992. It is interesting to note that the vote for the antitax party in Denmark is usually several percentage points higher than its opinion poll support. More to the point, in Britain in 1992, announcing even small tax increases gave the Conservatives the opportunity for stories about Labour irresponsibility and its "real" plans for huge tax increases for everyone. They seized the opportunity with vigour and repeated the same message over and over again: Labour was the party of large tax increases.

This was fertile ground. A Gallup poll at the end of February 1992 showed that, while 47 percent thought that Labour would be right to reverse the 1p tax cut expected in the Conservative budget, only 27 percent disapproved of Labour's spending and tax plans. Most important, 58 percent believed that their taxes would "go up a lot" under a Labour government.[22] The issue in the electorate's mind, therefore, seemed to be not small tax and spending increases, which they approved of as long as they were spent efficiently and on the right services, but large tax increases, which they feared if Labour were elected. Therefore, the Conservatives concentrated on their message about £1250 tax increases and reinforced it with their pictures of bombs, locusts, and double whammies.

The figure of £1250 was calculated on the basis of some questionable assumptions; besides, it was an average figure that took no account of the incidence of taxation. In fact, the tax proposals of the two parties were rather similar. A leading article of the *Financial Times* said there was not much to choose between them,[23] and the Institute for Fiscal Studies calculated that under Labour's tax plans four out of five families would gain, while 9 percent (those earning more than £30,000) would lose. Under the Conservative budget, the Institute found, 74 percent of families would gain, and 4 percent would lose.

Such figures have little popular resonance, and elections are fought on simpler messages. These the Conservative camp, both politicians and the press, hammered home. After telling its readers that "Labour votes to tax the poor," the *Daily Mail* followed up with "If you make it—they'll take it." The *Sun* said, "Labour to squeeze backbone of Britain," and the *Express* headline ran "Road to ruin with Kinnock." Michael Heseltine, who made most of the few good speeches of the campaign, told a meeting: "John Smith would squeeze national taxes not until the pips squeaked but until the oranges themselves ran blood-red under the weight of them. Now the Labour Party has presented the largest tax demand in history—its manifesto: short on ideas, wild on tax."[24] Much of this seems to have struck home with the public.

The economic situation was such that economic and tax issues dominated the campaign and drove out virtually every other competence issue. Matters such as defence, Europe, law and order, local government finance, transport, and energy barely made an appearance. Among competence issues, even the economy was essentially a valence issue about which there was no fundamental ideological division. If anything, the caring campaign was fought on an even narrower basis.

The Caring Campaign

At first the Conservatives presented their plans for a "Citizens' Charter." It was a strong personal favourite of Major and marked a further shift away from Thatcher's belief in pure market forces. Designed to improve the quality of public and privatized services, and covering fifteen areas from health, education, and tax to gas, electricity, telephones, and water, the charter promised to provide consumers with information about service standards and performance, to improve complaint procedures, and to strengthen the powers of the local ombudsman and the regulatory authorities of the privatised utilities. First launched in July 1991 as a "big idea" for the 1990s, and then relaunched in January 1992, the charter failed to catch the public imagination. To some extent, Major undermined his own case by opting out of the European Community's "social chapter," which had as its goals the same idea of citizen protection. Although the Citizens' Charter appeared in the Conservatives' election manifesto, the party did not press the idea very hard during the campaign.

The early stages of the Conservative campaign marked a further move towards the caring style of Conservatism, and more breaks with the Thatcher style. Her practice was to admit nothing and apologise for nothing, but under Major the government began to admit mistakes, if not apologise. Most notably, it admitted that the country was in a recession and later admitted that taxes had increased in the 1980s. Thatcher always claimed to have reduced taxes, but by this she meant that income taxes had been reduced, whereas in fact total taxes, including both income and indirect taxes, had increased. Even with Thatcher gone, however, the Conservatives did not find it easy to shed the uncaring image. In the spring of 1991, the chancellor of the exchequer, Norman Lamont, had said that unemployment was "a price worth paying" in the battle against inflation, a phrase often quoted against him by opposition speakers who suggested that he might set a good example himself by resigning.

To strengthen its caring case, the government turned to spending pledges in the four weeks before the election, with defence contracts, roads, health, and welfare figuring prominently in a package totaling £3.5 billion.[25] Despite the persistent claim of the Conservative government throughout the 1980s to have reduced public spending and its stated intent to continue doing so, and despite the somewhat parlous state of public finances, the government clearly wanted to send a message to voters in announcing this £3.5 billion spending package. Together with the £2.2 billion given away in the budget, the total was well over the £5 billion spent by Thatcher for the 1987 election. A national lottery with a £1.5 million jackpot was also announced.

Of the caring issues, the opinion polls showed that health was easily the most important—and a vote winner for Labour. Labour had, after all, set up the National Health Service (NHS) after the war and was still seen as its protector in 1992. There was also widespread concern that the Conservative's NHS reforms would, in effect, privatise parts of it and create a "two-tier" service for the rich and the poor. The government did its best to persuade the public that it had spent more on health than ever before, that hospital waiting lists had been reduced, and that its hospital trust reforms had worked and did not amount to privatisation. The public remained fixedly sceptical. An April 1992 poll found that 53 percent believed that the NHS was unsafe in Major's hands (38 percent thought it was safe), while 57 percent did not believe the government's claim that it would not privatise the NHS (32 percent did).[26] Labour maintained a large lead over the Conservatives on the health issue, and throughout the campaign Labour was judged the best party to handle the NHS by a majority of around two to one.[27]

Labour tried to capitalize on its advantage with a television programme on the NHS. Since this was the only time the campaign generated real drama, the broadcast and the events following it are worth considering in a little detail. The programme was in the form of a "docudrama" about two little girls. The parents of the first paid for private medical attention, promptly received, but the other, Jennifer, had her operation for a painful ear complaint delayed by lack of NHS funds. The programme was not supposed to present the facts about two real children but was loosely based on several case histories in the "faction" style. Nevertheless, the press discovered the real Jennifer's identity and ran stories about her and her family.

The Conservatives decided it was time to go on the attack to prevent Labour from capitalising on the health issue. Kinnock was accused of telling lies, of exploiting a small girl's pain, and of revealing her identity for political purposes. The Conservatives claimed that the programme demonstrated that Kinnock was totally irresponsible and unfit to hold public office; he was callous, cynical, and opportunist. The Conservative party chairman, Chris Patten, called the programme a "sleazy, contemptible broadcast." The health secretary, William Waldegrave, said that Labour was "trying to use techniques that would not have been out of place in pre-war Germany." At last the campaign had caught fire and in a way that put it beyond the control of the politicians. Here was a human-interest story with powerful political possibilities, and the Conservative tabloids seized their chance. "If Kinnock will tell lies about a sick little girl will he ever tell the truth about anything?" asked the *Sun* (26 March). A *Daily Express* headline ran: "The big lie. Kinnock on the run as TV fiction explodes in his face," and the *Daily Mail*'s was: "No regard for little girl: Fury over 'lies' in Labour's NHS broadcast."

What makes the "war of Jennifer's ear" important is the light it casts on several aspects of the campaign. First, it turned out that the programme was accurate in its claim that the real Jennifer's operation had been delayed for lack of NHS funds, a fact revealed in the published letter of a hospital official. After the tabloids' initial "big lie" assault, this was largely overlooked. Second, the Conservative campaign was not as alert as it might have been to take maximum advantage of the issue. At the height of the controversy, when the media were hungry for material, cabinet members were not available because they were lunching at the prime minister's country residence. Waldegrave, the solitary minister left to field the press conference, revealed the Conservatives' role in making public Jennifer's identity. Third, what was supposed to start a health service policy debate was immediately sidetracked into an issue about Labour's irresponsibility and then petered out in an argument about press irresponsibility. Matters of policy were scarcely discussed at all. Fourth, in the negative style of the whole campaign, the Conservatives managed to prevent Labour from capitalising on its NHS advantage. The electorate became impatient with the issue, and neither party gained.[28]

Two last comments should be made about the caring aspect of the campaign. First, the most important move the Conservatives made in the caring campaign was not in respect to any particular policy area, but in its election of Major as party leader. His personality and public image were so different from Thatcher's that the change was probably enough to cancel most of her uncaring reputation. Second, caring matters made little impact on the content of the campaign. On television, the topics of health and social services, education, the environment, housing, transport, and race took up 13 percent of news and election programme time. In the tabloids, they occupied only 7 percent of front-page space.[29] The effect cannot have helped Labour, since it was strong on these issues. Whether it influenced the election result is a different matter. Health and education were somewhat more prominent in 1987,[30] but Labour lost badly nonetheless.

The "war of Jennifer's ear" apart, the most notable feature of the caring campaign, as we have seen, was that it scarcely existed. If this is added to the earlier observation that the competence campaign was virtually monopolised by the economy, then it becomes clear that the 1992 campaign was exceedingly narrow in its range. It was a campaign of missing issues. The reason was mainly that the recession dominated everything. Given this, it was in Labour's interest to attack the soft target of the Conservatives' economic performance. The Conservatives thought they could best defend themselves by attacking Labour's tax plans and reputation for economic incompetence. When Labour tried to raise caring issues, such as the health services, it was in the Conservatives' interest to deflect the discussion and turn it into an argument about Labour's lies and untrustworthiness. The vacuum left by the missing issues was filled by political personalities, but even these were neither numerous nor large enough to raise the temperature.

The Leadership Battle

The dominance of Britain's parties has usually meant that the individual qualities and characteristics of the party leaders have not decided much in British elections. After all, Thatcher's average popularity throughout the 1980s was lower than that of any other postwar prime minister with the exception of Edward Heath (1970–74),[31] but she won a record three consecutive elections. In 1983 the Liberal leader, David Steel, was rated more highly than any other leader, but his party came third. In 1992, the Liberal Democrat leader, Paddy Ashdown, was similarly rated, but his party was also in third place in the polls. Nevertheless, the leadership of the two main parties in 1992 may have counted for more than usual. This was partly because weakened party identification during the previous twenty years left more room for party leadership to exercise an influence over voting behaviour. And, as an almost pure valence-issue election, 1992 may have left room for matters of style and competence to play a large role. Also, when the contest is as close as it was in 1992, matters of personality may weigh more heavily.

In any event, the parties were forced by circumstances to put a heavy stress on their leaders. The Conservatives had to erase the memory of Thatcher and put Major in its place. Given the state of the economy, they also had to make as much of Major's popularity as possible. Similarly, they had to attack what the opinion polls told them was one of Labour's weakest points—its leader, Neil Kinnock. Labour knew that it had to improve Kinnock's image if it was to have a chance of winning. There was some basis for this hope because in the 1987 election he had gained in popularity as a result of campaign exposure, and Labour was planning for a repeat performance in 1992. Because the Liberal Democrat leader, Paddy Ashdown, was one of the most popular and respected politicians in the country, his team was intent on using him to maximum effect.

For Major and Kinnock, a huge amount turned on the election; the loser would almost certainly lose his job as party leader. In contrast,

Ashdown's position seemed safe, partly because he was so popular with the electorate, and partly because there were few among his twenty-one Liberal Democrat colleagues in the House of Commons capable of filling his shoes. Even the "Paddy Ashdown scandal," if anything, did him good. The incident concerned the theft of documents referring to Ashdown's private life from the safe of his lawyer. Shortly after, he called a press conference in which he admitted to a brief affair with his secretary five years earlier. Major and Kinnock immediately backed him, saying it was a private matter, and Ashdown's own handling of the news enabled both him and his party to gain public support.

The three leaders played a dominant part in events. Major accounted for 30 percent of broadcast speech coverage for the Conservatives and for 40 percent of broadcast appearances. The figures for Kinnock were 41 percent and 47 percent. Ashdown accounted for 56 percent of the Liberal Democrat broadcast speech coverage. Compared with this, other leaders of the three parties appeared and spoke on television rarely. Among the Conservatives, Norman Lamont, Chris Patten, Margaret Thatcher, and Michael Heseltine (respectively chancellor, party chairman, ex-leader, and environment minister) were the most conspicuous. There was a rather broader spread on the Labour side among John Smith, Roy Hattersley, John Cunningham, Robin Cook, Bryan Gould, and Gordon Brown (respectively, shadow chancellor, deputy leader, campaign manager, and spokesmen on health, the environment, and trade and industry). But some senior government members, even some senior cabinet members, played only bit parts, including the home secretary, Kenneth Baker, and the foreign secretary, Douglas Hurd. The same was true for some senior figures on the Labour side, including the shadow foreign secretary Gerald Kaufman.[32]

The Conservatives almost overplayed their Major card. After the Gulf War, when he had a high standing, 45 percent of Gallup respondents thought he would make the best prime minister, compared with 25 percent for Kinnock, and 18 percent for Ashdown. Major maintained a lead of about 20 percent over Kinnock for the whole of 1991 and in fact by January 1992 had stretched it to 26 percent. From then onwards, however, the gap gradually narrowed as Kinnock picked up 6 percent and Major lost almost 10 percent. By election week, 39 percent said Major would make the best prime minister, compared with 28 percent who preferred Kinnock, a lead of 11 percent for Major (see table 5.5). In the four weeks before the election, fewer than 20 percent thought Major had campaigned most impressively, compared with 30–40 percent who nominated Ashdown, and 20–30 percent who named Kinnock.[33] Nevertheless, Major remained calm and confident throughout. Even in the last

TABLE 5.5
THE BEST PRIME MINISTER

Question: "Who would make the best prime minister?"

	Major	*Kinnock*	*Ashdown*	*Don't know*
1991				
January	48%	28%	10%	14%
March	45	25	18	12
June	42	25	20	13
September	47	24	17	11
December	42	25	21	12
1992				
January	48	22	18	12
17–18 March	42	24	17	17
24–25 March	39	28	16	17
31 March–1 April	36	28	19	17
2–3 April	38	26	21	15
7–8 April	39	28	18	15

SOURCE: *Gallup Political Index.*

two weeks, when poll after poll showed the Conservatives behind, and when the Conservatives were under fire for a poor campaign, Major maintained an outward assurance, repeating the claim that he would win in the end.

Notwithstanding the fact that Kinnock picked up support in 1992, as he had in 1987, there is evidence that the Labour leadership was a liability among some voters. Polling throughout the campaign showed that by far the most frequently cited reason for not voting Labour was the feeling that Kinnock would not make a good prime minister.[34] Many were conscious of his change of mind on important political matters (such as nuclear defence), and in interviews he often spoke in long and winding sentences. Fewer than a third believed he was a good Labour leader, compared with well over half who thought that Ashdown was a good leader for the Liberal Democrats and about half who were satisfied with Major. On most personal qualities except "caring," Kinnock was ranked well below Major by the public.[35] It is ironic that Kinnock's strongest point, his power as an orator who could move large audiences, was largely irrelevant to the media electioneering techniques of 1992, whereas Major's nice, caring, likeable, and reasonable features shone through best on television. It is also true that, as the Labour leader, Kinnock bore the brunt of the Conservative attack, the most personal, and quite possibly the most damaging, delivered by the Conservative press: "Nightmare on Kinnock St.—Taxes Up, Jobless Up, Warns Major" (*Daily Express,* 31 March); "Labour Leader Defends the Extremist Policies of Foot" (*Daily Mail,* 16 March); "Neil Kinnock Threatened the Biggest Pay and Prices Explosion since the Seventies" (*Daily Mail,* 19 March); "Kinnock ... the Least Qualified, Least Competent, and Least Experienced Leader in History" (*Daily Express,* 23 March).

Did the leadership battle affect the election outcome? It is extremely difficult to disentangle the effects of personality and policies, but the evidence, though circumstantial, suggests it did. Major was always more popular than Kinnock by a wide margin, although Kinnock's policies were better liked than Major's by a smaller margin. In the week before the election, 63 percent said they liked Major's personality, compared with 41 percent for Kinnock. At the same time, 46 percent said they liked Kinnock's policies, compared with 41 percent who liked Major's policies.[36] There seems to be a closer association between voting and approval of Major than between voting and approval of Major's policies.

The Media

The British media differ from most of those of the Western world in three main respects. First, the news media are highly centralised, and most people read a national daily and Sunday paper. Circulation figures are therefore often very large, and those of the four most popular dailies (the *Sun, Daily Mirror, Daily Mail,* and *Daily Express*) total over 10 million (see table 5.6) with an actual readership three times larger. The weekday circulation of the serious papers is about 2.5 million. Similarly, most people tune in to national television and radio news, although there are local news programmes. Second, most of the daily and Sunday papers are overtly party-political, and some of them are highly partisan, running news, opinion, and party propaganda together in the same stories. Third, the national press as a whole is biased towards the Conservative party. More than 70 percent of the dailies strongly support the Conservatives, 25 percent Labour, with the remaining 3 percent independent. The combination of large national circulations and strong party preference gives the press considerable potential influence in election campaigns. Its evident bias may give the Conservatives a significant electoral advantage.

The last point is much debated and is difficult to establish one way or the other. It is certainly true that a large proportion of newspaper readers appear to select a paper that fits their politics. It is equally

TABLE 5.6

NATIONAL NEWSPAPER CIRCULATION AND
PARTY SUPPORT

	Circulation (ooo)	Percentage of total	Party support
Dailies			
Mirror/Record	3,618.9	25.5	Labour
Sun	3,587.7	25.3	Conservative
Mail	1,667.6	11.8	Conservative
Express	1,517.7	10.7	Conservative
Telegraph	1,046.4	7.4	Conservative
Star	803.7	5.7	Conservative
Today	483.5	3.4	Conservative
Guardian	418.3	2.9	Qualified Labour
The Times	389.4	2.7	Conservative
Independent	374.2	2.6	Independent
Financial Times [a]	290.7	2.1	Labour
Sundays			
News of the World	4,716.8	29.6	Conservative
Sunday Mirror	2,782.4	17.4	Labour
People	2,141.2	13.4	Labour
Sunday Mail	1,974.7	12.4	Conservative
Sunday Express	1,679.3	10.5	Conservative
The Sunday Times	1,173.9	7.4	Conservative
Sunday Telegraph	560.1	3.5	Conservative
Observer	542.4	3.4	Labour
Independent on Sunday	386.7	2.4	Independent

a. Though normally regarded as a staunch Conservative paper, the *Financial Times* surprised its readers on election morning by advising them ("by a fine margin") to vote Labour.

true that particular papers appeal to particular markets (middle class/working class, young/old, men/women) and do their best to tailor their contents and style accordingly. For this reason, a large school of thought holds that the newspapers simply reinforce political attitudes and do not create them. Recent research, however, points out that a large minority select their newspaper for reasons other than its politics. Moreover, analysis suggests that, even allowing for the fact that some people pick their newspaper for its politics, and for the effects of such variables as party identification, social class, education, and attitudes towards key election issues, there is still a strong statistical relationship between party voting and newspaper reading. In other words, people with the same political views and the same social background, but who read different papers, will tend to vote for the parties their newspapers support.[37] This suggests that newspapers may, after all, exercise some influence over election results.

The main news programmes are watched regularly by 8 or 9 million people. In clear contrast with the newspapers, however, television is seen as a public service and is carefully regulated by law. This requires balance, accuracy, and impartiality in the treatment of politics, including a complete ban on political advertising and editorialising. The parties are allowed to broadcast their programmes but under carefully regulated conditions.

Both the print and the electronic media played a central role in the 1992 campaign, as they have in the last few elections. All three main parties organised themselves primarily around the requirements of sound bites, photo opportunities, television studios, and press conferences, and all three put a huge effort into trying to manipulate the news and its interpretation. The term "spin doctor," imported from the United States, entered common usage. Few public meetings were held, the candidates relying instead on carefully stage-managed meetings with the party faithful.

There was one notable exception, but this, too, quickly became a media event. In 1983 and 1987 Thatcher, taking a leaf out of the Nixon book, insulated herself almost completely from contamination by the general public, speaking only to hand-picked audiences. In 1987 Labour followed suit. But in 1992 Major held public meetings at which there were as many ordinary people as journalists and cameramen. After two encounters with hostile crowds in Bolton and Luton, he equipped himself (apparently against the advice of his campaign managers and the police) with a megaphone and a wooden "soapbox." The soapbox quickly became a news item in its own right, and what had started off as a series of public town-centre meetings in the old electioneering style quickly became a media event in the new, with the soapbox as the main item of interest.

In spite of Major's small forays into the almost-real world, the campaigns of the three main parties were mainly staged around the requirements of the media and their insatiable appetite for news. The media responded with a huge amount of campaign material. News and current affairs programmes were extended on radio and television, and all sorts of extra campaign programmes added.[38] The serious papers (the broadsheets) added special election supplements, and the popular papers (the tabloids) printed front-page election articles when they thought a dull campaign merited it (unless their political sympathies were embarrassed by the news, when they were relieved to be able to put shock–horror and gossip stories on the front pages). There are many examples, but one will suffice here. On March 20 *The Times, Daily Telegraph, Guardian, Financial Times,* and *Independent* made unemployment and taxation their headline news, but the *Daily Express, Sun,* and *Daily Mail* all led with royal gossip.[39]

Ironically, so long, dull, and uneventful was the campaign that, with the exception of "Jennifer's ear" and bad economic news, the media could not find a lot of news to report. They turned increasingly to news of opinion poll results and to news about how the media were covering the news. The economy and taxation consumed the lion's share of news time, but the progress of the election and poll results came an easy second.[40] Substantive issues such as education, crime, housing, the environment, and Europe were seldom discussed. Instead, news of the campaign—media-contrived events such as press conferences, announcements, posters, rallies, photo opportunities, commentary, and analysis of the campaign, and especially opinion poll results—were reported at great length.[41] Health, in the form of the Jennifer's ear controversy, made a brief appearance in the third week, and proportional representation, the consequences of coalition government, and Scottish devolution became issues in the last week.[42] But the economy and taxation apart, no substantive policy issue accounted for as much as 5 percent of broadcasting time or tabloid coverage.[43]

To go any further with the analysis, it is essential to distinguish between the print and the electronic media. As already mentioned, the impartiality and balance of the former are carefully regulated by law, whereas the papers are constrained only by "the golden chains of the market."

RADIO AND TELEVISION

As soon as the election was called, the BBC canceled an apparently controversial documentary on the Conservative government's contribution to the causes of the recession. Nevertheless, both television and radio news and current affairs programmes maintained a stopwatch fairness between the parties, and both continued to enjoy a substantial degree of public trust as reliable sources of news.[44]

The politicians, however, continued their usual rumblings about bias, particularly the Conservatives when they looked like losing. They blamed BBC television for their apparent predicament. One newspaper reported "intense and colossal bitterness" about the BBC's campaign coverage.[45] In large part, however, television simply reflected the poor quality of the Conservative campaign.[46] This was illustrated in the Conservatives' election broadcast showing John Major–Everyman returning to the scene of his boyhood in south London to buy tomatoes and kippers, and finding to his apparent surprise that his old house was still standing. The general public reacted negatively to all this. As one audience researcher said, "Major was seen as a bit of a wet. They don't deny that he is a nice bloke, but he came across as too soft." Labour's broadcasts were received with more enthusiasm, especially its references to abolishing the poll tax and to education. The audience also liked Labour's emphasis on "we"—Labour and the voters—compared with Major's talk of "I" and "you."[47] The Conservative presentation of the election manifesto was also dull and unexciting compared with Labour's slick—perhaps too slick—affair.

NEWSPAPERS

As usual, it is important to distinguish between the broadsheets and the tabloids. For the most part the broadsheets—*Guardian, Daily Telegraph, The Times,* and *Independent*—provided their customary full and detailed information. Perhaps the most notable aspect of the broadsheet coverage in 1992 was the increasing worry shown by *The Times* and *The Sunday Times* about the quality and effectiveness of the Conservative campaign as the polls reported a small but continuing Labour lead. But the only real surprise was the *Financial Times,* produced for financial and business leaders, which in the end advised its overwhelmingly Conservative readers to vote Labour. Its editorial on election day concluded: "The dangers of perpetuating in power a weakened and uncertain Conservative Party, set alongside the progress Labour has made in modernising itself, justify by a fine margin the risks of change."[48]

The role of the tabloids is more interesting and arguably far more important for the election outcome. The British take their tabloid papers for granted, as "natural" as bad weather. Foreigners accustomed to more objective and balanced reporting cannot believe what they are told about the British tabloids unless they see them for themselves, when they can scarcely believe what they read. An American journalist from the *Washington Post,* Glenn Frankel, was so struck by the British tabloid style and bias that he wrote, "in the tabloids, virtually every Tory has the stature of Winston Churchill, every Labourite is a lying Leninite and every 'fact' is a lethal weapon."[49] The *Daily Mirror,* a Labour paper, is as partisan as any, but the Conservative tabloids with sales of around 8 million dominate the tabloid market. Their role in the campaign was important in three main respects.

First, they mounted early attacks on Labour's economic competence and tax policies as well as on Neil Kinnock and other Labour leaders.

These attacks were sustained for months before the election with head-lines such as "Labour's Part Time Tax Shock" (*Daily Mail*, 20 January); "Kinnock's Policy Is 'Economic Suicide.' Ford Chief: 'Labour's Crazy Tax Plans'" (*Daily Mail*, 27 January),[50] "Greenfly on the Red Rose —Murdering the British Middle Class" (*Daily Express*, 18 March), "La-bour's Tax Rises Will Return Us to the Pay Jungle" (*Daily Mail*, 19 March), "Road to Ruin with Kinnock" (*Daily Express*, 20 March), and "Can You Really Afford Not to Vote Tory?" (*Daily Express*, 9 April).

Second, after initially criticising the Conservative campaign,[51] the tabloids threw everything into the last few days in their efforts to get the government reelected. Everything included the race card and the threat of immigrant hordes; Kinnock's dismal failure as a future prime minister, as a Labour leader, and as a human being; the huge tax, interest, and mortgage rate increases that would inevitably follow a Labour victory; the champagne socialist lifestyle of some Labour leaders; the return of the Winter of Discontent; how a Liberal Democratic vote would let La-bour in; how election reform and devolution would play into the hands of extremists; and trade union and extremist control of the Labour party.

The headlines included "Major Defies Labour Mobs" (*Daily Mail*, 21 March), "Threat of Return to Picket Terror" (*Sun*, 24 March), "La-bour to Ration Mortgages" (*Daily Mail*, 23 March), "The Kickback: The Secret Tax That Will Allow Labour to Reward Its Union Paymas-ters" (*Daily Mail*, 1 April), "Nazi Riots in Britain: PR Aids Fascists Claims Baker" (*Sun*, 7 April), "Baker's Migrant Flood Warnings: Labour Set to Open Doors" (*Daily Express*, 7 April), "The Winter of Shame: This Was the Face of Britain the Last Time Labour Ruled" (*Daily Mail*, 9 April, referring to the Winter of Discontent), "A Vote for Ashdown Will Let Kinnock into No. 10, Vote Conservative" (*Daily Express*, 9 April). Finally, there was the much-discussed *Sun* front page on election morning that showed a picture of Kinnock in a light bulb, with the words "If Kinnock Wins Today Will the Last Person to Leave Britain Please Turn Out the Lights?"

The third effect of the Conservative tabloids is debatable because it is difficult to establish, but it is worth discussing. The argument goes that Labour had to be very careful because the Conservative tabloids would punish its slightest mistakes and would seize on the hint of anything that could be presented as radical or "looney leftism." This contributed to the markedly cautious and negative nature of the Labour campaign. To have been more positive, to have been more passionate in style, and to have presented an image of a socialist future for Britain, as some com-mentators wanted,[52] would have risked delivering Labour into the hands of the Conservative press. Labour leaders, supremely conscious of the need to hang on to their small opinion poll lead, seem to have concentrated on the "safe" strategy of a technically well-organised and presented campaign that gave the Conservative press as little ammunition as possible. Labour also concentrated most of its efforts on television.

Many postelection analyses of the result turned on the influence of the Tory press, particularly its role in appearing to create a surprising and dramatic swing in the last few days. Indeed, the *Sun* claimed to have won the election on its own, with its headline "It's the *Sun* Wot Won It," implying that the Conservative campaign was not good enough to claim the credit. There is evidence to support this claim, including figures showing that the *Sun* had a high penetration in a few key Conservative-held marginals. For example, it was taken by 50.5 percent of homes in Basildon—72 percent above its national average—and Basildon registered only a small Labour swing.[53] But such evidence is at best circumstantial and is not supported by evidence from other Conservative marginals (such as Walthamstow, Hayes and Harlington, Erith and Crayford, and Feltham and Heston), where high sales of the *Sun* were accompanied by large Labour swings.

Another survey by MORI found that 4 percent of *Sun* readers switched their vote to the Conservatives in the final week before the election. At the same time, the survey found that 2.5 percent of the readers of the Labour *Mirror* also switched in the same direction, whereas only 2 percent of the staunchly Conservative *Daily Mail* did so.[54] It is true that the Conservative tabloids, with their daily circulation of around 8 million and a readership of well over 20 million, did conduct a wave of personal attacks on Kinnock and a concerted attempt to destroy the Labour case. This culminated in the "last heave" of the remaining days of electioneering, which must have been worth the equivalent of millions of pounds in advertising for the Conservative party. But the evidence that the late swing to the Conservatives was caused and created by the Tory tabloids is at best circumstantial and at worst implausible.

This is not to say that the newspapers had little or no effect on the election result, but it is not sensible to look for a newspaper effect in the final few days alone. The last-minute swing is unlikely to have been determined or created by short-term events. Opinions about election issues and feelings about voting intentions are built up over a longer period of time, and if the press plays a role in this process, it is because people read a partisan paper day in and day out over months, years, and decades. Attitudes and opinions may then be crystalized and mobilised at the moment of truth when the hard voting decision has to be made. If the Tory tabloids did swing the campaign in the last few days, they did so by reawakening fears and memories that had been sustained over a long period of time. For example, the Winter of Discontent is now an established folk memory. The form and content of the memory, however, is partly the creation of the tabloids' treatment of the events as they occurred in 1979 and as nurtured by them ever since. If the tabloid evocation of the Winter of Discontent had an effect on the voting, it was because the folk memory, created over the years, is based on a mixture of selective recall and media presentation, which was then triggered at the crucial time just before election day.

THE POLLS

A great many opinion polls were published covering almost every aspect of the election from voting intentions to attitudes towards the polls themselves. Indeed, the polls were a main news item in their own right and they got more attention than almost any substantive political issue, with the single exception of the economy and taxation.[55] "Horse-race journalism,"[56] which reports who is winning, who is losing, who has gained, and who has lost ground since the last poll, has become a main feature of modern British elections, as it has in the United States.[57] Public interest in the polls was also heightened because the two main parties were so close.

Another notable effect of polls in modern elections is that politicians concentrate so hard on the figures that they tend to become transfixed by them and react in an exaggerated way. A couple of poor results and morale dips. A run of good results and elation follows. The effects of this kind of poll fever showed clearly in 1992. Three weeks into the short campaign and still lagging slightly behind in most of the polls, the Conservatives were reported to be in disarray. "Top Tories Get Jitters as Campaign 'Wobbles'"; "Troubles? What Troubles? Asks Heseltine as Major Comes Under Attack," read the *Observer* headlines.[58] In comparison, Labour's small lead over the same period seems to have contributed to its "triumphalist" manner, culminating in the short-lived leads of 5–7 percent reported on the morning of 1 April (All Fools Day) and its last big rally in Sheffield on the same day. The rally was widely criticised for its "we have already won" style.

Ironically, there was little to choose between the polling results of the parties throughout most of the previous year (see table 5.3), and the gap during the short campaign was even narrower. In fact, for all its sound and fury, very little happened to voting intentions in the last weeks of political effort. Although most polls showed Labour in the lead for most of the time (table 5.7), the figure was rarely more than 1 or 2 percent and within the bounds of statistical error. The Conservatives were generally within striking distance, yet usually behind—that is, until

TABLE 5.7

RUNNING AVERAGE OF THE POLLS: SHORT CAMPAIGN

	Con.	Lab.	Lib. Dem.	Other	Lab. Lead
March					
11	38%	40%	17%	5%	2%
12	40	40	15	4	0
13	39	40	17	5	1
14	39	40	16	5	1
15	39	40	16	5	1
16	39	41	15	4	2
17	39	41	16	4	2
18	39	41	17	3	2
19	39	41	17	3	2
20	39	41	17	3	2
21	38	41	17	4	3
22	39	40	16	5	1
23	39	40	16	4	1
24	39	40	16	4	1
25	39	41	17	4	2
26	39	41	17	4	2
27	38	39	18	4	1
28	38	39	18	4	1
29	38	39	18	4	1
30	37	40	18	5	3
31	37	41	18	4	4
April					
1	36	40	18	5	4
2	36	40	19	5	4
3	37	39	19	4	2
4	37	40	19	4	3
5	37	40	19	4	3
6	37	40	19	4	3
7	37	40	19	5	3
8	38	39	19	3	1

SOURCE: *Guardian,* 9 April 1992, 1.

the very last days, when the gap closed. Election-day polls put the two parties neck and neck or Labour slightly in front. The campaign had been close fought and the climax would be a nail-biting affair, but a hung Parliament with Labour as the largest party was widely predicted, and everybody knew that the polls are usually right within small margins of error.

Campaign Analysis

The 1992 campaign was remarkable, not least because it presented a series of contrasts, if not contradictions. It was the longest since 1964, but it was not notably informative or educative. It was one of the closest in recent memory, yet it was one of the most boring and uneventful. It was fought at a time of great change in the world, but it was parochial.[59] On the domestic front the country was faced with many vital issues, but most were passed over. The central issue of economic recession might well have aroused political and ideological passions, but it was an almost pure valence-issue election about style, image, and managerial competence. Even on economic matters, the campaign focused mainly on taxation and had little to say about unemployment, training, investment, or strategies for economic recovery.

Perhaps one of the most surprising aspects of the whole affair was the poor quality of the Conservative campaign. In the last week *The Economist* reported that "the ineptness of the Tories' campaign has been raising eyebrows" and "a dismal campaign by the Conservatives has filled its supporters with dismay."[60] The broadsheets, even Conservative ones, went into details of the strategic and tactical mistakes in articles under headlines such as "Bombshell Too Far Gives Tories the Blues," "Soapbox Major Fails to Satisfy," and "Quest for a Tidal Wave: Tories Are Squabbling Over Whom to Blame for a Bad Campaign."[61] One is tempted to conclude that the campaign had no effect on the final result, but that would ignore the Conservatives' drumbeat theme of Labour's economic incompetence and its tax plans.

It is true that it was not a notably dirty campaign, as some had predicted, nor did the Conservative party (unlike at least one Conservative paper) play the race card, which some thought would be its last resort. Yet the campaign certainly did not go far to meet the requirements of liberal democratic theory that elections should inform and educate voters.[62] It was said of the 1988 presidential election in the United States that "there are no incentives at present for campaigners and the media to address tough problems of governance; the incentives all lead towards the use of symbols, and the creation of artificial drama through the emphasis on polls and strategic moves."[63] The same may be said of the 1992 British general election campaign.

Appendix: Campaign Diary

OCTOBER 1991

1   Labour ahead in polls. Major rules out a 1991 election.

2   Labour claims Major afraid of election. Morale high at Labour conference.

5   On last day of Labour conference Major claims Conservatives will win election because public trusts them to run economy.

8   Conservative Conference starts. Government said to be ragged and defensive.

9   First signs of NHS reform problems: London hospital changes delayed.

10   £1 million Hospital Trust deficit reported.

12   Inflation falls to 4.1 percent.

17   Treasury warns economy failing to pull out of the recession. Labour poll puts Labour at 4 percent lead but shows party still lags on economic competence, predicted to be main election battleground.

18   Commonwealth conference gives Major a world statesman role.

25   Reports that economy failing to recover, though recession may have bottomed out.

30   Disagreements in Conservative ranks over the forthcoming European Community Maastricht summit. Labour enthusiasm for EC increases.

NOVEMBER 1991

1   Chancellor Norman Lamont states in his Mansion House speech that worst of the recession over.

2   City responds gloomily to Mansion House speech.

4   Autumn (expenditure) statement gives extra £10 billion to health.

7   Chancellor predicts 2.75 percent growth in 1992, but cost of recession absorbs large part of the £11 billion growth in government spending.

7   Conservatives lose Kincardine and Deeside by-election to Liberal Democrats, Langbaugh to Labour.

15   Nineteenth consecutive monthly increase in unemployment, but smallest since September 1990. Bank of England claims signs of economic upturn.

16   Inflation falls to three-year low of 3.7 percent.

20   Pound falls against German mark, prompting fears of interest rate increase.

21   Thatcher calls for referendum on a single European currency, undermining Major's position that government should decide.

22   Government rules out referendum.

23   Pound falls to lowest level since United Kingdom joined exchange rate mechanism.

29   Kenneth Baker makes history as first home secretary found

	guilty of contempt of court (over extradition of an immigrant).
30	Department of Trade and Industry says recession is still biting hard.

DECEMBER 1991

10–12	Maastricht summit. John Major plays role of European statesman again and avoids splitting the Conservatives at cost of alienating most EC partners. Opposition parties attack government's semidetached role in Europe and lost opportunities.
16	Home repossessions in 1991 reported near 90,000.
17	Reports of 19 percent crime increase in 1991.
20	Pound under renewed pressure and official unemployment figure over 2.5 million (actual unemployment closer to 3 million).
21	Senior ministers reported to be doubtful of economic revival in time for election and said to be preparing the fall-back argument that recession is worldwide and would be worse under Labour.
24	Renewed rumours about need for interest rate rise to protect pound.
30	Consumer confidence falls in December from +3 to −17.
31	Reports of unemployment rises in Tory-held marginal seats.

JANUARY 1992

2	Major blames economic situation on world recession and admits that revival may be delayed.
6	Chancellor admits overoptimism about economic recovery, but attacks Labour's plans for tax increases. Labour announces it will increase the top rate of tax for those earning more than £30,000. Conservatives start to talk about a 10*p* tax increase under Labour. Story taken up by Tory tabloids.
7	Conservatives unveil poster showing large bomb and the slogan *"You'd Pay £1000 more tax a year under Labour."* Polls find that most voters would prefer higher public spending to pre-election tax cuts.
8	Labour announces plans for investment and positive government role in business support.
11	Housing market reported to be worst since war.
13	Kinnock warns against pre-election tax cuts to buy votes.
15	Conservatives take small poll lead. Labour's plans for National Insurance increases in some disarray. Kinnock admits they may be phased in. NHS gets an extra £200 million to reduce waiting lists.
17	Unemployment rises to four-year high. Party tax battle continues.
18	The Institute for Fiscal Studies says 8.7 percent of families would pay more tax, 46 percent less under Labour plans. Poll puts Labour 5 percent ahead of Conservatives, with Liberal Democrats at 12 percent.
19	Harris poll shows Conservatives ahead of Labour on tax

issues, but 40 percent want Chancellor Lamont sacked. Same poll shows that 43 percent blame recession on Thatcher's government, 28 percent on world recession, and only 9 percent on Major's government.

20   Major defends chancellor's courageous policies, but admits economic recovery will not start before election day.

22   Budget set for 10 March. Parties level in polls. City analysts Midland Montagu estimate Conservative election pledges at £335 billion, only £2 billion less than Labour.

23   Speculation about budget tax cuts.

24   Conservatives claim Labour's support for EC minimum wage of £3.40 an hour would result in extra 2 million unemployed. National Institute of Economic and Social Research says it would cost 120,000 to 170,000 jobs.

25   Two polls show narrow Tory lead.

28   1991 trade gap of £6 billion announced. Major relaunches Citizens' Charters.

29   Conservatives announce new union restrictions. Labour unveils its "Vatman" poster (showing Norman Lamont as an evil-looking Batman) and attacks Tory VAT increases. Kinnock extracts promise from Major not to increase VAT to pay for income tax cuts.

FEBRUARY 1992

2   The Sunday Times, News of the World, and (later) Daily Express print "Moscow Files" story about Kinnock's "private dialogues" with Kremlin. Observer leads with story about break-ins at Labour and Liberal Democrat offices and tampering with personal computers.

4   Governor of the Bank of England admits having been too optimistic about economic revival.

5   Paddy Ashdown scandal breaks.

7   Polls shows support for Ashdown, increase in Liberal Democrat support.

12   Main parties in dead heat in polls. Hung Parliament treated as a serious possibility.

13   Reports that recession is longest since the war. Conservatives trail the story of no tax cuts but increased public spending.

14   "Black Thursday": large increase in unemployment; Ford announces £920 million losses; manufacturing investment declines 15 percent; house repossessions increase to 75,000.

15   Inflation falls to 4.1 percent, but official figures show manufacturing output rose only 5 percent between 1979 and 1992. Polls put Conservatives two points ahead of Labour with Liberal Democrats improving to 17.5 percent. Opinion polls show many voters do not mind hung Parliament.

18   Conservatives attack Labour–trade union connection.

19   Substantial increases in long-term unemployment figures.

21   Revelation that surgeons paid up to £1000 for morning's work in attempt to cut hospital waiting lists. Conservatives unveil

	poster showing huge locust with slogan "Now Labour puts the bite on savings."
24	Reports that the public-sector borrowing requirement will rise to £30 billion. Kinnock again warns against tax cuts to buy votes. NOP/*Independent* poll puts Labour 4 percent ahead.
25	Conservatives unveil poster of policeman with one hand tied behind his back and the slogan "Labour's soft on crime."
28	December trade deficit of £409 million increases to £794 million in January.

MARCH 1992

5	Chris Patten, Conservative party chairman, states party has spent £440,000 donation from Asil Nadir, disgraced chairman of Polly Peck. Donation alleged to be illegal.
10	Budget Day. Taxes reduced, government borrowing doubled.
11	The pound and the markets wobble after the budget. Figures show a 16 percent increase in crime in 1991. Major announces 9 April as election day.
13	Major refuses TV debate with Kinnock. BBC cancels Panorama programme discussing government's role in creating recession.
15	Polls show two main parties close in the polls with Liberal Democrats at about 12 percent. Polls say voters are bored and impatient with negative campaigning of main parties. Liberal Democrats arouse least disdain.
16	Conservatives attack Labour as party of "permanent high tax," and accuse Liberal Democrats of cynicism.
17	Labour presents "alternative budget."
18	Tory and Labour manifestos published. Labour mentions neither class nor socialism. Conservatives launch criticized as amateur and boring. Two polls show 5 percent Labour lead. January industrial production fell 1.3 percent.
19	Gallup poll gives Conservatives 2 percent lead. Labour poster shows Major and Lamont hiding behind sandbags labeled "Tory defense policy" and the slogan "It's not our recession."
20	Official unemployment figures increase to 2.65 million (9.4 percent). Hostile crowds in Bolton force John Major to abandon first walkabout. Two-page advertisement for Natural Law party appears in broadsheets.
21	Thatcher makes a rare campaign appearance. Growing Conservative party and press concern over campaign.
23	Public spending set to exceed current revenues by £11.3 billion (on top of £28 billion PSBR), prompting stories of 5*p* income tax increase whichever party wins. Ashdown and Liberal Democrats claim their plans for 1*p* tax rise for education supported by most voters.
24	Government fails to rebut independent reports of £11.3 billion shortfall in public finances. Major rendered speechless by press conference questions. Polls disagree about which party has small lead.

25	Poll puts Labour 3 percent ahead. Labour election broadcast about "Jennifer's ear."
26	Conservatives attack Labour and Kinnock for lies and irresponsibility in "Jennifer's ear" programme.
27	Health minister admits Conservative role in making public Jennifer's identity.
28	Conservatives concerned about poor quality of party campaign. Hung Parliament increasingly seen as inevitable. Major's soapbox makes first appearance.
29	Polls report growing support for Liberal Democrats.
30	50 percent increase in business bankruptcies reported in past year. Major warns of "Nightmare on Kinnock St." and plans high-profile "walkabouts" with his soapbox. Two main parties level, but Liberal Democrats pick up 2 percent in the week.
31	Major promises progress towards 20p standard rate income tax, but Lamont claims little room for manoeuvre on taxing or spending in coming years. Lamont withdrawn from further media discussions with John Smith. Poll puts Labour 2 percent ahead and still points to a hung parliament.

APRIL 1992

1	ICM, Harris, and MORI polls give Labour 5–7 percent lead. "Glitzy" Labour rally in Sheffield. Liberal Democrats gain support.
2	Stock market and pound fall. Two main parties attack Liberal Democrats.
3	Polls return to slim Labour lead.
4	Conservatives warn of financial crisis and rioting if Labour wins.
5	Hung Parliament with Liberal Democrats holding balance makes proportional representation an election issue. Major flatly opposes it as "alien."
6	Party leaders face hostile questions from "Granada 500," electors selected from two marginal seats. Kinnock faces shouts of "Answer in English, not Chinese." Major hissed on poll tax. Ashdown accused of blackmail on proportional representation.
7	Poll gives Labour 2 percent lead. Nationalists appear to gain ground in Scotland. Constitutional reform becomes an issue. Major opposing devolution, proportional representation, and the dangers of a hung Parliament and weak government.
8	Main parties return to old themes of economy, tax, health, but Major softens position on proportional representation.
9	Election day. Polls put Labour marginally ahead or level with Conservatives. All point to hung Parliament.

Acknowledgements

I am most grateful to Steven Studd for research assistance and to Anthony King whose enormous patience with an early draft of the article greatly improved the quality of the final version.

Notes

1. For a recent and comprehensive review of economic voting, see Leif Lewin, *Self Interest and Public Interest in Western Politics* (Oxford: Oxford University Press, 1991), 29–59. A study of the 1987 general elections found that "electors with optimistic assessments of the past conditions and future prospects of the national economy were more likely to vote Conservative." William L. Miller et al., *How Voters Change* (Oxford: Clarendon Press, 1990), 252.

2. See, for example, Robert M. Worcester, *British Public Opinion* (Oxford: Basil Blackwell), 112.

3. *Gallup Political and Economic Index* 374 (October 1991): 4.

4. *Gallup Political and Economic Index* 364 (December 1990): 1.

5. Jan-Erik Lane, David McKay, and Kenneth Newton, *Political Data Handbook* (Oxford: Oxford University Press, 1991), 59–62.

6. *The Times*, 21 February 1992, 7.

7. The Gallup 9000 survey provides a monthly run of figures. See *Gallup Political and Economic Index*, 1991.

8. *Gallup Political and Economic Index* 374 (October 1991): 12–13.

9. This is not to say position issues played no part but that their role was small. Fundamental policy disagreement about the European Community is the most obvious example, but it was rarely brought into the open because ideological differences within the parties were as deep and wide as differences between them.

10. "Polls Strengthen Theory of Major Blunder," *Guardian*, 23 December 1991.

11. "Will Major Take an Early Plunge?" Anthony King, *Sunday Telegraph*, 10 March 1991.

12. "Tories Waver on Election Timing," *Independent*, 24 February 1992.

13. *Independent*, 14 February 1992, 1.

14. *Independent*, 15 February 1992, 6.

15. *The Times*, 21 February 1992, 7.

16. Speech to the House of Commons, 20 February 1992.

17. *Gallup Political and Economic Index* 378 (February 1992): 26.

18. *The Times*, 13 January 1992.

19. *Independent*, 11 March 1992, 12.

20. See *Guardian*, 3 March 1992, 2.

21. "Tax Cut 'Not a Vote-Winner,'" *Independent*, 7 January 1992, 1. The figure is consistent with most other surveys of this kind; see John Rentoul, *Me and Mine* (London: Hyman, 1989), 124–29, and Tom W. Smith, "Inequal-

ity and Welfare," in *British Social Attitudes: Special International Report,* ed. Roger Jowell et al. (Aldershot: Gower, 1989), 61–75.

22. *Gallup Political and Economic Index* 379 (March 1992): 18–19.
23. *Financial Times,* 17 March 1992.
24. *Observer,* 22 March 1992, 1.
25. "Tory Pre-Poll Promises to £3.5 Bn," *Guardian,* 6 March 1992, 2.
26. *Financial Times,* 1 April 1992, 11.
27. See, for example, *Gallup Political and Economic Index* 380 (April 1992): 6.
28. Over 80 percent thought that both parties had done "too much slanging" and strong disapproval of the Labour campaign doubled to 35 percent immediately after the health row. See "Slag-off Factor Stirs but Does Not Shake," *Independent,* 29 March 1992, 1, 23.
29. University of Loughborough, Communications Research Centre, *1992 Election Study for the Guardian* 5, table 2.
30. David Butler and Dennis Kavanagh, eds., *The British General Election of 1987* (London: Macmillan, 1988), 141, 183.
31. *Gallup Political and Economic Index* 380 (April 1992): 30. For a closer analyis of the impact of party leaders on the 1983 election, see Ivor Crewe, "How to Win a Landslide without Really Trying: Why the Conservatives Won in 1983," in *Britain at the Polls, 1983,* ed. Austin Ranney (Durham, N.C.: Duke University Press, 1985), 181–83.
32. For full details, see University of Loughborough, *1992 Election Study for the Guardian* 5, 1–9.
33. *Gallup Political and Economic Index* 380 (April 1992): 8.
34. Ibid., 27.
35. For popular images of Major and Kinnock, see *Gallup Political and Economic Index* 379 (March 1992): 21, 25.
36. *Gallup Political and Economic Index* 380 (April 1992): 26.
37. See William L. Miller, *Media and Voters* (Oxford: Clarendon Press, 1991); and Kenneth Newton, "Do People Read Everything They Believe in the Papers? Newspapers and Voters in the 1983 and 1987 Elections," in *British Elections and Parties Yearbook, 1991,* ed. Ivor Crewe et al. (Hemel Hempstead: Harvester Wheatsheaf, 1991), 51–74.
38. For details, see *Independent,* 12 March 1992, 10.
39. For more examples and discussion, see "Tabloids Suffer from Pollster's Droop," *Financial Times,* 4–5 April 1992, 6; and "Royals Relieve Beleagured Tabloids," *Guardian,* 19 March 1992, 16.
40. University of Loughborough, Communications Research Centre, *1992 Election Study for the Guardian,* table 1.
41. The same was true of the American presidential campaign of 1988. See Marjorie Randon Hershey, "The Campaign and the Media," in *The Election of 1988,* ed. Gerald M. Pomper (Chatham, N.J.: Chatham House, 1988), 96–100.
42. These became issues when, in the last few days, the polls showed the Conservatives running in third place in Scotland behind Labour and the Scottish Nationalists, and when a hung Parliament looked increasingly likely. Devolution and electoral reform were not important issues for the general public, but they excited interest among professional politicians.

43. University of Loughborough, Communications Research Centre, *1992 Election Study for the Guardian* 5, 6.

44. The great majority of viewers trust the BBC's impartiality, but among the minority who believe it is biased, more think it favours the Conservatives than think it favours Labour. For a recent survey, see *The Economist*, 26 October 1991, 39.

45. "Election 92," *The Sunday Times*, 5 April, 3. Bitter denunciations of the BBC predated the election campaign. However, see "The Siege of Our Screens," *Guardian*, 17 February 1992, 27.

46. An observer of American politics suggests that "this 'media-bashing' takes the form of asking for fair play or 'balanced treatment,' but its real aim is to insulate a candidate—or a President—from criticism." Wilson Carey McWilliams, "The Meaning of the Election," in Pomper, *The Election of 1988*, 181.

47. "Return to Brixton Proves a Turn-Off," *Guardian*, 21 March 1992, 3; "Kippers Star as Major Journeys to His Roots," *Independent*, 18 March 1992, 13; "Meter Voters Give a Mixed Reaction to Health Broadcast," *Guardian*, 28 March 1992, 4.

48. *Financial Times*, 9 April 1992.

49. Quoted in "Did the Tabloids Destroy Kinnock?" *Independent*, 15 April 1992, 15.

50. The Ford chief in question, Ian McAllister, wrote to Kinnock to apologise and deny the burden of the story, but by that time Chris Patten had quoted the *Mail* in the Commons and had been quoted, in turn, by the BBC. Thus the item became "news." A similar *Mail* "news" story concerned a split between Labour's deputy leader, Roy Hattersley, and the shadow chancellor, John Smith, and another concerned figures and stories in the *Mail* and the *Sunday Times* about Labour's minimum-wage proposals and resulting job losses. See "Tories Prime *Mail* for Shots at Labour," *Guardian*, 29 January 1992, 2.

51. The normally true-blue *Daily Mail*, which seems to have acted as the "official" Conservative newspaper, warned that the Conservatives deserved to lose if they did not "raise their game." *Daily Mail*, 28 March 1992.

52. See, for example, Charles Moore, "Nothing to Declare—That's What Is Wrong with Labour," *Daily Telegraph*, 14 February 1992.

53. "How the Newspapers Stand," *Marketing News*, 3 April 1992, 17.

54. "Did the Tabloids Destroy Kinnock?" The *Independent*, 15 April 1992, 15.

55. University of Loughborough, Communications Research Centre, *1992 Election Study for the Guardian*.

56. Anthony Broh, "Horse-Race Journalism: Reporting the Polls in the 1976 Presidential Election," *Public Opinion Quarterly* 44 (1980): 514–29.

57. Hershey, "Campaign and Media," 96.

58. 29 March 1992.

59. According to one study, "in recent weeks the UK has seemed to be hermetically sealed off from the rest of the globe." University of Loughborough, Communications Research Centre, *1992 Election Study for the Guardian* 5, 1.

60. *The Economist*, 4 April 1992, 27, 29.

61. Respectively, *Guardian,* 2 April 1992, 11; *The Sunday Times,* 5 April 1992, 17; and *Independent on Sunday,* 5 April 1992, 15.
62. The distinguished political columnist Hugo Young writing for the *Guardian,* repeatedly claimed that the campaign was fulfilling this vital democratic function.
63. Hershey, "Campaign and Media," 100.

6

Why the Conservative Party Won — Again

David Sanders

The 1992 election was undoubtedly one of the most extraordinary in recent British history. To the consternation of the opinion pollsters, whose findings throughout the campaign had predicted a hung Parliament, the Conservatives secured some 41.9 percent of the popular vote—a fraction down on its share in 1987—with Labour trailing at 34.3 percent and the Liberal Democrats at 17.8 percent. John Major's government was reelected with a twenty-one-seat majority in the House of Commons.

As we have seen throughout this book, the Conservatives' success was achieved in the most inauspicious of circumstances. Britain was in the grip of the longest recession since the early 1930s. Labour had moderated its policies and returned to the centre ground of British politics. The Liberal Democrats had declined. The poll-tax furore had left a legacy of resentment among large sections of the electorate. Margaret Thatcher, who had led the Conservatives to three resounding election victories, was gone. The Conservatives had been defeated in a long-running series of by-elections. And on top of all this, the opinion polls since the autumn of 1991 had indicated that support for the two major parties was running neck and neck, with Labour, if anything, slightly ahead.

The impression at the beginning of the campaign, on 11 March 1992, was that the parliamentary dominance enjoyed by the Conservatives since 1979 was about to end. This impression, moreover, was confirmed by the campaign itself. Forty-three of the forty-seven opinion polls conducted by the five main polling organisations during the campaign suggested that no single party would gain an overall Commons majority, with the result that constitutional specialists were consulted about the procedures that might be followed in the event of a hung Parliament. Labour and Liberal Democrat leaders gave public intimations of their preparedness to consider the possibility of coalition government. Yet, when the votes were finally cast, the Conservatives had won—again. They emerged with 336 seats—41 less than in 1987, but still sufficient for a secure working majority. Labour increased its seats from 229 in 1987 to 271. The Liberal Democrats—the former "Alliance" of Liberals and Social Democrats—obtained 20 seats, even though their share of the popular vote fell from 22.5 percent to 17.8 percent. Given the "hung Parliament" predictions of the polls, such a decisive Conservative victory suggested either that a very large swing to the government had taken place in the last twenty-four hours (four out of five polls conducted on the day before the election had given Labour a small lead) or that the polls had seriously, and consistently, underestimated the true level of Conservative support.

The swings between the parties varied considerably across the 651 constituencies, suggesting that local personalities and local conditions continue to be of some relevance in determining election outcomes. As in most postwar British elections, there were varying patterns of party support among voters with different social backgrounds and there were significant regional variations in swing. The regional breakdown of the Great Britain vote is summarised in table 6.1. Although the Conservative to Labour swing varied from −2.5 percent in Scotland to +6 percent in Yorkshire and Humberside, the overall picture of partisan support in 1992 was not substantially different from that in 1987: The Conservatives continued to dominate southern England, East Anglia, and the Midlands; Labour remained strongest in northern England, Wales, and Scotland; and the Liberal Democrats maintained a substantial presence in the South West. Notwithstanding any of these regional variations, the key to the Conservatives' success, as we later see, centred on their ability to convince sufficient voters that economic good times were just around the corner, provided that the incumbent government remained in office. The first part of this chapter demonstrates the profound effects that economic considerations exerted on the levels of support enjoyed by the major parties between the 1987 general election and the start of the official campaign five years later. The second part, based on the findings of two postelection surveys, explores a number of potential explanations for the voting behaviour of individual electors and concludes that, as in the preelection period, "pocketbook" calculations—though of a conditional and qualified sort—were crucially important in determining the outcome.

TABLE 6.1
REGIONAL SHARES OF THE GREAT BRITAIN
POPULAR VOTE, APRIL 1992

	Con.	Lab.	Lib.-Dem.	Nat.	Con.-Lab. swing
London	45.3%	37.1%	15.1%		+3.4%
South East	54.5	20.7	23.4		+3.2
South West	47.6	19.2	31.4		+2.6
East Anglia	41.1	18.0	19.5		+2.3
East Midlands	46.6	37.4	15.3		+4.7
West Midlands	44.8	38.8	15.0		+3.1
Wales	28.6	49.5	12.4	8.8%	+2.5
North West	37.8	44.9	15.8		+2.0
Yorkshire and Humberside	27.9	44.3	16.8		+6.0
North	33.4	50.6	15.6		+2.0
Scotland	35.7	39.0	21.5	13.1	–2.5
Overall Great Britain share	42.8	35.2	18.3		+2.1

The 1987 Parliament: The Major Parties' Varying Popularity

Figure 6.1 provides a summary of the changing support levels of the three main parties during the 1987 Parliament. The graphs show the monthly "poll of polls" ratings for each party based on quota sample surveys conducted by MORI, Gallup, Harris, ICM, and NOP. The monthly rating is the unweighted average of the percentage of respondents saying they would vote for the party in question "if there were a general election tomorrow," with "don't know"s excluded from the percentage base. Given the mismatch between the April 1992 opinion poll ratings and the actual election result, these measures clearly need to be treated with some caution. That said, there are three good reasons for considering the implications of such data. First, with the notable exception of 1970, the opinion pollsters, especially if their separate estimates are averaged, have predicted the outcomes of most postwar general elections reasonably accurately. Second, polls conducted at the many by-elections held during the 1987 Parliament generally provided a fairly accurate guide to the actual results. The polls thus did reflect popular feeling for much of the 1987–92 period. Third, election strategists in all three major parties interpret opinion polls' findings as a general indication of the state of party support. For the governing party in particular, the feedback that opinion poll ratings represent is an important ingredient in calculations about when an election should be called. And the timing of the 1992 general election was certainly a significant factor in the Conservatives' success.

Several things are immediately apparent from figure 6.1. First, the broad trends in Labour and Conservative support tend to move in opposite directions. When the trend in Conservative support is downwards (as between, say, the autumn of 1987 and the spring of 1990), the trend in Labour support is upwards; and vice versa. Liberal-Social Democrat

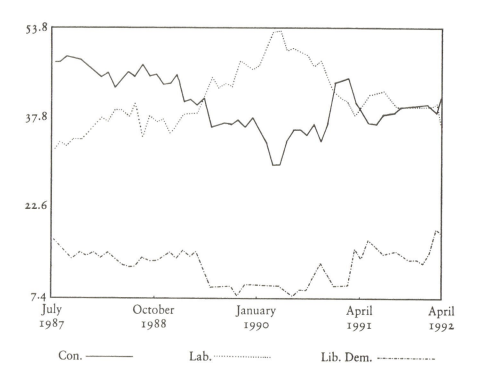

Con. ————   Lab. ················   Lib. Dem. ----------

FIGURE 6.1

VARIATIONS IN SUPPORT FOR THE CONSERVATIVE, LABOUR,
AND ALLIANCE/LIBERAL-DEMOCRAT PARTIES,
JULY 1987–APRIL 1992

SOURCE: The data shown are the unweighted monthly averages of the figures reported by Gallup, NORI, Harris, NOP, and ICM.

NOTE: Support for each party is measured as the percentage of respondents intending to vote for each party "if there were a general election tomorrow"; "don't know"s are excluded from the percentage base.

support drifted downwards in the immediate aftermath of the 1987 election, but then stabilised at around 15 percent until the spring of 1989. The rapid fall in support after April 1989 coincided with the divisive merger between the Liberals and the Social Democrats. As the Liberal-Democrats' identity began to develop, their support slowly recovered, though they temporarily lost ground following Thatcher's removal from office in November 1990.

A further observation that needs to be made about figure 6.1 concerns the impact of "significant political events." Three obvious candidates present themselves in the context of the 1987 Parliament: (1) the introduction of the poll tax in March 1990, (2) the accession of John Major to the premiership in November 1990, and (3) the Gulf War in February–March 1991.

1. *The introduction of the poll tax.* Whatever the actual merits and demerits of the community charge, there is no doubt that it was deeply unpopular. Indeed, at the time of its introduction, some 64 percent of respondents in a Gallup survey thought that the tax was "a bad idea," and 73 percent believed that they would be worse off as a result.[1] As figure 6.1 shows, at the time the tax was introduced, Conservative popularity, which had already been declining, dipped even further, reaching its lowest point (30 percent) during the Parliament. Labour popularity meanwhile soared, reaching its highest rating of 53 percent. The immediate effects of the introduction of the tax, however, seem to have dissipated rapidly. Within two months, both Labour and Conservative popularity had returned to their previous levels, suggesting that the long-term impact of the tax might have been less than was often popularly supposed.

2. *The accession of John Major.* Although Conservative popularity recovered moderately during the summer of 1990, perhaps as voters' memories of their poll-tax bills faded, by the autumn Conservative fortunes again appeared to be on the slide. A widely held view both within and outside the party was that a significant part of the problem was Thatcher herself. For one thing, she was seen as the prime mover behind the poll tax; it was identified in the public mind as *her* tax. For another, she seemed increasingly remote from the everyday cut and thrust of domestic British politics—a leader unprepared to listen either to the advice of her colleagues or to the criticisms of the electorate. All of this was reflected in Thatcher's personal poll ratings which, having been broadly in line with those of the Conservative party since the mid

1980s, consistently fell behind the party's ratings from the autumn of 1989 onwards.[2] By November 1990, Conservative MPs were ready to act. Fearful that the prime minister's personal unpopularity was adding to their own political difficulties, and fueled by opinion poll evidence that their party's ratings might rise by as much as ten percentage points under a different leader,[3] they abruptly removed Thatcher from office. True to the pollsters' predictions (and yet another reason for believing that their estimates are not entirely unreliable), Conservative popularity jumped an average of ten percentage points virtually overnight: in early December the Conservatives' average opinion poll rating stood at 47 percent. As figure 6.1 shows, however, this boost to Conservative fortunes (as well as the simultaneous damage to Labour's ratings) did not last more than a few months. By the late spring of 1991, Conservative popularity had fallen back below 37 percent, the point from which it had leapt so spectacularly in the wake of John Major's accession.

3. *The Gulf War.* From the time that Iraqi forces occupied Kuwait in August 1990, political observers began to speculate on the possibility that a successful Anglo-American military campaign against Saddam Hussein might have the same reviving effect on Conservative fortunes that Thatcher's campaign to recover the Falklands had had in 1982.[4] In the event, Thatcher's removal preempted any notion that a "bloody good war" was necessary to raise the government's popularity ratings: simply getting rid of her was enough. John Major's government nonetheless participated fully in the expulsion of Iraqi forces from Kuwait; and although the new premier pointedly avoided any sort of jingoistic triumphalism, his party's ratings remained high until March 1991. Nevertheless, those ratings had fallen below 37 percent by May 1991, suggesting that any Gulf War effect on Conservative popularity was very short lived. What all three episodes suggest is that the major political events of the 1987–92 period had only relatively ephemeral effects on the three parties' fortunes.

MODELING THE TRENDS IN PARTY SUPPORT, 1987–92

Far more intriguing than these temporary surges is the question of what determined the longer-term trends in support for the parties. Why did Conservative support fall so consistently until the spring of 1990, then slowly recover throughout 1991, even when the effects of Thatcher's fall and Major's election had apparently disappeared? Why did Labour's support rise and then fall on an almost identical time scale? This sort of decline-recovery trend in government support is familiar to students of recent British history.

One explanation for this decline-recovery pattern is that it results from the tendency of governments to introduce unpopular measures (especially if they involve unpalatable fiscal or monetary medicine) relatively early on in their periods in office, and to ensure, as far as circumstances allow, that the economy can be gently reflated in the run-up to the next general election. The Conservatives' problem during the 1987 Parliament was that, partly to counteract the potentially deflationary effects of the stock market crash of October 1987, the chancellor maintained a low interest rate policy for too long. The result of this policy was that Britain's inflation rate rose sharply during 1988 and 1989. To check this "overheating," the government was subsequently obliged to raise interest rates substantially from 1988 to 1990. Although base rates were progressively reduced after October 1990, the economic slowdown induced by the protracted period of high rates was so severe that both manufacturing output and gross domestic product fell for five successive quarters.

The government's high interest rate policies certainly appear to have adversely affected its popularity. Given the state of the British housing market, this was hardly surprising. Almost 70 percent of British voters own their own homes, and a large majority of that 70 percent pay for them through variable interest rate mortgages. As a result, base rate changes affect more than just the cost of consumer credit; they also have a direct, and often substantial, impact on the monthly outgoings of many British households, even in situations where monthly repayments are adjusted annually. Interest rates thus exert a very powerful pocketbook effect. One way in which this pocketbook effect is manifested is through the level of optimism that people exhibit about their financial prospects.

Survey data measuring the general sense of economic optimism among the British electorate have been collected on a monthly basis since the mid-1970s. Respondents are asked whether they think the financial position of their household over the next year will get better, get worse, or stay about the same.[5] Figure 6.2 shows how the overall balance of optimism–pessimism—the aggregate level of personal economic expectations—varied over the 1987–92 period. Previous studies have shown that fluctuations in these aggregate expectations are affected by a number of variables, including tax changes, inflation, and the way that the national press covers economic news,[6] but that interest rates are their most significant determinant. It seems reasonable to suppose, therefore, that the high interest rate policies of 1988–90 contributed substantially

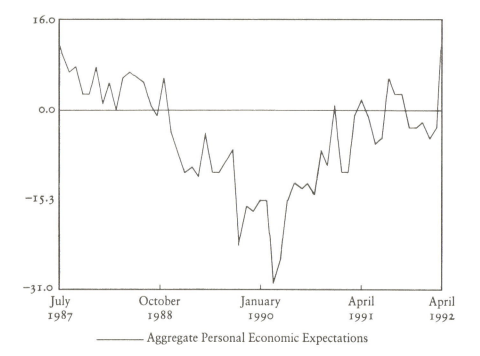

———— Aggregate Personal Economic Expectations

FIGURE 6.2

VARIATIONS IN AGGREGATE PERSONAL ECONOMIC EXPECTATIONS,
JULY 1987–APRIL 1992

SOURCE: Gallup.
NOTE: The data are derived from responses to the question, "How do you think the financial situation of your household will change over the next twelve months?" The monthly level of Aggregate Personal Economic Expectations is measured as the percentage of respondents who think their situation will get better minus the percentage who think it will get worse.

to the fall in aggregate expectations that occurred over the same period. By the same token, the sequence of interest rate reductions that was initiated in the autumn of 1990 probably played an important part in the recovery of expectations that occurred during 1991. A simple statistical model shows that, correcting for the sharp fall in expectations engendered by the introduction of the poll tax and the temporary boost associated with Thatcher's fall, a percentage point increase (reduction) in interest rates elicited on average during this period a two-point reduction (increase) in aggregate expectations in the following month.[7]

POPULARITY, PERSONAL ECONOMIC EXPECTATIONS, AND SIGNIFICANT EVENTS

The critical question, of course, is how far these changes in economic expectations might have affected the popularity of the Conservative government. There are certainly good reasons for supposing that they may have done. Many studies of the relationship between economics and political support have distinguished between "sociotropic" and "egocentric" motivations. Voters act sociotropically to the extent that their political judgements depend on their assessment of whether the government's economic performance has been good or bad for the country as a whole. They act egocentrically to the extent that their political judgements reflect the incumbent government's ability to deliver economic benefits to them personally. Most studies of economic voting in Britain, at least since 1979, have found that egocentric concerns tend to predominate over sociotropic ones.[8] The personal expectations index shown in figure 6.2 is quintessentially an egocentric measure. If voters are egocentric in this sense, then the measures in figure 6.2 might be expected to predict support for the government of the day on the argument that economic optimists, other things being equal, are likely to support the incumbent government to preserve the status quo they associate with optimism. I feel good about my own prospects; therefore, I feel good about the government. And vice versa.

Support for this sort of egocentric mechanism is certainly suggested by figure 6.3, which plots fluctuations in both aggregate personal expectations and government popularity during the course of the 1987 Parliament. As the figure indicates, although the fit between the two graphs is by no means perfect (the simple correlation is $r = .7$), the coincidence between them is good. Both declined during 1988 and 1989; both reached their low point in the spring of 1990 when the poll tax was introduced; and both then recovered slowly, peaking in time for the April 1992 election. It would clearly be simplistic to attribute the Conservatives' election victory to the government's ability to raise personal expectations purely on the basis of the sort of graphic evidence presented in figure 6.3. That said, more formal models of the impact of expectations on popularity likewise support the notion that expectations played a significant role in determining the level of support for the government during the 1987–92 period. They also bear out the conclusion that the direct political effects of the introduction of the poll tax and of Thatcher's removal were relatively short lived.[9]

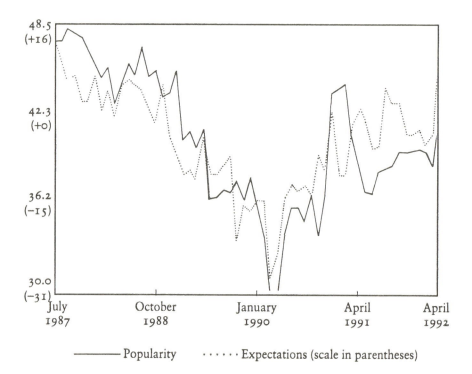

48.5
(+16)

42.3
(+0)

36.2
(−15)

30.0
(−31)

July   October   January   April   April
1987   1988   1990   1991   1992

——— Popularity   · · · · · Expectations (scale in parentheses)

FIGURE 6.3

VARIATIONS IN CONSERVATIVE POPULARITY AND VARIATIONS
IN AGGREGATE PERSONAL ECONOMIC EXPECTATIONS,
JULY 1987–APRIL 1992

SOURCES: The data shown are the unweighted monthly averages of the figures reported by Gallup, NORI, Harris, NOP, and ICM.

ELECTION TIMING, LABOUR'S REVIVAL,
AND A DELAYED RECOVERY

Given this apparently crucial role for economic factors in the determination of Conservative support, the government's reelection strategy from
1989 onwards focused on the need to wait until economic conditions
were right. Fortunately, or so it appeared at the time, most of the economic forecasts published in early 1990 anticipated that inflation would
fall sharply during 1991, permitting commensurate reductions in interest
rates, and also that the United Kingdom would be emerging from the recession by the end of that year. With such forecasts in hand, and with

current personal economic expectations still low, the obvious course of action was for the government to suspend Mrs. Thatcher's previous practice of seeking reelection every four years and to delay holding the election for as long as possible. The longer the government waited (and, legally, it could wait until July 1992), the greater would be its chances of conjuring up a strong "feel-good factor" among voters in time for polling day.[10]

What made waiting seem even more desirable to the Conservative Central Office planners was the disturbing revival of the Labour party. As figure 6.1 shows, Labour's popularity ratings had been improving slowly ever since late 1987, but with the publication of *Meet the Challenge, Make the Change* and the Policy Review in May 1989, the party's support surged to over 40 percent for only the second time in nearly a decade.[11] The rejection of unilateralism and nationalisation, together with a newfound enthusiasm for the European Community (EC), seemed to mark Labour's return to the political mainstream. In the period between May 1989 and April 1992, Labour's poll ratings fell below 40 percent in only two months: in March and September of 1991, when its ratings were 38.5 percent and 39.5 percent. As table 6.2 indicates, the average level of Labour support between May 1989 and April 1992 was 44 percent—a restoration of the sort of popularity that the party enjoyed prior to the SDP breakaway in September 1981.

The Policy Review's success lay not just in the more moderate policy positions it proposed. Labour throughout the 1980s had been widely seen as extremist, irresponsible, and disunited. The Policy Review and Kinnock's style of leadership generally reversed these perceptions. Within months of the review's publication, the widely felt sense that Labour

TABLE 6.2

AVERAGE MONTHLY OPINION POLL SUPPORT[a]

FOR THE LABOUR PARTY, 1979–92

June 1979–September 1981	(SDP split)	43.4%
October 1981–June 1983	(general election)	30.9
July 1983–June 1987[b]	(general election)	35.4
July 1987–April 1989	(Policy Review published)	36.9
May 1989–April 1992	(general election)	44.0

a. Percentage intending to vote Labour, excluding "don't know"s, averaged from the polls conducted by Gallup, MORI, Harris, Marplan/ICM.

b. Splitting the 1983–87 parliamentary term into two periods equivalent to that for 1987–92 yields July 1983–April 1985, 35 percent; May 1985–June 1987, 35.8 percent.

"had become too extreme"[12] had all but disappeared. Similar transformations occurred in mass attitudes towards Labour's "responsibility"[13] and "unity."[14] While it would be unwise to attribute all these changes in mass perceptions to the effects of the Policy Review, there can be no doubt that the review was an important symbol of Neil Kinnock's new model party. What concerned Conservative party managers was that Labour now looked, and felt, "electable" in a way that had seemed impossible as recently as 1987. Its policies were moderate, its leaders serious and sober. The wild men of the left, if they had not been expelled altogether, had either been silenced or were keeping their own counsel in deference to the need to secure a Labour victory.

This image of Labour electability, combined with the fragile state of the economy during 1990 and 1991, had profound consequences for the timing of the election. There was a brief interlude when John Major might have called an early election in the hope of taking advantage of a temporary surge in opinion poll support for the Conservatives. As table 6.3 shows, between December 1990 and March 1991, the Conservatives—benefiting in part from John Major's "honeymoon" and in part from the allied victory over Iraq—were briefly ahead of Labour. Major's publicly expressed reason for not calling a "khaki election" in these circumstances was that he wished to establish his own credentials in office before appealing to the electorate. It seems more likely that Conservative

TABLE 6.3

AVERAGE MONTHLY CONSERVATIVE LEAD OVER LABOUR
JANUARY 1990–APRIL 1992[a]

1990		1991		1992	
January	−11.1%	January	+3.2%	January	+0.2%
February	−16.0	February	+3.8	February	−0.2
March	−22.8	March	+2.5	March	−2.0
April	−23.0	April	−1.3		
May	−15.5	May	−4.9		
June	−13.7	June	−5.4		
July	−13.3	July	−4.2		
August	−13.7	August	−2.5		
September	− 9.7	September	−1.0		
October	−13.7	October	+0.1		
November	− 7.5	November	−0.1		
December	+ 1.9	December	+0.1		

a. Popularity ratings derived from Gallup, MORI, Harris, NOP, and ICM.

strategists advised him that with the economy still firmly locked in recession, the party's lead was in danger of evaporating in the heat of a three-week campaign. With one eye on the forecasts of economic improvement towards the end of the year, therefore, Major postponed the election until at least the autumn.

Even by October, however, neither the opinion polls nor the condition of the economy augured particularly well for the government. The "green shoots of recovery," which Chancellor Lamont had been promising throughout 1991, had failed to appear. The forecasters, moreover, were still predicting some sort of improvement by the late spring of 1992, though the projections were certainly more pessimistic than they had been a year earlier. In these circumstances, it made sense for Major to wait until 1992, particularly as he could justify delay on the grounds that the vitally important negotiations over the future of the EC, scheduled for Maastricht in December 1991, needed to be completed satisfactorily before he could put his case for reelection to the electorate. This combination of circumstances—Labour's apparently continuing strength and the promise of economic recovery in 1992 in spite of the current recessionary difficulties—explains why the British general election was held in the spring of 1992.

Explaining Individual Electors' Votes

The claim of this chapter is that the Conservatives won the 1992 election because they convinced enough voters (1) that a non-Conservative vote would return a Labour government, possibly in coalition or in a minority; and (2) that the modest recovery in their personal economic prospects that they had recently experienced was more likely to be sustained under a Conservative government than a Labour one. Before this claim can be elaborated and justified, however, a brief digression is necessary. The opinion polls' apparent failure to predict the election outcome must be considered.

THE PROBLEM OF THE OPINION POLLS

We noted earlier that at the end of the campaign the five major polling organisations estimated that support for the two major parties was running neck and neck—broadly the same pattern that they had been reporting for the previous four months. The average ratings of the parties, excluding Northern Ireland, in the four polls conducted (by ICM, MORI, Gallup, and NOP) on 7 and 8 April were: Conservative, 38.4 percent; Labour, 39.2 percent; and Liberal Democrat, 19.2 percent. The actual result (again excluding Northern Ireland) was Conservative, 42.8 percent; Labour, 35.2 percent; Liberal Democrat, 18.3 percent. Such a huge disparity between estimate and actuality clearly demanded explanation. The pollsters themselves advanced the notion of a "very late swing": 4 to 5 percent of voters simply switched their preference from Labour to Conservative on election day itself, something that even the most sophisticated polling techniques could not have anticipated.[15] In support of this claim, the pollsters could point to the considerable individual-level variations in party support they had occasionally observed. An NOP panel study for the *Independent on Sunday,* for example, found that 18 percent of voters had changed their party preferences during the first two weeks of the campaign.[16] The problem with these intimations of individual volatility was that they nevertheless resulted in a high level of aggregate stability—a stability that had been observed throughout the preceding months. Indeed, according to the NOP panel, the net effects of voters switching during the campaign were negligible, if anything suggesting a movement towards Labour rather than away from it, as the "late swing" hypothesis would imply.

There were two further problems with the "late swing" explanation. First, such a huge late swing had never been observed in a British general election before. Labour's opinion poll lead during the 1970 campaign had certainly been reversed in the final days before the actual vote, but polling had effectively stopped the weekend before the election, and the scale of the swing observed then was nothing like that observed between 8 and 9 April 1992. Second, and perhaps most alarming of all for the pollsters, two out of three "exit polls" conducted on election day itself—polls that asked very large numbers of respondents, as they came out of the polling stations, how they had just voted—still got the result terribly wrong. A third estimated that the Conservatives had secured a four percentage point lead over Labour—half the actual lead they achieved.[17] Unfortunately, there was no convincing explanation available as to why these exit polls—usually a reliable guide to what has actually happened—had been so inaccurate. With the honourable exception of Harris, the pollsters still underestimated the Conservative share of the vote and overestimated Labour's—even when their respondents had just voted. This in turn casts some doubt on the claim that all of the mismatch between the pollsters' predictions and the actual election outcome can be explained in terms of a large, pro-Conservative late swing.

Inevitably in these circumstances, a number of other explanations have been advanced to account for the mismatch. Of the explanations that follow, 1 through 5 are all consistent with the idea that the polls, certainly during the official campaign and perhaps for a few months before it, simply misrepresented "true" opinion. Explanations 6 and 7 are consistent with the polls being in some sense "correct" in their representation of opinion throughout a campaign that then unpredictably changed course in the last twenty-four hours.

1. The quota sampling techniques used by the polling agencies somehow undersampled Conservative voters, who were either disproportionately unavailable at the selected sampling points or else more likely to refuse to be interviewed when approached.
2. Labour support was overestimated because people who had not registered to vote, in order to avoid being sent a poll-tax bill, were more likely to be Labour supporters.
3. Some Conservative voters, fearful of being seen by interviewers as uncaring and selfish, were too shy to reveal their "true" voting intentions.
4. Some respondents, perhaps resentful of the way that political debate often seemed to be dominated by opinion poll findings, deliberately misled the pollsters.
5. Some respondents used the opinion polls as a sort of "cost-free referendum" on the government's record, which allowed them to "punish" the government with poor ratings even though they intended to vote for it in the real poll.
6. Insufficient attention was paid to the "don't know" and "won't say" respondents, whose nonresponses were either downplayed or, more usually, simply excluded from the percentage base when calculations about vote share were being published.
7. Some voters were "poor predictors of their own behaviour"[18]—in replying to the pollsters before the election, they did not fully weigh all the calculations that they would eventually make when they entered the voting booths.

Unfortunately, it is simply not possible to establish which of these explanations, if any, are correct. The evidence necessary for a convincing empirical evaluation of any of them would inevitably rely on survey-based sources—and there is, of course, no guarantee that any such sources would themselves be free of the very contaminants whose effects they sought to evaluate. Two implications follow from this condition of necessary ignorance. First, all that can be said with confidence is that there may have been a massive and unprecedented late swing to the Conservatives, Conservative support may consistently have been higher than the polls reported, or both. If this conclusion seems unusually timid, then so be it. Second, considerable caution needs to be exercised in deciding which opinion polls should be consulted in order to determine why particular electors voted the way they did. The present analysis focuses on the results of two polls: the Harris "exit" poll referred to earlier, which slightly underestimated Conservative (and overestimated Labour) support, but which at least forecast the correct winner by a clear margin; and a Gallup survey conducted on the two days following the election that (when the 4 percent of respondents who refused to disclose their voting record are excluded) produced a vote distribution (Conservative, 43 percent; Labour, 36 percent; Liberal Democrat, 18 percent) that almost exactly mirrored the actual outcome.[19]

THE FLOW OF THE VOTE AND "SOCIAL BACKGROUND CHARACTERISTICS"

The percentage of votes cast for each party in the 1987 and 1992 general elections is shown in table 6.4. The figures distinguish between the votes cast in Great Britain excluding Northern Ireland and in the United Kingdom as a whole. Partly because of the security problems in Northern Ireland, survey data for the entire United Kingdom are unavailable. As a result, the ensuing discussion follows the standard practice of excluding the Northern Ireland electors and parties from the various calculations. No special reference is made either to the Scottish and Welsh nationalist parties. This is not to suggest that these parties are unimportant—on the contrary, their increased share of the vote over the last few elections suggests they are increasingly important—merely that their British vote share is so small that the attitudes and characteristics of their supporters cannot be estimated accurately from a national sample of under 2000 electors.

TABLE 6.4
VOTE SHARES OF THE THREE MAJOR PARTIES IN THE
1987 AND 1992 GENERAL ELECTIONS

	Great Britain[a]		United Kingdom	
	1987	1992	1987	1992
Conservative	42.8%	43.3%	42.3%	41.9%
Labour	35.2	31.5	30.8	34.3
Alliance/Liberal Democrat	18.3	23.1	22.5	17.8

a. Excludes Northern Ireland.

Table 6.5 shows how voters claim to have switched their party preferences between 1987 and 1992. Following the pattern established in previous elections, approximately three-quarters of Conservative and Labour supporters voted the same way on both occasions, with 5 to 7 percent switching to each of the other two major parties. Almost two-thirds of 1987 Alliance supporters voted Liberal Democrat in 1992, with 14 percent shifting to Labour and 10 percent to the Conservatives. Just over 10 percent of supporters of each party in 1987 did not vote in 1992. The Conservatives attracted a slightly larger share of the votes both of those who decided not to vote in 1987 and of those who were too young to vote in that year, though a large number of newly eligible electors, 35 percent, failed to vote at all. Whatever these figures indicate, they show that although the aggregate Conservative share of the vote changed very little between 1987 and 1992, this aggregate stability concealed considerable individual-level change.

There are two ways of approaching the question of why these individual-level changes occurred. One is to concentrate primarily on the switchers—the voters who changed their party choice between 1987 and 1992. These are the people who changed: what, if anything, differentiated them from those who did not? The problem with analysing switchers, unfortunately, is that with a sample size of under 2000 their number is relatively small. For example, the 5 percent of Conservatives who

TABLE 6.5
THE "FLOW OF THE VOTE" IN THE 1987 AND 1992
GENERAL ELECTIONS

	1987 vote						
	Con.	*Lab.*	*Alliance (Lib. Dem.)*	*Other*	*Eligible but did not vote*	*Too young to vote*	*Don't know / refused*
1992 vote							
Con.	75%	5%	10%	0%	18%	25%	22%
Lab.	5	74	14	26	15	21	18
Lib. Dem.	7	6	64	26	7	15	18
Other	1	2	0	48	1	4	3
Nonvoter	11	13	12	0	57	35	54
Total	99	100	100	100	98	100	115
N	631	522	189	19	206	200	27

SOURCE: Gallup postelection survey, 10–11 April 1992.

switched to Labour in 1992 are represented by only 31 individuals. Sensible generalisations about the characteristics or motives underlying the behaviour of such a small number of individuals simply cannot be made, especially when it is recognised that respondents cannot always recall accurately how they voted on previous occasions (in turn suggesting that "switchers" may not always be accurately identified in the first place).[20] This is not to say that "switchers" will be entirely ignored in what follows, merely that any discussion of their distinctive characteristics must play a secondary analytic role.

An alternative way of approaching the question of what might cause individual-level change is to examine the overall profile of each party's supporters and, where appropriate, to assess how that profile might have changed between the last and the most recent election. Table 6.6 makes a first pass at this task. The table shows how the support for the parties varied across different social and economic groups, comparing the 1992 position with that of 1987. The 1992 figures broadly confirm what has long been known about the British electorate's political preferences: that the Conservatives tend to draw their support disproportionately from older voters, nonmanual workers, nonunionised workers, owner-occupiers, and people employed in the private sector; that, in contrast, Labour support tends to be stronger among the young, manual workers (particularly if they are employed in the public sector), trade unionists, and council tenants; and that the Liberal Democrats tend to draw their (lower levels of) support from all groups more or less evenly.

There are several distinctive features of the table that need to be emphasised. First, the 1992 election seems to have reopened the gender gap in British electoral politics. Between 1964 and 1979, the Conservatives consistently obtained greater support from women than from men. During the 1980s, however, this gap gradually disappeared—perhaps because women were particularly antagonised by Thatcher—so that by 1987 there was virtually no gender difference in party support at all. In 1992 the "traditional" position was restored, with support for the Conservatives some five percentage points higher (and support for Labour three points lower) among women than among men. The precise reasons for this reopened gender gap are difficult to specify, though the fact that 48 percent of women (compared with 42 percent of men) thought that the Conservatives had "the best leaders" may have been partly responsible.

A second noteworthy feature of table 6.6 concerns the preferences of the different age groups. In 1987, aggregate support for the Conservatives increased progressively with age (36 percent of the under-25s voted Conservative; 38 percent of the 25–34s; and so on), supporting the fa-

TABLE 6.6

VOTING PATTERNS BY SOCIAL BACKGROUND CHARACTERISTICS
IN THE 1987 AND 1992 GENERAL ELECTIONS
(ROW PERCENTAGES)

	1987			1992		
	Con.	Lab.	Lib. Dem.	Con.	Lab.	Lib. Dem.
Gender						
Men	44%	32%	23%	40%	38%	17%
Women	44	31	23	45	35	18
Age						
Under 25	36	40	22	38	35	22
25–34	38	36	25	37	41	18
35–44	44	28	26	38	38	21
45–64	47	29	22	44	35	19
Over 65	49	27	23	49	33	14
Occupational class						
Professional / managerial (AB)	52	15	31	56	20	21
Routine nonmanual (C1a)	54	21	23	49	28	20
Skilled manual (C1b/C2)	38	41	20	39	40	18
Unskilled manual (D/E)	31	47	22	30	51	14
Trade union membership						
Self or spouse in union	33	39	26	28	50	18
Neither in union	50	27	22	49	31	18
Housing tenure						
Owner-occupier	51	23	25	49	23	19
Council tenant	21	58	19	23	58	14
Private tenant	37	35	27	38	37	19
Employment sector						
Private sector	44	32	23	42	36	18
Public sector	40	34	25	41	37	19
Employment sector and class						
Nonmanual, private sector	50	17	22	61	19	19
Nonmanual, public sector	49	23	26	45	30	22
Manual, private sector	33	45	22	31	50	18
Manual, public sector	29	50	21	35	47	16

SOURCES: The 1987 figures (N = 3204) are taken from Ivor Crewe, Neil Day, and Anthony Fox, *The British Electorate, 1963–1987: A Compendium of Data from the British Election Studies* (Cambridge: Cambridge University Press, 1991). The 1992 figures (N = 1880) are taken from the Gallup postelection survey, except for those relating to occupational class, which are calculated by averaging the breakdowns reported in the Harris exit poll (N = 4701) and the Gallup postelection survey. All figures exclude "don't know"s/"refused to say" from the percentage base.

miliar "life-cycle" adage that voters tend to become more conservative as they get older. In 1992, however, the youngest cohort was more pro-Conservative (38 percent support) than pro-Labour (35 percent), while the 25–34 cohort was more pro-Labour (41 percent) than pro-Conservative (37 percent). This suggests that two rather different "cohort" effects may have operated in addition to the traditional life-cycle effect: that as the under-25 voters of 1987 aged, they retained their support for Labour, whereas "new" voters—politically socialised during an unbroken period of Conservative government—were clearly more Conservative than their chronological age would imply.

Three other aspects of table 6.6 are worth highlighting. As the table reveals, the occupational class composition of party support in 1992 was not noticeably different from that in 1987. Both Labour and the Conservatives made some progress among professional/managerial groups —mainly at the expense of the Liberal Democrats—and Labour increased its share of the vote among routine nonmanual and unskilled manual workers. None of these changes, however, was markedly different from the three percentage point improvement in its vote share that Labour enjoyed overall. Only among the skilled manual workers—the so-called C2s who were famously "won over" to the Conservatives by Thatcher in 1979 but who slowly drifted back to Labour in 1983 and 1987—did Conservative support increase, albeit by only one percentage point. Support for Labour did increase disproportionately among trade unionists; however, this greater apparent commitment to Labour may reflect a tendency for Conservative trade unionists to be overrepresented among the ranks of the large number of comrades who deserted the movement between 1987 and 1992.[21] Finally, owner-occupiers broadly tended to remain loyal to the Conservatives. Presumably, the pain of higher mortgage interest rates, which so damaged the Conservatives' popularity ratings during 1989–91, had been sufficiently relieved by the time of the election, or overridden by other considerations, for such voters to "forgive and forget."

The overall picture presented by table 6.6 is fairly clear. With minor exceptions, voters across the different categories tended to shift their aggregate support for the parties between 1987 and 1992 in broadly similar ways. Across most—though, obviously, not all—of the categories, Conservative support fell slightly, Liberal Democrat support fell moderately, and Labour support increased moderately. In simple terms, the national swing away from the Liberal Democrats and towards Labour was reproduced across most social groups. But if the results reported in table 6.6 indicate *how* the different groups of voters shifted (or failed to shift), they do not really explain *why* particular electors, or groups of electors, cast their votes as they did. Notwithstanding the remarks made earlier about the unreliability of the data available on "switchers," the social-background profiles of the recruits to, and defectors from, each of the three major parties were examined systematically to see if they differed markedly from the general profile shown in table 6.6. Although the findings are not reported here, the results of this analysis showed that switchers' profiles did not differ significantly from those of nonswitchers. This relative uniformity of swing across different voter types suggests in turn that efforts to explain the election outcome need to focus on factors other than voters' social-background characteristics. It is these other factors that are now examined.

The Role of Voter Perceptions

If variations in voters' social-background characteristics do not, empirically, seem to offer a very compelling explanation for their patterns of voting behaviour, it clearly makes sense to examine voters' perceptions of the political parties, of the current state of the country, and of their own personal circumstances to see whether an explanation can be found there. Unfortunately, examining voter perceptions and attempting to link them to voting choices is not a straightforward task. The central problem is that it is often difficult to establish whether a particular attitude should be interpreted as a cause of a particular behaviour or whether the attitude constitutes a rationalisation of it. Table 6.7 presents a good illustration of this problem. Respondents who thought that "the last thirteen years" (of Conservative government) had been "good for Britain" were much more likely to vote Conservative; those who thought that the period had been "bad for Britain" were more likely to vote Labour or Liberal Democrat. But did people vote Conservative *because* they thought the Conservatives had been good for Britain? Or had they already decided, for entirely separate reasons, to vote Conservative—a prior preference that itself determined their "good for Britain" response? Unfortunately, there is no foolproof way of answering these questions: what is cause and what is effect cannot be definitively resolved. In these circumstances, it becomes a matter of judgement as to whether a particular empirical finding identifies a "real" cause underlying voters' behaviour or whether it merely represents an obfuscating rationalisation of it. With this caveat very much in mind, the potential impact of voter perceptions is examined in three main areas: leadership factors, the principal issues, and the economy.

TABLE 6.7

PERCEPTIONS AS TO WHETHER THE LAST THIRTEEN YEARS
HAVE BEEN GOOD OR BAD FOR BRITAIN, BY
MAJOR PARTY VOTE, 1992

Question: "Have the last thirteen years been good or bad for
Britain overall?"

	All respond-ents	Conservative voters	Labour voters	Liberal Democrat voters
Good	47%	86%	12%	35%
Bad	48	10	85	37
Don't know	5	4	4	7

SOURCE: Harris exit poll, 9 April 1992. N = 4071.

LEADERSHIP FACTORS

Voters obviously need to have confidence in the judgement of those
whom they elect, but in the British context, party support does not always move directly in line with the ratings of individual party leaders. As
table 6.8 indicates, in the months before the 1992 election—at a time
when the Conservative and Labour parties were both receiving around
40 percent support in the opinion polls and the Liberal Democrats were
trailing a poor third—the satisfaction ratings for the individual party
leaders showed Ashdown clearly performing best (around 70 percent satisfied), though Major (50–60 percent) was consistently ahead of Kinnock
(about 40 percent). Although being satisfied with a prime minister's performance is clearly not the same as being satisfied with an opposition
leader's, there can be no doubt that the leadership perceptions indicated
in the table did not match those for party support as a whole. This in
turn suggests that leadership perceptions could not have been particularly important as determinants of voting intentions in the year or so before the 1992 election. Once the election was announced, however, the
continued weak showing of the Liberal Democrats confirmed expectations that Ashdown's strong personal image would not affect many voters' preferences because the real choice for prime minister lay between
Major and Kinnock. In this "two-horse" race, Major's ten-point advantage over Kinnock may well have played some part in some people's voting decisions, though the precise extent of any such effect is almost impossible to specify.[22]

TABLE 6.8

OPINION POLL RATINGS OF THE MAIN PARTY LEADERS,
MAY 1991–APRIL 1992

	Percent satisfied with Major	*Percent that think Kinnock is doing a good job*	*Percent that think Ashdown is doing a good job*
1991			
May	59	42	73
June	57	43	73
July	59	41	73
August	60	40	72
September	62	38	72
October	69	44	71
November	56	40	73
December	55	37	68
1992			
January	54	37	71
February	53	39	72
March	51	39	74

SOURCE: Gallup. Figures for Major refer to satisfaction with his performance as prime minister. Figures for Kinnock and Ashdown refer to whether each of them is doing "a good job." "Don't know"s excluded from the percentage base.

There is certainly indirect evidence that "the Kinnock factor" harmed Labour's political fortunes to some extent. First, only 28 percent of respondents to Gallup's election survey considered that Labour had "the best leaders," compared with an equivalent figure for the Conservatives of 53 percent. Second, when respondents to the same survey were asked how they would have voted if John Smith had been Labour's leader, the responses suggested that in such circumstances Labour would have increased its vote share by roughly three percentage points, taking one extra point from the Conservatives and two from the Liberal Democrats.[23] While it would be foolish to place too much reliance on the responses to this sort of hypothetical question, it would be equally foolish to dismiss "the Kinnock factor" as having been of no electoral consequence. If Labour had secured an extra 3 percent of the popular vote, the Conservatives would almost certainly have been robbed of their overall Commons majority.

POLICY POSITIONS AND ISSUES

It is sometimes said that voters make fairly rational assessments of the policy positions adopted by the parties on certain key issues (whatever they may be). The party that comes closest to the individual elector's own position and/or which is expected to perform best on these key issues can expect to receive his or her vote. The evidence from the 1983 and 1987 elections, however, does not seem to bear out this "issue voting" hypothesis. Heath, Jowell, and Curtice showed that if in 1983 voters had supported the party they considered best able to handle the issue they believed to be most important, the Labour and Conservative parties would have received equal shares of the vote; but the actual result gave the Conservatives a fifteen percentage point lead over Labour.[24] Crewe repeated the calculation for 1987 and found that under the same assumptions, Labour should have enjoyed a two-point lead over the Conservatives; but the actual result left Labour eleven points adrift.[25] Strictly comparable data were not available for the equivalent calculations to be made for 1992, but the role of issues in 1992 can nevertheless be examined.

Table 6.9 shows which party respondents thought had "the best policies." On the face of it, the table lends considerable support to the issue-voting hypothesis. The overall percentage of respondents thinking that each of the major parties had the best policies broadly corresponds with the vote shares that the parties actually received; and the vast majority of Conservative (96 percent), Labour (90 percent), and Liberal Democrat (71 percent) voters thought their party had the best policies. The difficulty is that these responses may merely reflect the cause/rationalisation problem alluded to earlier. Respondents may cite party X as having "the best policies" because they have already decided to vote for party X and wish, consciously or unconsciously, to appear to be consistent. Indeed, when the issue-based evidence is examined more closely, the case for a causal effect of issue preferences on party support is considerably weakened.

Table 6.10 shows the disparity between voters' perceptions as to which party is best able to handle major problems and their actual voting behaviour. For ease of interpretation, the Liberal Democrats are excluded from the table, and only the five most important issues (defined as issues regarded as important in their voting decisions by 10 percent or more of respondents) are considered. Several observations need to be made about the table. First, the three issues picked out most frequently as being important—the National Health Service (by 41 percent of respondents), unemployment (36 percent), and education (23 percent)

TABLE 6.9

PERCEPTIONS AS TO WHICH PARTY HAS
"THE BEST POLICIES," BY MAIN
PARTY VOTE, APRIL 1992

Question: "Taking everything into account, which party has the best policies?"

	All voters	*Conservative voters*	*Labour voters*	*Liberal Democrat voters*
Conservative	46%	96%	6%	25%
Labour	37	2	90	11
Liberal Democrat	14	2	3	71
Other	2	0	0	3
N	1521	620	526	263

SOURCE: Gallup postelection survey; "don't know"s excluded from the percentage base.

—were all issues on which Labour enjoyed a big lead. The Conservatives' two best issues—inflation and taxation—were considered important by only 11 percent and 10 percent of electors respectively. Defence and law and order, traditionally two of the Conservatives' strongest suits, failed to figure significantly at all.[26] Second, there is for each issue a clear mismatch between respondents' perceptions as to which party is best able to handle the situation and which party they voted for. For example, 60 percent of the 779 individuals who cited health as one of the two most important issues affecting their voting decision believed that Labour was the party best able to handle health. Yet, of those same 779 people, only 49 percent actually voted Labour. In other words, some 11 percent of the people who, on the basis of their stance on the health issue might have been expected to vote Labour, failed to do so. The same pattern is evident in all the other issue areas. Sixty-three percent of those who considered unemployment important favoured Labour's ability to handle it, yet only 47 percent of them actually voted Labour. Labour's policies on education were favoured by 57 percent of those who thought education an important issue, yet only 43 percent voted Labour. The same problem even afflicted the Conservatives. Of the 203 respondents who considered inflation important, some 77 percent favoured Conservative policies, yet only 66 percent voted Conservative.

TABLE 6.10

PARTY PREFERENCES BY ISSUE IMPORTANCE IN VOTING DECISION

Issue	Column 1:[a] Percentage of all respondents saying that this issue was one of the two most important affecting their voting decision	Column 2:[b] Percentage who believe this issue is important and that the Conservative party is best able to handle it	Column 3: Percentage who believe this issue is important and that the Labour party is best able to handle it	Column 4: Percentage who believe this issue is important and who voted Conservative	Column 5: Percentage who believe this issue is important and who voted Labour
Health Service	41 (N = 779)	29	60	27	49
Unemployment	56 (N = 680)	32	63	34	47
Education	23 (N = 439)	27	57	30	43
Inflation	11 (N = 203)	77	14	66	17
Taxation	10 (N = 197)	85	10	76	13

SOURCE: Gallup postelection survey.

a. Entries in column 1 do not add to 100 because respondents can specify two issues as being "most important" in their voting decision.

b. Entries in column pairs 2–3 and 4–5 are row percentages, excluding "don't know"s/"did not vote." These pairs of numbers do not add to 100 because Liberal Democrat and other parties' shares are excluded.

What all this suggests is that once the connections between issue preferences and voting patterns are analysed issue by issue the significance of the strong aggregate correlation between "best policies" and vote set out in table 6.9 dissipates considerably. If the parties' issue positions had really mattered in electors' voting decisions, the fact that Labour possessed such a huge lead on the three most important issues would almost certainly have produced a Labour victory. Indeed, extrapolating from respondents' positions on the ten most frequently cited issues, it can be estimated that, if electors had voted exclusively on their issue preferences, Labour's vote share would have been in the region of 44 percent, with the Conservatives well behind at 33 percent.[27] The fact that the actual outcome was so different from this issue-preference outcome casts considerable doubt on the issue-voting hypothesis. Many individuals certainly did vote in ways that were consistent with their issue preferences, but there were too many who simply did not to permit the conclusion that issues were of anything more than marginal significance in determining the 1992 outcome.

THE ECONOMY

The condition of the domestic economy has been a crucial factor in determining the outcome of many democratic elections. A booming domestic economy, though not necessarily a guarantee of success, is always a useful foundation for any incumbent government seeking to persuade voters to reelect it. As discussed earlier, John Major's problem in the spring of 1992 was that, although an economic recovery was in prospect, it had not yet arrived. There was, moreover, an intriguing element of paradox in his position. His government's chances of securing a further term of office would be enhanced if recovery preceded the election; but the recovery itself was unlikely to occur until the political uncertainty surrounding the election had itself been dispelled. In the event, the Conservatives did manage to conjure an appropriate set of perceptions about the economy in the minds of sufficient voters to ensure their reelection. In order to see how this came about, it is necessary to unpack the notion of "the economy," since different aspects of economic circumstances can clearly pull electors in different, and sometimes contradictory, directions.

Consider, first, the two economic indicators that have traditionally been associated with the objective performance of the economy as a whole: inflation and unemployment. As noted earlier, inflation was considered a major election issue by only 11 percent of the electorate, some two-thirds of whom voted Conservative and only 17 percent Labour. Insofar as inflation mattered, therefore, it helped the Conservatives. But in circumstances where the annual inflation rate had been falling steadily throughout the previous year and was forecast to remain low, it clearly did not matter very much. Unemployment, in contrast, was very much a Labour issue. Of the 36 percent of voters who rated it an important issue, 47 percent voted Labour, compared with only 34 percent who supported the Conservatives. Among the unemployed themselves, there was certainly disproportionate backing for Labour (53 percent), though Conservatives also received a surprisingly high level of support (34 percent).[28]

Further insights into the impact of unemployment on voting patterns can be gained by examining table 6.11. The table shows the regional variations in swing from Conservative to Labour between 1987 and 1992 and the percentage change in unemployment in each region between December 1990 and December 1991. A comparison of the two sets of figures clearly demonstrates that it was London, the South East, and the West Midlands (all with increases in unemployment above 3 percent) that were hardest hit by the 1991–92 recession. As the table also shows, four of the six regions with a less-than-average increase in unemployment also experienced a regional swing to Labour that was less than average. Similarly, four of the five regions subjected to a greater-than-average increase in unemployment also experienced a greater than average swing to Labour. Although these figures clearly need to be interpreted with caution, they imply that the rise in unemployment during the 1987 Parliament did inflict a small amount of damage on the government's electoral fortunes—though clearly not enough to prevent its reelection.

Inflation and unemployment, however, are not the only economic factors that might impinge on the behaviour of voters. How most voters perceive both their own economic position and that of the economy as a whole may fluctuate quite independently of these particular objective variables. As shown earlier, for example, the aggregate level of personal economic expectations can rise markedly, even while unemployment is rising, if enough employed people are feeling better off as a result of interest rate cuts. Voters' economic perceptions can be divided into three broad categories: whom voters hold responsible for current macroeconomic successes or failures; whether they think the main opposition party is likely to manage the economy more effectively than the incumbent government; and how far they believe their own personal financial interests are likely to be maximised if they support the incumbent government.

ATTRIBUTING RESPONSIBILITY FOR ECONOMIC SUCCESS AND FAILURE

The overriding feature of the British economic landscape in the run-up to the 1992 election was undoubtedly the recession—the longest period of continuously falling GDP since the 1930s. The available evidence, how-

TABLE 6.11

CONSERVATIVE TO LABOUR SWING, 1987–92, AND CHANGE
IN THE PERCENTAGE RATE OF UNEMPLOYMENT,
DECEMBER 1990–DECEMBER 1991

Region	Regional swing from 1987 to 1992	Percentage point change in unemployment, 1990 to 1991
London	+ 3.4%	+ 3.3%
South East	+ 2.5	+ 3.2
South West	+ 3.2	+ 2.6
East Anglia	+ 3.7	+ 2.3
East Midlands	+ 4.7	+ 2.5
West Midlands	+ 3.1	+ 3.2
Wales	+ 2.5	+ 2.2
North West	+ 2.0	+ 1.9
Yorkshire and Humberside	+ 6.0	+ 2.0
North	+ 2.0	+ 1.5
Scotland	– 2.5	+ 1.1
Average	+ 2.78	+ 2.34

CONSERVATIVE TO LABOUR SWING BY AVERAGE
INCREASE IN UNEMPLOYMENT

	Less than average increase in unemployment	Greater than average increase in unemployment
Less than average swing from Conservative to Labour	Scotland North North West Wales	South East
Greater than average swing from Conservative to Labour	East Anglia Yorkshire and Humberside	East Midlands South West West Midlands London

SOURCE: *Employment Gazette.*

ever, suggests that the electorate did not hold John Major's government responsible for it. As table 6.12 shows, a Gallup question designed to elicit respondents' attribution of blame was asked in each month between January and April 1992. The import of the responses in table 6.12(*a*) is clear. Roughly half of respondents consistently blamed the world recession for Britain's economic difficulties and about 40 percent

TABLE 6.12
ATTRIBUTION OF RESPONSIBILITY FOR THE
RECESSION, BY VOTING INTENTION

Question: "It is now generally agreed that Britain's economy is in recession. Who, or what, do you think is most to blame for the recession: the
worldwide economic recession, the Thatcher government's policies, or
the Major government's policies, or what?"

*(a) The changing aggregate pattern, January–April 1992
(column percentages)*

	January	February	March	April
Worldwide recession	50%	50%	46%	48%
Thatcher government	38	42	46	43
Major government	2	4	4	4
Other/don't know	10	4	6	6

*(b) Attribution of blame, by voting intention, April 1992
(column percentages)*

	Worldwide recession	Thatcher government	Major government
Conservative	61%	11%	9%
Labour	13	60	63
Liberal Democrat	17	21	14

SOURCE: Gallup. Gallup did not ask the question in its postelection survey. The
April figures are taken from the preelection poll conducted on 7 and 8 April, which is why
voting intention, rather than "vote," is employed. Other/"don't know"s included in
percentage base but not reported.

blamed the Thatcher government; only 4 percent blamed the Major government. The consistency of the responses over time, moreover, suggests
that electors drew a sharp distinction in their own minds between the
Thatcher and Major governments. But as table 6.12(*b*) indicates, the
electoral consequences of that distinction were not particularly marked.
Among respondents who blamed either Major or Thatcher for the recession, the proportions supporting Labour (63 percent and 60 percent respectively) were almost identical. By far the most important distinction
shown in table 6.12(*b*) is that between respondents who did not blame
the Conservatives for the recession and those who did. Among the former, the ratio of Conservative to Labour supporters was 61:13; among
the latter, it was 10:61. In short, the attribution of blame for Britain's

economic difficulties correlated strongly with Conservative *versus* Labour patterns of support. Those who held the Conservatives culpable for the recession tended to vote Labour; those who did not tended to vote Conservative.

WHO IS BEST ABLE TO MANAGE THE ECONOMY?

Even in the depths of a recession for which the incumbent government is widely held responsible, it is still possible for a majority of electors to believe that conditions would be even worse under another government. This possibility raises the obvious question of which party electors regard as the most competent—or least incompetent—manager of the country's economic affairs. A survey question seeking to tap this sense of comparative competence was asked regularly between May 1991 and April 1992. The responses, reported in table 6.13(*a*), suggest that the Conservatives consistently enjoyed a lead over Labour of at least twelve percentage points. Moreover, although the lead was gradually diminishing during the first three months of 1992, it reopened dramatically in April so that, by the end of the election campaign, the Conservatives' competence rating stood at +19—the widest gap since the end of Major's honeymoon a year before.

The close association between perceptions of managerial competence and voting is shown in table 6.13(*b*). Although around a quarter of those respondents who thought the Conservatives best able to handle Britain's economic problems defected to other parties, fully 76 percent voted Conservative. Likewise, 86 percent of those who preferred Labour's economic management in fact voted Labour, with only 13 percent defecting.[29] Purely on the basis of this evidence, of course, it is not possible to conclude definitely that many people voted Conservative or Labour because they considered that the Conservatives or Labour represented the best available management team. Nonetheless, the strong empirical connection between perceptions of managerial competence and party preference in two such different conceptual domains does suggest that these perceptions were of some relevance in influencing voters' behaviour.

THE "POCKETBOOK" FACTOR

It was argued earlier that pocketbook factors—operationalised as aggregate personal economic expectations—were an important influence on variations in government popularity during the 1987 Parliament. It was noted, moreover, that aggregate expectations increased sharply in April 1992, thus facilitating the sort of pocketbook conditions likely to be con-

TABLE 6.13

PERCEPTIONS OF PARTY COMPETENCE IN THE
HANDLING OF ECONOMIC PROBLEMS,
1991–92

Question: "With Britain in economic difficulties, which party do you
think could handle the problems best—the Conservatives under John
Major, or Labour under Neil Kinnock?"

(a) Variations in responses, March 1991–April 1992 (column percentages)

	Conservatives best	Labour best	Conservative advantage
1991			
March	53%	29%	+24%
April	49	28	+31
May	45	31	+14
June	44	31	+13
July	45	29	+17
August	36	23	+13
September	47	28	+19
October	45	31	+14
November	45	31	+14
December	44	29	+15
1992			
January	44	31	+13
February	43	31	+12
March	40	33	+13
April	52	31	+21

*(b) Perceptions of party competence, by Conservative/Labour vote
(column percentages)*

	Conservatives best (52% of all respondents)	Labour best (31% of all respondents)	Neither/don't know (17% of all respondents)
Conservative	76%	1%	10%
Labour	7	86	31
Liberal Democrat	15	10	52
Other	2	2	6
	100	100	100

SOURCE: Gallup. April figures taken from Gallup postelection survey, 10 and 11
April. "Don't know"s are included in the percentage base in (*a*); nonvoters are excluded
from the percentage base in (*b*).

ducive to a Conservative victory. Unfortunately, in their immediate post-election survey, Gallup failed to ask a question about respondents' personal economic expectations. But a question was asked designed to tap the same sort of considerations: "Taking everything into account, do you think you and your family would be better off under a Labour government led by Mr. Neil Kinnock than you are now, worse off, or would it not make any difference?"

This question had in fact been asked at monthly intervals since May 1991. As a result, it is possible to compare aggregate responses to the "better off–worse off" question with aggregate personal expectations. This comparison is shown in figure 6.4. As the figure indicates, the two indexes tended to rise and fall together (the simple bivariate correlation is $r = .7$). Crucially, both rose sharply between March and April of 1992, suggesting not only an increase in expectations but also an increase in the proportion of voters who feared they would be worse off under a Labour government.

Table 6.14 is also revealing. It shows the strong connections between respondents' perceptions as to whether they would be better or worse off under Labour and their intended and actual voting pattern. Consider first the right-hand segment of the table. This shows that 80 percent of respondents who thought they would be better off under Labour voted Labour, and 79 percent of respondents who thought they would be better off under the Conservatives voted Conservative. This suggests that around 76 percent of Labour and Conservative supporters voted in accordance with their pocketbooks,[30] a very strong indication that egocentric voting played an important role in the election.

A comparison of the left- and right-hand segments of table 6.14 also casts light on the "late swing" phenomenon referred to earlier. The left-hand segment shows the response pattern on the two days before the election; the right-hand segment shows the pattern two days after it. The "better off under Labour" column displays remarkable stability across the two segments. Indeed, the pattern of partisan support is identical, despite the large differences in the number of respondents interviewed. There are two noticeable differences between the pre- and postelection polls, however. First, among those who considered they would be worse off under Labour, actual Conservative voting (79 percent) was four percentage points higher than had been intimated in the preelection poll (75 percent). The fact that there was a four-point decline in Liberal Democrat support (down from 18 percent in the preelection poll to 14 percent postelection) suggests that a straight switch in support from the Liberal Democrats to the Conservatives may have occurred.

A second difference between the two surveys reported in table 6.14

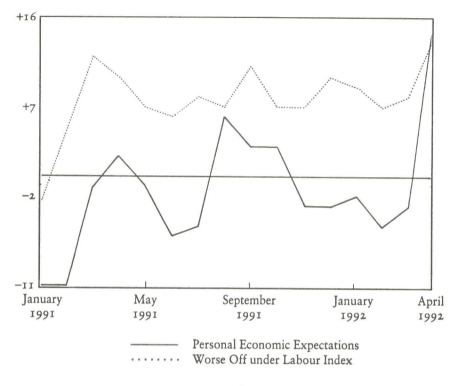

FIGURE 6.4

VARIATIONS IN AGGREGATE PERSONAL ECONOMIC EXPECTATIONS
AND IN AGGREGATE WORSE OFF UNDER LABOUR INDEX
JANUARY 1991–APRIL 1992

NOTE: Aggregate Personal Economic Expectations are measured as explained in
figure 6.2. The Aggregate Worse Off under Labour Index is derived from the following
question: "Taking everything into account, do you think you and your family would be
better off under a Labour government led by Mr. Neil Kinnock than you are now, worse
off, or would it not make any difference?" The Worse Off under Labour Index is constructed by subtracting the percentage who think they would be better off under Labour
from the percentage who think they would be worse off under Labour.

was, however, more substantial in its effects. The proportion of voters
who thought they would be better off under Labour fell from 36 percent
in the preelection poll to 32 percent afterwards. Simultaneously, the proportion who thought they would be worse off rose from 42 percent before the election to 47 percent after it. Taken together, these two shifts
opened up a significant gap (fifteen percentage points, rather than six)

TABLE 6.14

RESPONDENTS' PERCEPTIONS AS TO WHETHER THEY WOULD BE
BETTER OFF OR WORSE OFF UNDER LABOUR; COMPARISON
OF PREELECTION AND POSTELECTION POLLS
(COLUMN PERCENTAGES)

	Preelection survey			*Postelection survey*		
	Better off under Labour	*Worse off under Labour*	*No differ-ence*	*Better off under Labour*	*Worse off under Labour*	*No differ-ence*
Conservative	4%	75%	27%	4%	79%	27%
Labour	80	4	37	80	5	42
Liberal Democrat	2	18	7	2	14	6
N	792	910	490	440	634	280
N as percentage of cases in survey	36	42	22	32	47	21

SOURCE: Gallup. The preelection survey was conducted on 7 and 8 April; the postelection survey on 10 and 11 April. Nonvoters and minor parties included in the percentage base.

between voters' expectations of what the Conservative and Labour parties would be able to deliver for them. Moreover, the stability of the responses in the two "better off under Labour" columns referred to earlier strongly suggests that this widening gap was not simply caused by sampling fluctuations. What the Conservatives achieved in the last twenty-four hours of the campaign was a decisive shift in voters' perceptions of their personal economic prospects under a Labour government. After the final opinion polls had been conducted, some 5 percent more voters became convinced (or realised consciously for the first time) that they would be worse off under Labour—and roughly 80 percent of them proceeded to vote Conservative. By the same token, 4 percent fewer voters became convinced that they would be better off under Labour, thereby significantly reducing the pool of potential egocentric Labour supporters. The critical question, of course, is why such a shift in economic perceptions should have occurred. One possible explanatory factor that certainly merits investigation is the question—much talked about during the election—of taxation.

THE ROLE OF TAXATION

It was noted earlier that only 10 percent of Gallup's postelection survey respondents identified taxation as one of the two most important issues affecting their voting decisions. It was also noted that three-quarters of that group voted Conservative. The taxation issue, in essence, had two key characteristics: (1) it was apparently not very important overall (a feature presumably compounded by the general weakness of issue-based voting in Britain); but (2) insofar as it mattered at all, it was an issue that strongly favoured the Conservatives.[31]

In one sense, this preference for the Conservatives on the tax issue was odd. Since the mid 1980s, there had been an increasing sense among the British electorate that public services should be extended, even if this meant increasing taxes. From February 1985 onwards, more than 60 percent of British electors consistently expressed a preference for extending services and increasing taxes instead of cutting taxes and reducing services.[32] Even though British voters had reelected a tax-cutting government in 1987, the Labour party, in preparing its 1992 campaign, seemed to take this evidence to heart. Within a week of Chancellor Lamont's March budget being presented—in which the Conservatives had reduced income tax for very low wage earners from 25p to 20p in the pound and expressed their intention eventually to extend this lower rate to all taxpayers—Labour's shadow chancellor, John Smith, presented a Labour "shadow budget" that promised to raise income tax rates substantially for high earners and to increase National Insurance contributions for middle-income groups. Labour's justification for these increases was that more investment was needed in Britain's education and training system, in its transport infrastructure, in its housing stock, in its industrial base, and in the National Health Service. All this could be achieved only through higher taxation.

The Conservatives' response, ably assisted by the editors of the mainly pro-Conservative national press, was to strive to make the question of taxation a major election issue. In terms of the express responses to survey questions posed by the pollsters, they were not very successful in this endeavour. Yet, even though taxation was not specified as being important by many voters, it could still have been important. After all, on the three issues cited as the most important most frequently (unemployment, education, and health), Labour enjoyed a substantial lead, yet far more people actually voted Conservative. This to some degree must discredit the express responses that voters provided in relation to specific issues. That taxation—and particularly Labour's shadow budget taxation plans—was important is certainly implied by the evidence presented in table 6.15. As the table indicates, while only 30 percent of voters thought they would benefit from Labour's tax proposals, fully 49 percent believed they would be worse off, and over three-quarters of this latter

TABLE 6.15

PERCEPTIONS OF LABOUR'S TAX AND
BENEFIT POLICIES, BY VOTE

Question: "Would you be better off or worse off under Labour's tax and benefit policies?"

	Better off under Labour	Worse off under Labour	No difference
Conservative	4%	76%	19%
Labour	82	7	50
Liberal Democrat	13	17	31
	100	100	100
N	1336	2236	829
N as percentage of cases in survey	30	49	19

SOURCE: Harris exit poll, 9 April. Nonvoters and minor-party voters excluded from the percentage base.

group voted Conservative. In essence, if taxation was in fact an important election issue, and the evidence of table 6.15 suggests it may well have been, then it worked very much in the Conservatives' favour.

ECONOMIC PERCEPTIONS AND
POLITICAL JUDGEMENTS

Our discussion of the role of economic factors in determining voting preferences in Britain in 1992 can be summarised as follows. First, although rising unemployment during 1991–92 inflicted some damage on the government, its effects were not as marked as they might otherwise have been because a significant proportion of the electorate blamed the worldwide recession, rather than Conservative policies, for Britain's economic difficulties. Second, voters' overall level of personal economic optimism increased gradually during 1991–92 as interest rates were reduced. Optimism accelerated sharply during late March and April of 1992. It is difficult to be certain why this increase in optimism occurred, but Chancellor Lamont's promise to reduce taxation, as well as the prime minister's insistence that economic recovery was being delayed only by the uncertainty of the election outcome, probably had something to do with it. Although it is not yet possible to demonstrate this empirically, the pro-Conservative popular newspapers probably played a part in helping to generate this increased sense of optimism. Previous research certainly suggests that their efforts in this regard met with some success in 1983.[33] Third, the Labour party, by announcing explicit tax and spending plans for the coming financial year even before the official campaign began, presented the Conservatives with a convenient political hook on which to hang their claims that many people would be worse off under Labour. As table 6.14 indicates, the conviction that they would indeed be worse off under Labour came very late to many people. Whether the delay was because it took some time to assimilate the Conservatives' message, or whether it simply took the discipline of the voting booth to make voters aware of their real political preferences, is impossible to say. In any event, there *was* a decisive swing away from Labour at the very end of the campaign, and it was undoubtedly a result, in part, of the growing perception that a Labour government would damage people's personal economic prospects. Electors' personal expectations had recently been raised. The Conservatives were able to convince them that under a Labour government, those raised expectations would in all probability be dashed. In these circumstances, it was not surprising that the Conservatives were able to secure sufficient votes to achieve reelection.

This analysis can be taken one step further. Economic factors were decisive in convincing voters that they would be worse off under Labour. It seems likely, however, that these doubts about Labour's economic competence spilt over into the noneconomic sphere as well—that there was a reduced sense of Labour's general competence to govern in comparison with the Conservatives. That such a generalised sense of Labour's limitations did develop in the last twenty-four hours of the campaign is suggested by the results reported in table 6.16. The table shows how electors between the immediate pre- and postelection periods shifted their views about which party, Labour or the Conservatives, was best able to handle a series of different issues. The importance of the reported figures lies not in the absolute percentage of respondents who preferred the Conservatives to Labour, or vice versa, on a particular issue. Rather, it lies in the systematic change in aggregate perceptions that occurred between 7–8 and 10–11 April. In every issue area apart from homelessness, the percentage of respondents favouring the Conservatives rose (on average, by just under six percentage points) and the percentage favouring Labour fell (on average, by three points) between the pre- and postelection polls.

There are at least three potential explanations for this extraordinarily consistent pattern of change. One is that it was simply due to sam-

TABLE 6.16

PRE- AND POSTELECTION SURVEY FINDINGS ON
VOTERS' PERCEPTIONS OF THE BEST PARTY
TO HANDLE KEY ISSUES

	Best party to handle it	Pre-election survey	Post-election survey	Shift[a] to Con.	Shift[a] to Lab.
Environment	Con. best	21%	26%	+5%	
	Lab. best	25	21		−4%
Europe	Con. best	46	55	+9	
	Lab. best	26	21		−5
Transport	Con. best	25	29	+4	
	Lab. best	46	42		−4
Taxation	Con. best	43	49	+6	
	Lab. best	31	29		−2
Homeless-ness	Con. best	20	23	+3	
	Lab. best	48	48		+0
Law and order	Con. best	41	47	+6	
	Lab. best	29	25		−4
Inflation	Con. best	45	54	+9	
	Lab. best	30	25		−5
Unemployment	Con. best	26	30	+4	
	Lab. best	48	46		−2
Defence	Con. best	52	59	+7	
	Lab. best	22	18		−4
Strikes	Con. best	48	54	+6	
	Lab. best	30	27		−3
National Health Service	Con. best	26	32	+4	
	Lab. best	51	49		−2
Education	Con. best	27	33	+6	
	Lab. best	41	39		−2
Pensions	Con. best	29	35	+6	
	Lab. best	47	44		−3
Status of women	Con. best	23	28	+5	
	Lab. best	38	35		−3

SOURCE: Gallup preelection survey, 7–8 April 1992; Gallup postelection survey, 10–11 April 1992.

a. Shift from 7–8 April to 10–11 April.

pling fluctuations; the postelection poll sampled a more pro-Conservative group of respondents. The problem with this interpretation is that the preelection poll was very much in line with the three other preelection polls published on the same day; and the postelection poll, as noted earlier, produced a vote distribution that almost exactly mirrored the actual election outcome. A second possible explanation is that the changes resulted from a genuine shifting of respondents' opinions on each issue—that in the last twenty-four hours of the campaign voters suddenly became convinced that the Conservatives would pursue better policies than Labour on the environment, Europe, transport, taxation, law and order, and the rest. The inadequacy of this explanation speaks for itself. It seems extremely unlikely that in the final hours of the campaign, large numbers of voters could have yet again weighed the relative merits of the Conservative and Labour parties in each of the fourteen issue areas shown in table 6.16 and then altered their assessments of which party was best able to handle the problems associated with each of them.

It is far more likely—and this is the third explanation—that the changes summarised in table 6.16 were themselves the result of voters having already decided that they would vote Conservative because the Conservatives, in a very generalised way, were just better than Labour at running things. There was nothing specific that occurred in the last days of the campaign (or, indeed, at any stage of the campaign) that might have caused 5 percent more voters suddenly to believe that the Conservatives had the best policies on the status of women, or 9 percent more voters suddenly to believe that the Conservatives were to be trusted on Europe. These changes did not result from a considered and rational assessment of the parties' relative merits in each of these areas. The fact that perceptions shifted so markedly in all fourteen issue areas simultaneously suggests that the observed responses were largely rationalisations. They derived from decisions—to support the Conservatives—that had already been taken and that themselves reflected fears about personal economic well-being and the general ability of Labour to govern. Labour had made itself appear electable from at least the time of the Policy Review, and the electorate had duly appeared to reward it with increased support. At the very last moment, however, the Conservatives had been able to conjure up a set of circumstances that promised widespread personal prosperity combined with a widespread perception that the fulfillment of this promise would be seriously prejudiced by the return of a Labour government. This was an argument that proved too powerful for waverers to resist. Once inside the voting booths, they voted Conservative in sufficient numbers to ensure John Major's reelection.

Summary and Conclusions

Most political acts have multiple causes. When 30 million votes are cast in a general election, the full causal picture is necessarily one of enormous complexity. In these circumstances, although some sort of reductionism is inevitable, the analyst always hopes that he or she has not engaged in reductio ad absurdum. The causes of the Conservative victory in April 1992, of course, were many and varied. Indeed, some of the causes were so obvious in their effects that, having operated remorselessly over previous elections, they have been barely mentioned here. Partisan identification, for example—the general affective attachment that different individuals feel towards particular political parties—has been paid scant attention because identification patterns changed very little between 1987 and 1992.[34] This does not mean that the identifications acquired over the years by large numbers of voters were unimportant as predisposing influences on their voting behaviour. Part of the explanation for the Conservatives' success undoubtedly lies in the reservoir of support built up by the party over many years past.

But what is the essential nature of the explanation for the Conservative victory offered here? The first part of the chapter sought to show that one important causal strand derived from the government's response to its own midterm unpopularity. That unpopularity had resulted partly from the fact the economy had first overheated and then, just as domestic counterinflationary policies had begun to bite, a further dose of deflation had been administered by the general downturn in the world economy. A second factor underlying the government's low midterm poll ratings was the fact that Margaret Thatcher had fallen increasingly out of touch with both parliamentary and public opinion—a remoteness that was symbolised by her insistence that the poll tax must be introduced in spite of all the opposition it engendered. The Conservatives—the most formidable election-winning machine in twentieth-century British politics—responded professionally to both difficulties. The reductions in interest rates introduced by Chancellor Lamont during 1990–91 gradually restored spending power to consumers and, in particular, to the mortgage-holding owner-occupiers, a large and traditionally pro-Conservative sector of the electorate. The solution to Thatcher's unpopularity was rather more radical. She was simply removed from office by her colleagues, and her much-resented community charge was abandoned with all speed.

In addition to addressing its own midterm unpopularity, the Conservative government also responded effectively to the electoral threats posed by Labour's new image. With the 1989 Policy Review, Labour had shifted its policy stance back to the centre ground of British politics. Potentially, this left the radicalism of the Thatcherite right exposed to the accusation of extremism. John Major's premiership did not involve a complete return to the consensual centre so abhorred by Margaret Thatcher. But it did represent a move in that direction. As chancellor of the exchequer, Major had already stolen Labour's more moderate European clothes by taking Britain into the ERM in October 1990. As prime minister, his unequivocal statements in support of the National Health Service represented a partial renewal of the Conservative party's commitment to the principles of Beveridge—to the welfare state. Similarly, Norman Lamont's massive increase in public borrowing at the height of the 1991–92 recession—though not accompanied either by Keynesian rhetoric or a by commitment to full employment—constituted a departure from the strict monetarist principles espoused by the Thatcherites and, in effect, a return to the demand-management techniques advocated by Keynes himself. Moreover, in addition to shifting its own ground in order to present a more caring face to the electorate, Major's government lost no opportunity to attack Labour at what it saw as its weakest point: Neil Kinnock. With the support of large sections of the popular press, the opposition leader's character, judgement, and abilities were insistently questioned; and with some success. Kinnock's ratings in the opinion polls consistently lagged far behind those of both Major and Ashdown. And although it is almost impossible to demonstrate this empirically, it seems likely that Kinnock's weak image was in part responsible for the consolidation of Conservative support that appeared to take place at the very end of the campaign.

The critical factor underpinning the Conservatives' victory, however, was the fact that enough people, drawn from all social groups, were moved to vote according to their pocketbooks. Many voters were irritated with the Conservatives for imposing a lengthy period of high interest rates upon them. They were concerned about the length of the recession and the fact that unemployment was still rising. But in the nine months or so before the election, the beneficial effects of the interest rate reductions initiated in October 1990 were starting to feed through to people's pockets. Economic optimism was rising and even began to accelerate quite sharply in the final weeks of the campaign. The Conservatives' political triumph was to make the satisfaction of these rising expectations conditional on a Conservative victory. By the end of the campaign, almost half the electorate believed they would be worse off under Labour's taxation policies; and a large proportion of them—most of them, falsely, avowing to the pollsters that taxation had not been an issue affecting their vote—duly voted Conservative.

There was, to the dispassionate observer, a considerable irony in all this. As far as John Major had been concerned, to be obliged to call an election while the economy was still in recession was highly undesirable, if not downright dangerous. Yet, paradoxically, the fact that the election was held under recession conditions may actually have helped the Conservatives. The opinion polls predicted a hung Parliament throughout the campaign. This in turn implied that, after the election, either a coalition or a minority government would be in power. In either event, political uncertainty would prevail: if there were a coalition, because British politicians had had no real experience of coalition government;[35] if there were a minority government, because the parties would engage in endless jockeying in anticipation of another election being called in the near future. The obvious danger was that any such continuation of political uncertainty would further delay Britain's economic recovery as consumers postponed their major spending decisions until more stable—and predictable—political conditions had emerged. Sustained political uncertainty, moreover, could weaken sterling on the foreign exchanges, thereby provoking a renewed rise in interest rates aimed at protecting sterling's position in the ERM. In these circumstances, a non-Conservative vote looked perilously like a vote for prolonging the recession. Voters who may well have wanted to punish the Conservatives for their generally poor economic record during the 1987 Parliament found themselves in a position where such gestures might well prolong, or even intensify, their own economic discomfort. There were signs that the Conservatives had just about turned the economic corner and that good times were again close at hand. It was better, in this situation, to vote for the devil you knew than the devil you didn't. It was better to vote Conservative—just to be on the safe side.

APPENDIX TO CHAPTER 6
DATA FOR FIGURES 6.1 – 6.4

Observation	Con.[a]	Lab.[a]	Lib.[a]	PEXP[b,c]	PERS[d]	WORSELAB[e]
87 July	47.6000	32.5000	17.5000	15.0000	47.7781	n.a.
87 August	47.6000	34.0000	16.0000	10.0000	45.9558	n.a.
87 September	48.5000	33.5000	15.0000	7.0000	44.8624	n.a.
87 October	48.3000	34.5000	14.0000	8.0000	45.2269	n.a.
87 November	47.9000	34.5000	15.0000	3.0000	43.4045	n.a.
87 December	47.1000	35.5000	14.5000	3.0000	43.4045	n.a.
88 January	46.1000	37.0000	15.0000	8.0000	45.2269	n.a.
88 February	45.0000	38.0000	14.0000	1.0000	42.6756	n.a.
88 March	45.7000	37.5000	15.0000	5.0000	44.1335	n.a.
88 April	43.2000	39.5000	14.0000	.0000	42.3111	n.a.
88 May	44.6000	39.5000	13.0000	6.0000	44.4979	n.a.
88 June	46.0000	38.5000	12.5000	7.0000	44.8624	n.a.
88 July	45.2000	40.5000	12.5000	6.0000	44.4979	n.a.
88 August	47.1000	35.0000	14.0000	5.0000	44.1335	n.a.
88 September	45.1000	38.5000	13.5000	1.0000	42.6756	n.a.
88 October	45.5000	37.5000	13.5000	-1.0000	41.9467	n.a.
88 November	43.7000	38.0000	14.0000	6.0000	44.4979	n.a.
88 December	44.0000	35.5000	15.0000	-4.0000	40.8533	n.a.
89 January	45.5000	36.6000	13.9000	-7.0000	39.7599	n.a.
89 February	40.7000	38.7000	15.4000	-11.0000	38.3020	n.a.
89 March	41.3000	38.9000	14.3000	-10.0000	38.6665	n.a.
89 April	40.2000	39.0000	15.0000	-12.0000	37.9375	n.a.
89 May	41.5000	41.5000	12.0000	-4.0000	40.8533	n.a.

Observation	Con.[a]	Lab.[a]	Lib.[a]	PEXP[b,c]	PERS[d]	WORSELAB[e]
89 June	36.6000	45.0000	9.0000	−11.0000	38.3020	n.a.
89 July	36.7000	43.3000	9.2000	−11.0000	38.3020	n.a.
89 August	37.2000	43.9000	9.2000	−9.0000	39.0309	n.a.
89 September	37.0000	43.4000	9.2000	−7.0000	39.7599	n.a.
89 October	37.8000	47.8000	7.4000	−24.0000	33.5639	n.a.
89 November	36.5000	47.1000	9.3000	−17.0000	36.1152	n.a.
89 December	38.1000	46.3000	9.3000	−18.0000	35.7507	n.a.
90 January	36.0000	47.1000	9.3000	−16.0000	36.4797	n.a.
90 February	34.0000	50.0000	9.0000	−16.0000	36.4797	n.a.
90 March	30.0000	52.8000	9.2000	−31.0000	31.0127	n.a.
90 April	30.0000	53.0000	9.1000	−26.0000	32.8350	n.a.
90 May	34.0000	49.5000	8.1000	−16.0000	36.4797	n.a.
90 June	36.0000	49.7000	7.4000	−13.0000	37.5731	n.a.
90 July	36.0000	49.3000	8.4000	−14.0000	37.2086	n.a.
90 August	35.0000	48.7000	8.4000	−13.0000	37.5731	n.a.
90 September	37.0000	46.7000	11.1000	−15.0000	36.8441	n.a.
90 October	34.0000	47.7000	12.9000	−7.0000	39.7599	n.a.
90 November	37.0000	44.5000	11.1000	−10.0000	38.6665	n.a.
90 December	44.0000	42.1000	9.1000	1.0000	42.6756	n.a.
91 January	44.4000	41.2000	9.2000	−11.0000	38.3020	−3.0000
91 February	44.7000	40.9000	9.4000	−11.0000	38.3020	4.5000
91 March	41.0000	38.5000	15.5000	−1.0000	41.9467	12.0000
91 April	39.0000	40.3000	13.8000	2.0000	43.0401	10.0000
91 May	37.1000	42.0000	16.9000	−1.0000	41.9467	7.0000
91 June	37.0000	42.4000	15.8000	−6.0000	40.1243	6.0000
91 July	38.6000	42.8000	14.5000	−5.0000	40.4888	8.0000

Observation	Con.[a]	Lab.[a]	Lib.[a]	PEXP[b,c]	PERS[d]	WORSELAB[e]
91 August	38.8000	41.3000	14.9000	6.0000	44.4979	7.0000
91 September	39.0000	40.0000	15.0000	3.0000	43.4045	11.0000
91 October	40.0000	40.0000	14.0000	3.0000	43.4045	7.0000
91 November	40.0000	40.0000	13.5000	-3.0000	41.2177	7.0000
91 December	40.1000	40.0000	13.5000	-3.0000	41.2177	10.0000
92 January	40.2000	40.0000	13.0000	-2.0000	41.5822	9.0000
92 February	40.0000	40.0000	15.0000	-5.0000	40.4888	7.0000
92 March	39.0000	40.5000	19.0000	-3.0000	41.2177	8.0000
92 April	43.0000	35.0000	18.0000	16.0000	48.1426	14.0000

a. Figure 6.1: Raw scores are Con. (Conservative), Lab. (Labour), and Lib. (Liberal Democrat).
b. Figure 6.2: Raw scores are PEXP (Aggregate Personal Economic Expectations).
c. Figure 6.3: Raw scores are Con. (Conservative government popularity) and PEXP (Aggregate Personal Economic Expectations). But note that it may be easier to plot Con. and PERS, then to adjust the vertical axis labels. PERS is an artificially constructed aggregate personal expectations variable for use with software (i.e., mine) that allows only one scale on each graph.
d. Figure 6.4: Raw scores are PEXP and WORSELAB (percent worse minus percent better under Labour).

Notes

1. The *Gallup Political Index* for October 1989 reported that 64 percent of respondents thought that the poll tax was a bad idea. By February 1990, 73 percent of respondents thought they would be worse off as a result of the tax; only 11 percent thought they would be better off.

2. During the second quarter of 1989, the difference between the percentage of respondents who were "satisfied" with Thatcher and the percentage who intended to vote Conservative was zero. By the fourth quarter of 1990, Thatcher's satisfaction ratings were running six percentage points behind the party's ratings. See *Gallup Political Index.*

3. An opinion poll for the *Sunday Correspondent* for 23 March 1990 found that if Michael Heseltine were leading the Conservatives, 41 percent of respondents said they would "vote Conservative if there were a general election tomorrow." This compared with a figure of 28 percent support for the Conservatives under Mrs. Thatcher. Similar differences were observed in equivalent contexts throughout the summer and autumn of 1990.

4. The Falklands War certainly gave an immediate boost to Conservative popularity, which leapt from 33 percent support to 42 percent within a month of the Argentine invasion. Whether the long-term effects of this boost lasted through to the 1983 election is a matter of some debate. For discussion, see Helmut Norpoth, "The Popularity of the Thatcher Government: A Matter of War and Economy," in *Economics and Elections: The Calculus of Support,* ed. Michael Lewis-Beck, Helmut Norpoth, and Jean-Dominique Lafay (Ann Arbor: University of Michigan Press, 1991), 141–60; David Sanders, Hugh Ward, and David Marsh, "Macroeconomics, the Falklands War and the Thatcher Government: A Contrary View," ibid., 161–84.

5. Gallup asked their respondents: "How do you think the financial situation of your household will change over the next twelve months?" The response options were: "get a lot better," "get a little better," "stay about the same," "get a little worse," "get a lot worse."

6. See David Sanders, Hugh Ward, and David Marsh, "Government Popularity and the Falklands War: A Reassessment," *British Journal of Political Science* 17 (April 1987): 281–313; David Sanders, "Government Popularity and the Next General Election," *Political Quarterly* 62 (April 1991): 235–61; David Sanders, Hugh Ward, and David Marsh, "The Political Impact of Newspaper Coverage of the UK Economy, 1979–87," *British Journal of Political Science,* forthcoming.

7. If the level of Aggregate Personal Expectations at time t is denoted PE_t, the following empirical estimates are observed:

$$PE_t = 22.4 + 0.39(PE_{t-1}) - 2.1(\text{Interest Rates}_{t-1})$$
$$- 16.2(\text{Poll Tax dummy [March 1990]})$$
$$+ 11.6(\text{Major's accession dummy [December 1990]})$$
$$+ \varepsilon_t$$

Adjusted $R^2 = .77$ $LM(12)X^2 = 8.8$ $N = 58$ $DW = 2$
Sample: July 1987–April 1992

where ε_t is a random error term; all the coefficients are significant at the .01 level; and the model passes the standard CUSUM, CUSUMSQ, and serial correlation tests.

8. David Marsh, Hugh Ward, and David Sanders, "Modelling Government Popularity in Britain, 1979–1987: A Disaggregated Approach," in *British Politics and Election Yearbook*, ed. Ivor Crewe and Pippa Norris (London: Simon and Schuster, 1991).

9. Estimating the effects of Personal Expectations (*PE*) on government popularity in a simple lagged endogenous variable model yields:

$$\text{Popularity}_t = 13.6 + 0.68(\text{Popularity}_{t-1}) + 0.15(PE_t) + \varepsilon_t \quad \text{(Eq. 1)}$$

Adjusted $R^2 = .86 \quad LM(12)X^2 = 16.0 \quad N = 58 \quad DW = 1.85$
Sample: July 1987–April 1992

where ε_t is a random error term; all the coefficients are significant at the .01 level; and the model passes the standard CUSUM, CUSUMSQ, and serial correlation tests.

To take account of the possibility that expectations in the recent past may also be important as influences on popularity, the Personal Expectations term, *PE*, can be expressed as a weighted average of expectations at time t, $t - 1$, $t - 2$, and $t - 3$. In these circumstances, the weighted average, $PE_{t..t-3}$, is defined as:

$$PE_{t..t-3} = (PE_t + \rho PE_{t-1} + \rho^2 PE_{t-2} + \rho^3 PE_{t-3})/4$$

where ρ is the "discount rate" defined by the coefficient on PE_{t-1} in

$$PE_t = 0.98 + 0.79(PE_{t-1}) + \varepsilon_t \quad \text{(Eq. 2)}$$

Adjusted $R^2 = .64 \quad LM(12)X^2 = 12.8 \quad N = 58$
Sample: July 1987–April 1992.

Using this weighted average term for personal expectations yields:

$$\text{Popularity}_t = 18.16 + 0.57(\text{Popularity}_{t-1}) \quad \text{(Eq. 3)}$$
$$+ 0.27(PE_{t..t-3}) + \varepsilon_t$$

Adjusted $R^2 = .85 \quad LM(12)X^2 = 17.8 \quad N = 58 \quad DW = 2.13$
Sample: July 1987–April 1992

where ε_t is a random error term; all the coefficients are significant at the .01 level; and the model passes the standard CUSUM, CUSUMSQ, and serial correlation tests.

Adding to (Eq. 3) dummy variable terms for the introduction of the poll tax (March 1990) and for Major's accession yields:

$$\text{Popularity}_t = 16.26 + 0.62(\text{Popularity}_{t-1}) \quad \text{(Eq. 4)}$$
$$+ 0.27(PE_{t..t-3}) - 3.56(\text{Poll Tax})$$
$$+ 6.00(\text{Major}) + \varepsilon_t$$

Adjusted $R^2 = .88 \quad LM(12)X^2 = 14.6 \quad N = 58 \quad DW = 2.13$
Sample: July 1987–April 1992

where ε_t is a random error term; all the coefficients are significant at the .01 level; and the model passes the standard CUSUM, CUSUMSQ, and serial correlation tests.

The coefficient on the lagged dependent variable, Popularity$_{t-1}$, measures the rate at which "shocks" to popularity are discounted. The relatively low value (.62) of this coefficient in (Eq. 4) indicates that, as suggested earlier, the effects of such shocks dissipate rapidly. For example, according to (Eq. 4), over and above the effects of expectation, the boost to government popularity from Thatcher's removal was worth six percentage points in December 1990; $6 \times .62 = 3.72$ points in January 1991; $6 \times .62^2 = 2.3$ points in February; $6 \times .62^3 = 1.43$ points in March; and so on.

10. See Sanders, "Government Popularity and the Next General Election."
11. The only other occasion was in September 1984 when Labour's "poll of polls" rating was 40.3 percent.
12. In April 1987, 67 percent of Gallup respondents agreed with the statement that "Labour has become too extreme"; only 24 percent disagreed. In September 1989, the first time that the question was posed after the review, only 29 percent of respondents agreed with the statement, whereas 61 percent disagreed. See *Gallup Political Index.*
13. In September 1987, 31 percent of Gallup's respondents thought that Labour was "becoming more responsible," compared with 19 percent who considered it "less responsible." The corresponding figures for August 1989 were more responsible, 49 percent; less responsible, 9 percent. See *Gallup Political Index.*
14. During the first quarter of 1989, 17 percent of Gallup respondents considered that Labour was united; 73 percent considered it divided. By the last quarter of 1989, 48 percent regarded Labour as united and only 41 percent described it as divided. See *Gallup Political Index.*
15. See, for example, MORI chairman Robert Worcester's reported comments in the (London) *Evening Standard,* 4 April 1992, under "Polls Have Never Got It So Wrong" by Flora Hunter and Colin Adamson.
16. Peter Kellner, "Slag-Off Factor Stirs but Does Not Shake," *Independent on Sunday,* 29 April 1992.
17. The exit-poll estimates of party vote share in the election were as follows:

	% Con.	% Lab.	% Lib. Dem.	Number of cases
ICM for Sky News	38	41	18	20,000+
Harris for ITN[a]	41	37	18	20,000+
NOP for the BBC	39	39	17	18,000+
"Poll of exit polls" (average)	39.3	39.0	17.7	
Actual result	42.8	35.2	18.3	

NOTE: All three exit polls were conducted on 9 April 1992 as respondents emerged from the polling stations.

a. Harris asked over 20,000 respondents how they had just voted. They interviewed 4701 of these respondents in more detail. Subsequent references to "the Harris exit poll" relate to this *sub*sample of 4701 respondents.

18. I am grateful to Anthony King for suggesting this phrase to me.

19. For a discussion of the failure of the opinion polls, see Ivor Crewe, "A Nation of Liars? Opinion Polls and the 1992 Election," *Parliamentary Affairs* 45 (October 1992).

20. See, for example, Bo Särlvik and Ivor Crewe, *Decade of Dealignment: The Conservative Victory of 1979 and the Electoral Trends of the 1970s* (Cambridge: Cambridge University Press, 1983).

21. In 1987, the Trades Union Congress (TUC) had 9,243,297 affiliated members. By 1992, the figure had dropped to 7,757,000.

22. The mass-circulation and strongly pro-Conservative *Sun* newspaper conducted a highly charged series of personal attacks on Kinnock during the last few days of the campaign. Its editor certainly believed that the electorate's doubts about Kinnock's competence needed as much reinforcement as possible. In the immediate aftermath of the election, the *Sun* claimed that its campaigning, particularly against Kinnock, had played a major role in the Conservatives' reelection.

23. Of the 1880 individuals interviewed by Gallup, 44 who voted Liberal Democrat and 28 who voted Conservative thought that they "would have actually voted Labour if Mr. Smith had been Labour leader." At the same time, 16 Labour voters thought that they would *not* have voted Labour under these circumstances (44 + 28 − 16 = 56, or 3 percent of the 1880 total respondents).

24. Anthony Heath, Roger Jowell, and John Curtice, *How Britain Votes* (Oxford: Pergamon Press, 1985).

25. Ivor Crewe, "Why Mrs. Thatcher Was Returned with a Landslide," *Social Studies Review* 3 (January 1987): 2–9.

26. Defence was mentioned as important by 3 percent of respondents; law and order by 2 percent.

27. The actual numbers of people citing each issue as one of the two most important in determining their voting decision (total number of voters = 1521) are given in table N.27 (p. 221).

28. Unemployed respondents to Gallup's postelection survey voted as follows: Conservative, 34 percent; Labour, 53 percent; Liberal Democrat, 7 percent; other/did not vote, 4 percent.

29. Not surprisingly, Liberal Democrat support was greatest among those who thought neither Labour nor Conservative could "handle the problems best."

30. The calculation here is (1) 601 voted Conservative + 516 voted Labour = 1117; (2) 351 of those who believed they would be better off under Labour voted Labour; (3) 499 of those who believed they would be worse off under Labour voted Conservative; (4) 351 + 499 = 850; (5) 850 as a percentage of 1117 = 76 percent.

31. It is, of course, possible, that the 5 percent of the electorate identified in table 6.14 who "switched" at the eleventh hour from believing they would be better off under Labour to believing they would be worse off were strongly represented in the 10 percent who considered taxation an important issue. Unfortunately, given that the pre- and postelection surveys did not interview the same set of respondents, it is simply not possible to assess the validity of this proposition.

TABLE N.27

	N	Number who thought Labour best	Number who thought Conservatives best
National Health Service	779	467	226
Unemployment	680	428	218
Education	439	250	118
Inflation	203	28	156
Taxation	197	20	167
Homelessness	134	66	17
Pensions	110	60	25
Defence	59	3	52
Law and order	40	6	25
Strikes/unions	16	4	11
Total		1332	1015

NOTE: Divide each total by 2 because respondents were asked to specify the *two* most important issues in their voting choice:

Total $N/2$	666	507
Total $N/2$ as a percentage of 1521	44	33

32. Since 1979, Gallup polls have frequently asked their respondents: "People have different views about whether it is more important to reduce taxes or keep government spending. How about you? Which of these statements comes closest to your own view?"

Taxes should be cut, even if it means some reduction in services.

Things should be left as they are.

Government services should be extended even if it means increases in taxation.

In February 1985, 16 percent of respondents favored cutting taxes, while 59 percent favored extending services. In April 1992, 10 percent favored cutting taxes and 63 percent favored extending services.

33. Sanders, Ward, and Marsh, "Political Impact of Newspaper Coverage."

34. As table N.34 (next page) indicates, some 90 percent of 1992 respondents identified with one of the three major parties, compared with an equivalent figure of 94 percent for 1987. This small decline in the overall level of partisanship, however, has to be set against two other factors. First, the overall percentage of respondents identifying with the different parties changed very little between 1987 and 1992 (43.3 percent identified with the Conservatives in 1987 compared with 43.6 percent in 1992; and so on). Second, the percentage of respondents identifying either "very" or "fairly strongly" with each party increased noticeably between 1987 and 1992. Although it is difficult to draw any firm conclusions from this clear empirical tendency, it does suggest that voters in 1992 were, on average, rather more attached to their preferred party than they had been in 1987.

TABLE N.34

PARTY IDENTIFICATION PATTERNS AT THE TIME OF
THE 1987 AND 1992 GENERAL ELECTIONS [a]

	1987		1992	
Conservative				
Very strong	10.3		14.9	
Fairly strong	22.4		21.1	
Not very strong	10.6		7.6	
Subtotal		43.3		43.6
Labour				
Very strong	9.4		15.5	
Fairly strong	15.6		17.5	
Not very strong	11.3		4.3	
Subtotal		36.3		37.3
Liberal Democrat				
Very strong	2.0		3.7	
Fairly strong	8.4		8.7	
Not very strong	10.0		6.6	
Subtotal		20.4		19.0
		100.0		99.9

a. Figures reported are column percentages. The 1987 figures are taken from Ivor Crewe, Neil Day, and Anthony Fox, *The British Electorate, 1963–1987: A Compendium of Data from the British Election Studies* (Cambridge: Cambridge University Press, 1991). Figures for 1992 are from the Gallup postelection survey. The base N for the 1992 calculations is 1327—the respondents who expressed an identification in response to the question: "Leaving aside this particular election, would you say you generally think of yourself as Conservative, Labour, Liberal Democrat, or what?" Respondents were then asked: "And would you call yourself very strong ... [party] ... fairly strong or not very strong?"

35. The Labour–Liberal pact of 1977–78, which helped sustain the Callaghan government in power after it lost its Commons majority, was not a formal coalition. The Liberals had no ministerial portfolios.

7

The Implications of One-Party Government

Anthony King

The British people, including most British politicians, greeted the results of the 1992 election with their usual phlegm. The campaign had been fought, the Conservatives had won, Labour had lost, and that was that. Within a few weeks the 1992 campaign seemed a distant memory, and most people, including most politicians, went about their business as though nothing had happened. Everything appeared normal.

But in fact everything was far from normal. The 1992 election established two records. One concerned the long-term duration of the Labour party's electoral difficulties. In 1992 Labour became the first major political party since World War II to fail to poll as much as 40 percent of the popular vote in six consecutive elections. Not since the 1920s and 1930s had any opposition party fared so consistently badly; and at that time Labour was only just establishing itself as the main opposition party to the Conservatives. When Labour lost three elections in a row to the Conservatives in the 1950s, its average share of the popular vote was 46.3 percent. Losing four elections in a row between 1979 and 1992, its average share of the vote was a mere 32.4 percent. Labour did worse in 1992 than it had in 1935, in the midst of the Great Depression.[1]

The other record established in 1992 was of even greater significance. It had once been an axiom of British politics that the electoral pendulum swung from time to time and that, as a result, the two major political parties alternated in office. The swing of the pendulum was, of course, by no means regular, but the alternations in office were reasonably frequent. Before the 1980s, there had been no decade for more than a century in which one party held office throughout. Now, in 1992, the pendulum seemed to have stopped swinging. The Conservatives' victory was their fourth in succession. No party had achieved that feat since the Tories under Lord Liverpool won four in a row between 1812 and 1826;

and that was long before Britain became a democracy. By the time of the next general election, in 1996 or 1997, the students entering Britain's colleges and universities for the first time will not have been born when any party other than the Conservatives last held power at Westminster.

One commentator wrote soon after 9 April: "Following last Thursday's election, Britain no longer has two major political parties. It has one major party, the Conservatives, one minor party, Labour, and one peripheral party, the Liberal Democrats."[2] He may have been exaggerating, but the fact remains that the British party system in 1992 began to show signs of being what Sartori calls a "predominant-party system"—that is, one in which a single party both controls an absolute majority of seats in the legislature and is able to govern on its own, without the need of coalition partners, for a prolonged period of time. As it happens, Sartori suggests that a reasonable working definition of "a prolonged period of time" is at least four consecutive legislatures.[3] The Conservatives are now well into their fourth consecutive legislature.

Modern Britain is quite unusual in this respect. Very few other countries have now, or have ever had, predominant-party systems on Sartori's definition of the term. In the United States the Democratic party held the presidency for twenty consecutive years from 1933 to 1953, but the Democrats' control of the executive branch was punctuated by a two-year period (1947–49) when the Republicans had a majority in Congress. The Christian Democrats in Italy have been the dominant party since the end of the war, but they have never had a parliamentary majority and have always had to share power with others. Better examples of predominant-party systems are India for a substantial portion of its postindependence history, Sweden under the Social Democrats for most of the period between 1932 and the 1970s, Canada under the Liberals between 1935 and 1957, and, above all, Japan, where the Liberal Democrats and their predecessors have held power almost continuously since 1948. Elsewhere in the democratic world, coalition governments or the alternation of parties in power are the norm. In the 1990s Japan and Britain are more or less alone in being "democratic one-party states."

The Conservatives' continuing dominance at Westminster is reinforced by another feature of the British political system that is easy to overlook. Britain is one of the very few countries in the democratic world in which there are no autonomous centres of political power apart from the national government. Britain's system of government is unitary, and there are therefore no states or provinces to act as a check on, and an alternative to, the national government. Local government exists but is weak. In the absence of a written constitution and a bill of rights, the courts have only a limited capacity to interpret statutes and to question the actions of the government of the day. The legislative and oversight roles of the opposition parties in Parliament are similarly limited. Moreover, Britain's political culture, at least at the national level, is not a bipartisan or nonpartisan culture. On the contrary, cooperation across party lines at Westminster is relatively rare, and the operative principle of the British system is winner-take-all. "We are the masters now," a Labour MP cried in the aftermath of Labour's 1945 election victory. Today in Britain the Conservatives are the masters. They have been so since the late 1970s. They will remain so until at least the late 1990s.[4] Only the European Community acts as a kind of outside check.

The fact that Britain appears to be emerging as a predominant-party system is worth pausing over for a number of reasons. One is that few people, even in Britain, seem to have noticed what is happening (The Conservatives are reluctant to appear triumphalist, Labour to appear defeatist.). Another is that this new development cuts athwart so much of the conventional wisdom about British politics and government.

The textbook writers of a generation ago painted a picture of the British political system that was both simple and, to many observers, highly attractive.[5] The two major parties, the Conservatives and Labour, contested elections every four or five years. They did so on more or less equal terms. Sometimes one party would win, sometimes the other. In effect, the two took turns in having a parliamentary majority and controlling the government. Admittedly, the Conservatives were in power during most of the 1950s, but during the 1960s and 1970s the partisan composition of the government changed no fewer than four times (in 1964, 1970, 1974, and 1979). Textbook writers took the alternation of parties in power so much for granted that they seldom emphasised it.

They were aware, however, of the advantages it appeared to offer the British system as a whole. Governments, knowing they could be defeated, always had to "run scared." They had to be sensitive to public opinion, and they had also to pay close attention to the views of the opposition parties in the House of Commons because there was always a chance that opposition MPs were reflecting the views of crucial "swing" elements in the electorate. The closeness of party competition also helped ensure governmental moderation and restraint. Most voters held moderate opinions and rejected both ideological extremes. The party leaders therefore had to offer them moderate policies (and only occasionally gave way to the grassroots activists' more radical demands). Finally, the frequent alternation of parties in power meant that the opposition front bench always had on it a considerable number of men and women with ministerial experience, often extensive experience. The available pool of political talent was constantly recycled.

To be sure, parts of this picture began to be false to reality in the 1970s, when both parties' policies began to polarise, and there was always the danger that the parties' extreme sensitivity to the electorate might lead to immobilism and a paralysis of policy; but most politicians and political observers on the whole approved of what they saw—and the traditional textbook picture still lingers on in many people's minds.[6]

But what happens to a country's political life when its party system ceases to be a competitive two-party system, as Britain's was during most of the postwar period, and becomes—or shows most of the signs of becoming—a predominant-party system? In the aftermath of the 1992 election, the question needs to be asked. It would be remarkable if such a profound change in the pattern of party politics did not have widespread ramifications throughout the British system.

Some of our answers will inevitably have to be speculative because democratic Britain has had no previous experience of sustained one-party government; but about one implication of the 9 April result we can already be clear. By the time of the next election, very few people on the opposition front bench will have had any practical experience of governmental office.

Labour's Cumulative Loss of Experience

The group of men who occupied the senior offices in the last Labour government have all now quit the scene. The prime minister, James Callaghan, retired from the House of Commons at the 1987 election. His closest associates—the chancellor of the exchequer, Denis Healey, the foreign secretary, David Owen, the home secretary, Merlyn Rees, and the leader of the House of Commons, Michael Foot—retired in 1992. Only six members of the Callaghan cabinet—Tony Benn, Roy Hattersley, John Morris, Stan Orme, Peter Shore, and John Smith—remain in the House of Commons, and only the new party leader, John Smith, remains on the front bench. Smith served as a junior minister from 1974 to 1978, but his only experience of cabinet office was the six months he spent as secretary of state for trade between November 1978 and May 1979.

The post-1992 Labour party's dearth of ministerial experience can be expressed in another way. A total of 271 Labour MPs were returned to Parliament at the election. In addition to the 6 former cabinet ministers already mentioned, a further 16 of the 271 had served in the last Labour government as junior ministers. The total of 22 might seem not too unsatisfactory; but it is in fact highly misleading. By the time of the next election, all but 7 of the 22 will be aged sixty or over, and apart from John Smith, only 3 of them—Margaret Beckett, John Cunningham, and Michael Meacher—are likely to remain on the front bench. The element of continuity between the last Labour government and any future Labour government will thus be minimal. If Labour were to win in 1996 or 1997, the new administration would be the least experienced since that of Ramsay MacDonald in 1924, when Labour took power for the first time.

Labour's cumulative loss of experience may not harm the party electorally. Most voters do not distinguish clearly, if at all, between the holding of ministerial office and membership of the House of Commons; in their eyes, anyone who has sat for a long time in the House of Commons and whom they see frequently on television must, almost by definition, be "experienced." But the loss is likely to manifest itself in more subtle ways. People who have never been ministers are not even honorary members of what Heclo and Wildavsky years ago dubbed the "Whitehall village."[7] They do not know civil servants; they do not know the ways of government departments, the Cabinet Office, and Number 10; and they do not know, except in the abstract, how business is transacted in the European Community. More than that, they have had no firsthand experience of the substantive problems with which modern governments are forced to deal. It is one thing to formulate an interest-rate policy or a social security policy in opposition, quite another to implement either of them in practice.

One consequence is that if Labour wins again, the new Labour government will have to ascend an unusually steep learning curve, as novice ministers (surrounded by other novice ministers) discover that the worlds of government and opposition are quite unlike each other. For a time, at least, the new ministers are likely to be heavily dependent on their civil servants; and Labour's activists in the country, as well as many of those who voted Labour, are likely to suffer disappointments as not all of Labour's promises are fulfilled. Another consequence is that, in the meantime, the Labour party as a parliamentary opposition is in danger of being progressively enfeebled. Experience increasingly confronts inexperience across the despatch box; knowledge (if not wisdom) confronts ignorance. Even before the 1992 election, Conservative ministers often commented privately that they were able to get away with too much on the floor of the House of Commons. As in the case of the poll tax, they were conscious of winning arguments even when they did not deserve to win them. They themselves felt—and are likely to feel increasingly as time goes on—that such an imbalance between ministers and opposition spokesmen is not in the end conducive to good government.[8]

The Conservatives' prolonged dominance tends to enfeeble the opposition. It also has important consequences for the conduct of both governmental business and political debate in Britain.

Over-the-Shoulder Politics

Between the end of World War II and the early 1980s, political debate in Britain consisted almost exclusively of debate between the major political parties. The issues that aroused controversy among people in Britain interested in politics—liberty versus equality, taxation, the nationalisation of industry, spending on the welfare state, comprehensive education —were also the issues that separated the Conservative and Labour parties. To know that a particular politician favoured more state ownership of industry was to know that he was a Labour supporter and to know his views on most of the other issues of the day. Conversely, to know that another politician favoured a gradualist approach towards granting independence to Britain's African colonies was also to know that he was a Conservative and that he probably favoured, for example, a tough anti-inflationary policy. People's views came in neatly tied bundles, and the bundles were tied in blue and red ribbon. To be sure, there were sometimes differences of opinion within parties (Labour was deeply divided over German rearmament in the 1950s), and very occasionally issues arose that cut across party lines. But by and large the lines of public debate and the lines of party–political debate on major issues ran in parallel.[9]

This simple partisanship of postwar political debate in Britain was well captured by politicians' behaviour in the House of Commons. The leading figures in the two main parties faced each other across the despatch box day after day and were cheered on by the backbenchers arrayed along the green benches behind them. The confrontation of politicians matched the confrontation of ideas and points of view. The one stood as a metaphor for the other. The paramount political battle was the party–political battle.

The structure of political debate in Britain still has, as the 1992 campaign showed, a large party–political component. The Conservative and Labour parties confronted each other during the campaign on the traditional issues of taxing and spending, inflation and interest rates, and the state of the National Health Service and the nation's education. No one dropping in on the 1992 campaign from the 1950s or 1960s would have felt particularly disoriented (though Labour's failure to mention nationalisation might have occasioned a certain amount of surprise). The two parties' emphases were the traditional emphases, and both parties exhibited a genuine passion in emphasising their differences.

But in fact the campaign, as a guide either to what British politicians believe to be the important issues of the 1990s or to the parties' stands on those issues (insofar as they have them), was both partial and misleading. It did not reflect the underlying patterns of political controversy and discussion in late-twentieth-century Britain. And the same is true of British party politics more generally. The old boxes are still there, but the new issues do not fit into them. There is now a considerable disjunction between real politics and traditional two-party politics.

The future of Britain in the European Community is the paradigm case. The European issue raises all kinds of questions: about further European integration, about the European Monetary System, about the Common Agricultural Policy, about the extent of "subsidiarity" (the powers that are to remain devolved to national governments), about the future role of the European Parliament, and, not least, about the enlargement of the Community to include the Nordic states and Austria on the one hand and the newly emerging democracies of eastern Europe on the other. All these questions are of immense importance and are acknowledged to be so by every politician in the country. Yet they hardly figure in the traditional party–political debate. Both major parties claim to be "pro-European," but on almost all the questions just listed both parties are deeply divided (or else lack a clear vision of the way forward). As a result, the debates become in-group and arcane, and clear choices are not offered to the electorate.

Europe is the paradigm case of this breakdown of the traditional two-party pattern, but it is by no means the only one. Environmental issues equally unsettle both major parties, with environmental claims pitted against the interests of both taxpayers and producers. Women's issues likewise pit traditionalists against feminists in both parties. And there are similar blurrings of historic party lines on defence, agriculture, constitutionalism, electoral reform, Northern Ireland, teaching methods in schools, and how best to deliver high-quality services throughout the public sector. In other words, the domain within which the traditional Conservative–Labour party debate still holds sway has shrunk considerably; outside that domain, the parties have ceased to put down anything like unambiguous markers.

This new and less overtly partisan pattern of political debate is probably not in any way a cause of Britain's emerging pattern of one-party domination; the first signs of the development of important cross-cutting cleavages on policy issues, not least on Europe, were becoming evident as early as the 1960s, long before the start of the Conservatives' present hegemony. But the existence of one-party government has an important bearing on the way in which political disputes under the new dispensation are resolved.

Putting it very simply, Britain's voters once chose between two major political parties with differing policies and philosophies, and the party that won then proceeded to try to put its policies and philosophy into practice. There was a direct, albeit crude, electorate–government link. Now, however, in the 1990s, the voters choose between two political parties, neither of which has clearly stated views on a wide range of issues, and the normally victorious Conservative party then proceeds, within itself, to try to work out policy on the most contentious issues. The voters have not been disfranchised; they could still vote for another party. But the combination of policy ambiguity and one-party dominance means in practice that the voters' involvement in the policy process is now much less direct. Political scientists sometimes speak of "sites" or "arenas" at which or within which the most important policy decisions are made. What has emerged as easily the most important site or arena in contemporary British politics is the Conservative party, especially Conservative ministers but also backbench Conservative MPs, who are increasingly lobbied by pressure groups and who are now, far more than in the past, the focus of media attention.

The most vivid illustration of this point occurred, not at the time of the 1992 general election, but seventeen months before, at the time of the Conservative leadership election, when a combination of Conservative cabinet ministers and backbenchers succeeded in toppling Margaret Thatcher. The regicide, as it was called, was the result of widespread Conservative fears of losing the next election—a proof that Conservative dominance of British politics has not yet become total—but also of longstanding tensions within the party, between "wets" and "dries" and between the beneficiaries and nonbeneficiaries of Thatcher's ministerial patronage. Whatever occasioned the coup, however, no outside forces were directly involved—and its policy consequences were far more important than those of any recent general election. The community charge, or poll tax, the "flagship" of Thatcher's third term, was abolished. The British government's tactics in its dealings with the European Community were changed fundamentally.

Once again, Europe is the paradigm case of the new within-party politics. Europe scarcely featured in the 1992 election because both major parties accepted, or claimed to accept, the broad outlines of the Maastricht treaty that John Major had helped negotiate in December 1991. Labour objected only to the government's insistence on opting out from the treaty's so-called social chapter. In fact, however, the treaty itself had been brokered (that is probably the right word) not only among Britain and the other eleven members of the European Community but among the conflicting points of view within the Conservatives' ranks. The prime minister saw each member of his cabinet individually to find out what would and would not be acceptable to them at Maastricht, and he kept in close touch at all stages with opinion on the back benches. Major was in the business of consensus building, and the consensus he most needed to build was within his own party.

Since the election, and especially since Denmark's rejection of the Maastricht accord in May 1992, the debate about Britain's future in Europe, and what the future of the European Community as a whole should be, has continued to be a debate essentially among the various factions, groupings, and tendencies within the ruling party. The debate sees Conservative "Euro-federalists" pitted against Conservative "Euro-skeptics" (with a large body of party opinion somewhere in between). It takes the form of private and sometimes secret meetings, of selective leaks to the press, of television and radio interviews, of coded statements by cabinet ministers, and of the competitive signing of early day motions in the House of Commons. Labour, itself divided on the issue, takes no part. The only outsiders who appear to be involved are the leading Conservative-inclined national newspapers, such as the *Daily Telegraph,* and Conservative periodicals like the *Spectator.* The general public watches, if at all, from a respectful distance.

This new politics of one-party government has, like the old, its own visual metaphor. A generation ago, frontbench spokesmen of the two major parties confronted each other face to face across the despatch box. They still do; but their confrontations are increasingly a ritual, a form that has to be gone through for form's sake.[10] Far more important today are the exchanges that take place between ministers standing at the despatch box and the government backbenchers seated behind them. To address their own backbenchers ministers have to look over their shoulders. In an era of one-party government, British politics is increasingly over-the-shoulder politics.

Dependency Relations

Politics follows power. When a party has been in power for a very long time, and looks like remaining in power more or less indefinitely, then those who want something from government, or are dependent on government, increasingly focus their attention on the party in power. They increasingly neglect the parties that are out of power; or, if they do pay attention to them, it is only out of politeness or possibly a desire to be seen as behaving in a fair-minded, nonpartisan way. Within hours of the Conservatives' election victory in 1992, a quartet of Britain's most prominent trade union leaders, pillars of the Labour establishment, were to be seen on television declaring their willingness, indeed their eagerness, to establish good working relations with the new round of Conservative ministers. The Labour party might be exiled from power; they had no intention, if they could avoid it, of sharing that exile.

Small signs of Labour's and the Liberal Democrats' exile are to be found everywhere in British political life. Neil Kinnock, Labour's leader during the election, announced immediately afterwards that he would stand down as soon as a new leader could be chosen. In an earlier era, the ensuing leadership contest would have attracted considerable media attention. After all, the party would be choosing someone who in all probability would be a future prime minister. But in the circumstances of 1992 the election aroused little interest. Coverage of the contest, even in the national broadsheet newspapers, was limited in quantity and was more dutiful than enthusiastic in tone. The journalists did not give the impression that they thought they were covering "a big story." Coverage of Labour's internal debate about the party's future was likewise minimal. Much of the debate was conducted in the correspondence columns of the *Guardian*.

The media manifested their loss of interest in the opposition parties in other ways. Throughout the postwar period, until the early 1980s, the post of labour correspondent or industrial correspondent on one of the heavyweight national newspapers had been much coveted. The trade unions were news; the unions' dealings with the Labour party were news; Labour and industrial correspondents were senior journalistic figures, who had no trouble getting their copy into their papers. In the 1990s, all that has changed. With the decline in importance of both the unions and the Labour party, the status of labour correspondents has correspondingly declined, and their copy finds its way into print less and less. Similarly, the political editors of national newspapers and the television networks typically in the 1990s assign relatively junior members of their staffs to cover Labour and Liberal Democrat affairs. The real action is with the Conservatives and the government.

More important signs of the Conservatives' continuing predominance can be found in the activities of Britain's pressure groups and other organisations that have a large stake in the government's goodwill and the content of government policy. Ministers listen to those they want to, or feel they have to, listen to. The groups and organisations, for their part, have no choice but to listen to the government. To adapt a phrase used by the American journalist Samuel Lubell in the 1950s, the Conservative party and government in the 1990s are increasingly a sun around which the interest groups and the other political parties revolve like so many captive moons.[11]

The political columnist of the London *Economist,* "Bagehot" (Andrew Marr), has pointed out the extent to which in Conservative-dominated Britain the pressure groups concentrate their efforts on government ministers and civil servants and virtually ignore both the opposition parties and, for the most part, the rituals of party politics at Westminster. "Here," he writes, "is a cheeky comparison":

> Greenpeace, an international environmental lobby, has 411,000 British supporters in 210 local groups; it had an income of around £8 million ($14.5 million) last year; and it influences government thinking. The Labour Party has only 254,000 paid-up individual members. In 1990, the last year for which figures are available, its income was £6 million. It has next to no influence on government. In the real world, which organisation cuts more ice?[12]

He goes on to note the influence in Whitehall of other bodies —Friends of the Earth, the Council for the Preservation of Rural England, the Institute of Directors, the Institute for Fiscal Studies, the Child Poverty Action Group—that can make trouble or, alternatively, have in their possession ideas and facts that ministers find useful. British pressure groups have always tended to focus on the governing party and the executive branch of government; but their focus has recently become more exclusive, and the ongoing links of many of them with a single political party, the Conservatives, have become considerably more intimate.

Organisations that are dependent on the government have likewise had to accommodate themselves to the fact of continuing Conservative predominance. The government's ethos becomes their ethos. They cannot look to any other party to save them. The BBC, whose charter is due to be renewed in 1996, continues to maintain its traditional impartiality in the reporting of political news, but in all its decisions about internal organisation and management it is conscious that the government ultimately has the power to redefine its role or even stop it from broadcasting altogether. The Independent Broadcasting Authority and the individual television companies function under similar constraints, and the same is true of Britain's universities, all of which are heavily dependent on state funds, of managers in the National Health Service, of the various arts organisations, and of local government bodies such as the Association of County Councils and the Association of Metropolitan Authorities. For all these organisations, the British state is now effectively a one-party state.

The government feels obliged to listen to some influential pressure groups, such as Greenpeace and the Council for the Preservation of Rural England, but its reliance on such groups, and the extent to which they can influence government decisions and policy, has declined substantially since the 1960s and 1970s. Throughout the postwar period, British governments of all parties pursued interventionist economic policies, and the scale of their interventions tended to increase as time went on. By the end of the 1970s, the British government was engaged in something called "economic planning" (or the pursuit of "industrial strategy"); it was the author of a succession of incomes policies designed to restrain wage and salary increases, and it was the owner on a prodigious scale, not merely of almost all the country's public utilities (e.g., electricity, gas, water) but of a substantial proportion of its manufacturing industry as well (e.g., steel, ships, airframes, aeroengines, motor vehicles). In its role as planner, wage regulator, and employer, it needed at least the consent and ideally the active cooperation of both private-sector employers and the trade unions—of what were known in the jargon of the time as "both sides of industry."

The institutional expression of the government's dependence on private industry and the unions during the 1960s and 1970s was a variety of arrangements and continuing discussions loosely lumped together under the heading of "tripartism" (or, occasionally, "corporatism"). Government representatives talked to the private-sector employers. They talked to the unions. Frequently all three met together. At the apex of this loose system of consultation and negotiation was the National Economic Development Council, established by Harold Macmillan's Conservative government in 1961 and made up of representatives of the government, the Confederation of British Industry (CBI), and the Trades Union Congress (TUC). The council met monthly in an imposing office block on the north bank of the Thames.

Margaret Thatcher abhorred this whole approach. She did not believe in economic planning. She did not believe in incomes policies. She did not believe in the government ownership of industry. All three violated her free market, private enterprise principles. Thatcher especially disliked the habits of mind and the institutions of corporatism. She believed that the freely elected government of the day had no business sharing its power and authority with unelected bodies like the CBI and the TUC. Instead, in the manner of Charles de Gaulle in France, she believed that no self-appointed "intermediaries" should be allowed to interpose themselves between her and the British people. She disliked the TUC far more than the CBI, but in fact she had considerable disdain for any pressure group that sought to negotiate with the government on anything like an equal basis. During her twelve-year premiership, Thatcher abandoned economic planning, abandoned incomes policy, and privatised a majority of the previously state-owned industries. Having abandoned economic planning and incomes policy, she was also in a position to abandon tripartism. Thatcher as prime minister held meetings with trade union leaders no more than twice during her entire twelve years in office. She was more cordial in her relations with industrialists, but she greatly preferred to meet them as (successful) individuals rather than in the form of organised deputations.

The result was to marginalise all interest groups, especially the trade unions (whose powers were further undermined by union-curbing legislation and rising levels of unemployment) but not only them. John Major in November 1990 inherited a system in which the government talked to interest groups on a strictly ad hoc and need-to-know basis. The government might on occasion be influenced by interest groups, but it no longer shared its power with them in anything like the way it had. It was certainly no longer in thrall to them. In other words, Britain's pressure groups increasingly focus their attention on the government and the party in power, and at the same time the government's power vis-à-vis the groups has, thanks to Thatcher, been substantially increased. Britain's one-party state is, by European and North American standards, a very powerful state indeed.

One oddity of the Thatcher years was that she allowed the National Economic Development Council, that symbol of the tripartite era, to linger on. It continued to meet, but did nothing. Then suddenly, in mid-June 1992, the chancellor of the exchequer, in a brief statement in the House of Commons, announced that it was to be abolished forthwith. More than a year and a half after the fall of Thatcher, the triumph of Thatcherism over tripartism was complete.

Sweden and Japan

We remarked earlier that Britain is not only a country with a dominant party but is also one with both few autonomous centres of political power and a highly partisan, winner-take-all political culture. In Britain, the party that is in is in. The party that is out is out. Full stop. There are no separated institutions sharing powers and virtually no checks and balances. Against this background, it is interesting to compare Britain's one-party system of government in the 1990s with one country that used to have such a predominant-party system, Sweden, and with one country that still has, Japan. How does modern Britain resemble, and differ from, these two countries?

The Swedish Social Democratic party dominated Swedish politics and largely controlled the Swedish government for forty years after 1932 (far longer than the Conservatives have thus far been in power in Britain). Moreover, the Swedish Social Democrats were a highly disciplined party, fully capable of forcing their legislation through the Swedish Riksdag whenever they chose. Yet to read accounts of Swedish politics during the Social Democratic hegemony is, by comparison with Britain in the 1990s, to be transported into a completely different world.[13]

Swedish politics during that era differed from Britain's today in five main respects. In the first place, Sweden's political culture was one that emphasised the rational adaptation of means to ends. Whereas British politicians, faced with a problem such as education or nationalisation versus privatisation or the National Health Service, have in recent years usually reached for the ideologically correct solution, the Swedes were almost invariably pragmatic. Proposals that seemed unlikely to achieve their desired objectives, or were likely to achieve them only at too great a cost, were quietly dropped—or, more commonly, having been tested against reality, were never introduced in the first place. The Social Democrats, for example, fought the 1944 election on a programme of extensive nationalisation of industry but then, during the ensuing four years, abandoned the policy completely in the face of intense opposition pressure.

The Swedish political climate was, and is, suffused with "the old ideal of *saklighet*—objectivity, unprejudiced respect for evidence, a spirit of cool rational appraisal ... an essentially liberal faith in the capacity of unemotional reasoned argument to winnow out the best possible solution to any given problem."[14] Elder reports that Swedish government departments "show an almost Platonic care in setting out the rationale of, and the background to, government propositions."[15] Certainly every government legislative proposal is accompanied by voluminous documentation, occasionally running to thousands of pages. British governments are not so fastidious.

Second, and associated with the spirit of *saklighet,* was the spirit of accommodation. Every writer about Sweden agrees that the Social Democrats, despite their dominant position, adhered to the Swedish norm of consensus seeking. The aim was not to defeat one's political opponents but, if possible, to do a deal with them so that everyone felt that he or she had been consulted and no one felt too aggrieved. As Anton remarks, the behaviour of Swedish leaders was characterised by "a highly pragmatic intellectual style, oriented towards the discovery of workable solutions to specific problems [that structured] a consensual approach to policy making."[16] Elder refers to the Swedes' "essentially conservative belief that the national interest is best served by co-operation across factional boundaries in a spirit of national unity."[17] Hancock likewise writes:

> As persistent norms of political behavior, conciliatory attitudes among political antagonists have yielded a contemporary elite political culture ... of restraint, rational calculation, and a willingness to bargain with others in the pursuit of party or group goals. These characteristics apply to formal political processes as well as interaction among pluralist forces within Sweden's broader socioeconomic system.[18]

Once again, restraint and a willingness to bargain and accommodate are not now, if they ever were, British norms.

Third, this spirit of elite accommodation led to a considerable spirit of nonpartisanship, even when the Social Democrats were firmly in control. Accommodation included accommodation across party lines. Opposition MPs frequently chaired powerful Riksdag committees. The reports of these committees, even ones dealing with important government legislation, were frequently unanimous. And on foreign policy issues the government invariably sought, and listened to, the views of the influential Advisory Council on Foreign Affairs, composed of representatives of all the main parties in the Riksdag. As though to symbolise the Swedish desire to keep partisanship within bounds, MPs in the Riksdag were, and are, seated not by party but by province. The spirit of nonpartisanship extended even to matters of political patronage. The chief executive in each of Sweden's twenty-five provinces is the provincial governor, appointed by the national government. At the height of the Social Democrats' ascendancy, between 1945 and 1965, the government in Stockholm appointed forty-nine governors. Only thirteen were Social Democrats. Twelve were members of other parties. The remaining twenty-four were civil servants or other nonpartisans.[19] The question "Is he one of us?" does not seem to have been asked.

The fourth striking contrast between one-party Sweden and one-party Britain concerns the process of legislation. As in Britain, the dominant party in Sweden ultimately controlled the bulk of legislation, and discipline among the dominant Social Democrats was tight. Unlike in Britain, the Swedish government's aim was to prepare legislation with almost exhaustive thoroughness, to amass every available relevant fact, to consult widely, and to try, in the end, to enact a bill that had the widest basis of parliamentary and public support. Royal commissions and other consultative procedures, usually involving members of the opposition, were employed extensively at the prelegislative stage. Interest groups were centrally involved. When proposals were ultimately introduced into the Riksdag, they were subjected to rigourous and often prolonged scrutiny—and were reported on at length—by committees of MPs with access to nongovernmental expert advisers. The Swedish pattern was not the British one of behind-closed-doors governmental decision making on legislation followed by sometimes perfunctory parliamentary scrutiny with tight whipping in the division lobbies from the beginning.[20]

Finally, the process of parliamentary and public scrutiny of government, including one-party government, in Sweden is facilitated by the Swedish norm of openness. Subject to a limited number of exceptions —relating, for example, to national security, crime detection, and personal privacy—the norm in Sweden, reinforced by a series of Freedom of the Press acts dating back to the eighteenth century, is that all official documents are to be made freely available for consultation by members of the public. The onus is on the government to show why anything should be withheld. In practice, the norm of openness does not greatly inhibit behind-the-scenes discussions of future government policy—ministers and civil servants can always talk on the phone, and anyway confidential papers circulated in connection with the preparation of business are not considered "official documents"—but the norm does affect legislation (as well as the rights of the citizen). All the papers collected by, and emanating from, the royal commissions and the other forms of prelegislative inquiry are made available to the press and MPs. As Elder remarks:

> The [publicity] rule enables a considerable amount of informed debate to take place when draft legislation and commission reports are being circulated on remit between the various administrative authorities concerned. Divergences of view between these authorities are brought to light and an opportunity is given for facts that have been overlooked to be taken into consideration. At the same time the opposition parties are provided with a variety of material for use against the government in debate.[21]

Needless to say, the Swedish openness norm is not operative in Britain. The British norm is one of governmental secrecy.

One-party government in Sweden between 1932 and the 1970s thus operated under a number of constraints. Even in the heyday of the Social Democrats' power, there was never talk of Sweden enduring an "elective dictatorship."[22] The style of Swedish politics was inclusionary rather than exclusionary; interest groups were consulted; and partisanship was kept within bounds. The process of making policy in Sweden was conducted painstakingly, with ample opportunities for public discussion and participation.

The experience in Japan is different again. It is particularly worth attending to because the Japanese political system resembles the British in many respects. The prime minister, cabinet, and civil service are the country's principal policy makers. The Diet in Japan, like the British Parliament, is essentially subordinate. Party discipline in both houses of the Diet is strict. And in Japan, as in modern Britain, there are almost no important centres of political power apart from the national government. Indeed the resemblances between the Japanese and British systems are not entirely accidental. As Japanese parliamentary institutions developed during the first three decades of this century, Japanese politicians had the British system very much in mind; and after World War II, the American occupation authorities, for reasons that are still not entirely clear, imposed a new, democratic constitution that was much more British than American in its basic principles.[23]

The Liberal Democratic party (LDP) has dominated Japanese politics almost continuously since the war, and there is one respect in which one-party government in Japan and one-party government in Britain resemble each other quite closely. Both systems tend to exclude—not, of course, from the ballot box but from more direct participation in governmental policy making—those groups that are not part of the governing party's informal "coalition" or set of support groups. These excluded groups in Britain include the trade unions, to a considerable extent Labour-controlled local authorities, and many of the bodies that claim to speak on behalf of the poor. Such groups may be allowed, as it were, to say their piece; but they are seldom effectively heeded. The same pattern recurs in Japan, and few writers on Japanese politics do not refer to it in one form or another. The American scholar T.J. Pempel describes Japan as "a democratic regime in which a cohesive conservative social coalition has remained relatively unchecked in its control of the strong state institutions." And he adds: "It is also a regime from which organised labor has been consistently excluded."[24] Richardson and Flanagan likewise draw attention to "the partial exclusion of the left and labor unions" from Japanese political life and to the cumulative effect these exclusions have had on the pattern of Japanese public policy.[25]

In a number of other respects, however, Britain and Japan differ —and look like they will continue to differ into the indefinite future. One concerns corruption. Whether the definition used is Western or Japanese, Japan's politics and government are probably the most corrupt in the democratic world. Japanese politicians buy votes, they buy influence in government, and they buy political advancement. In turn, they themselves are bought. All Japanese politicians need large sums of money to finance their election campaigns; some of them become rich. Scandals are frequent; kickbacks on government contracts are endemic. It has been said that "corrupt practices are woven so deeply into the fabric of Japanese politics that reform programs are virtually doomed to failure short of a radical purging and restructuring of the entire system."[26]

By contrast, national politics and government in Britain are, and seem likely to remain, virtually corruption free. British cultural values are inimical to corruption; there are no cultural norms in Britain, unlike in Japan, of "reciprocity, exchange of favours, and gift-giving."[27] And British norms of financial propriety are reinforced by the independence of the civil service and by the presence of watchdog bodies like the parliamentary Public Accounts Committee, chaired by a member of the opposition. Large donations to the Conservative party may buy honours and invitations to 10 Downing Street, but there is no evidence that they affect, for example, the building of roads, the awarding of government contracts, or the distribution of state subsidies. A junior minister in the late 1940s was forced to leave public life when he accepted a gift of as little as two bottles of whisky. There is no reason to think that one-party Britain will be any more open to corruption than two-party Britain.

Another important difference between Britain and Japan concerns the civil service in the two countries. In both countries, the senior civil service consists of able men and women (mostly men) chosen on a highly competitive basis and drawn mainly from elite educational establishments. The devotion to duty of civil servants in both countries is unquestioned. The British civil service, however, remains strictly neutral in politics, despite the recent prolonged period of one-party government. British officials take positive pride in their willingness to work with politicians of all political parties. Few of them are publicly identified with the Conservatives, and many of them undoubtedly vote Liberal Democrat or Labour. Had Labour won the 1992 election, many British civil servants would have relished the opportunity to display their political and administrative skills for the delectation of new masters.

The relationship between the Japanese civil service and the dominant party in Japan is considerably more ambiguous. At one level, Japanese civil servants, on "descending from heaven" at the age of fifty or fifty-five, frequently become involved in LDP politics or the affairs of interest groups closely associated with the LDP; there have been times in postwar Japan when more than half the cabinet was composed of men who had recently been civil servants.[28] At another level, the LDP has been in power so long that the interests and outlook of the LDP and the interests and outlook of the Japanese civil service seem gradually to have melded, so it becomes hard to tell where "the government" in the party sense ends and "the government" in the bureaucratic sense begins. Pempel writes of there having occurred almost a "fusion" between the two.[29]

Moreover, unlike in Britain, the Japanese civil service has *never* had experience of working with a government other than one dominated by the LDP. "Thus one has no real sense of what would happen within the state bureaucracy if, say, a socialist government came to Japan. Would new socialist policies be introduced and implemented with comparative ease, or would the bureaucracy effectively resist changing past practices?"[30] The answer is that no one knows. Japan, in that sense, is a much more fully developed one-party state than Britain seems likely to be in the near future.

In one respect, however, Japanese politics and government somewhat resemble Sweden's. In Japan as well as in Sweden, though not in Britain, considerable emphasis is placed on consensus building. All accounts of Japanese politics—and of Japanese life generally—lay considerable emphasis on the Japanese desire to arrive at the largest possible quantum of unforced agreement and, if at all possible, to do so without anyone having lost face or been seen too publicly to have been beaten. Elder describes the Swedish legislative process as "leisurely, thorough," and frequently very time-consuming.[31] Reischauer likewise describes the political decision-making process in Japan as "flexible, careful, and thorough," though he adds that it "moves very slowly."[32]

New policy proposals in Japan are discussed extensively in the LDP and its factions, committees, subcommittees, and task forces, among different government departments, among the government departments, the LDP, and interest groups, and, not least, in the committees of the Diet, where opposition Dietmen can have their say. This entire process is underpinned by a network of some 250 advisory councils, appointed by the ministries and made up of academics and representatives of interest groups and the media. "Perhaps," Pempel notes, "only Sweden outdoes Japan in the prevalence given to such bodies."[33] The effect is that most new laws adopted in Japan have a wide basis of support. A large proportion of the bills passed by the Japanese Diet, including bills on important subjects, are passed unanimously.

The desire in Japan to build as wide a consensus as possible, and the LDP's fear of being presented by the media as high-handed and dictatorial, has led to a curious (and very un-British) practice in the Japanese legislature, which two American observers have dubbed "the de facto opposition veto."[34] Although the LDP since the war has almost always had the power to steamroller its entire legislative programme through the Diet, it has frequently yielded to opposition objections, and the fear of opposition obstruction, and agreed to withdraw contentious bills. A total of nine such bills were withdrawn in the Diet sessions between 1970 and 1974.[35] Reischauer does not use the term "de facto veto," but he writes along similar lines:

> It [is] imperative for the party in power to limit the number of controversial bills presented in the Diet as much as possible. Less controversial matters are carefully tailored to avoid any serious controversy, and the important controversial issues are made as palatable to the opposition as possible and are strictly limited in number. For many years, for example, there has been a Liberal Democratic consensus on upgrading the Defense Agency to the status of a Defense Ministry, but year after year the measure has been shelved as more symbolic than substantive and therefore not worth the political price that would have to be paid for it.[36]

The Swedish and Japanese experiences, taken together, thus suggest that one-party government need not necessarily or invariably mean either winner-take-all government or a policy-making process dominated totally by the governing party. Consensus building is possible, and opposition groups and parties need not be entirely excluded from influence. The British style in the 1990s is not the only possible style.

Opportunities and Dangers

The Conservative party's fourth general election victory in a row presents both the party and Britain as a whole—unused to one-party government—with two dangers and a potential opportunity.

One of the dangers is that after so many years in power, the Conservative government will become complacent, stale, and out of touch, that it will respond to its own needs rather than the country's, and that it may even come to misconstrue what is in its own best interests. By 1996 or 1997 John Major will have held office continuously, as either a government whip or a minister, for the better part of fourteen years. He will long since have ceased to drive his own car, answer his own phone, or worry about the mortgage on his house. His experience of life in Britain in the 1990s will increasingly be both vicarious and out of date. The majority of his colleagues will be in the same position. The danger is in some ways greater for the Conservatives than it would be for Labour, since so many Conservative ministers, being financially well-off, have had little or no experience in their own lives of, for example, working women with children, parents struggling to pay for their children's education, or children trying to look after ageing parents. In the words of Bagehot in *The Economist:* "Some of the Tories who staggered, blinking, out of their Whitehall offices to fight the 1992 election seemed as if they had lost touch with reality years ago. How will they seem five years hence?"[37]

The greater danger, from the country's point of view as well as the Conservatives', is that of authoritarianism. Power easily becomes self-justifying. The Conservatives may come to believe that they govern as of right, that opinions other than their own are not worth listening to, and indeed that non- or anti-Conservative views are somehow illegitimate ("How dare they ...?"). Thatcher undoubtedly exhibited authoritarian tendencies; they contributed to her growing public unpopularity and eventually to her fall. Major, however, exhibits no such tendencies. On the contrary, he is a good listener and appears, temperamentally, to be liberal minded. The worry must be that anyone in power for a very long time, possibly angry, frustrated, or in adversity, may be tempted to take shortcuts through liberal democratic processes. Even if Major does not succumb to temptation, others around him may. The Canadian Liberal party after two decades of continuous power became increasingly authoritarian and contemptuous of Parliament.[38] In Britain, the danger is made more real by the fact that so much power is concentrated in the national government in Whitehall. In their dealings with ministers, very many institutions in Britain are supplicants rather than in any sense equals.

The potential opportunity held out by a long period of one-party government is for substantial continuity of government policy. It has often been said, and is probably true, that an important source of Britain's relative economic decline over the past four decades has been the numerous and often erratic changes in government economic policy. The structure of taxation has changed. Tax rates have changed. Exchange rates and interest rates have fluctuated wildly. Companies have been in private ownership, then nationalised, then returned to private ownership. The laws relating to trade unions have been reformed, re-reformed, and then re-re-reformed. It has often not been clear for prolonged periods what the nature of Britain's relationship with the European Community was going to be. Part, at least, of these wild gyrations of policy has been attributed to "adversarial politics," to the alternation in power of parties with radically differing policies, each determined to abandon the policies of its predecessor and to substitute its own, ignoring the fact that policy changing, in itself, carries costs. Businessmen already live in a risky, uncertain world. They have found their risks and uncertainties gratuitously increased by government. Insofar as this analysis has validity, a sustained period of one-party government contains within it the possibility of a sustained period of policy calm, enabling individuals, organisations, and companies to plan with a little more certainty for the future. All that ministers have to do is resist the temptation to tinker. Unfortunately, British politicians, even Conservative politicians, love to tinker. They seem to think that is what they are there for.

The Future

One of the few certain consequences of the 1992 election was the discrediting, at least temporarily, of the opinion polls. They got it wrong; they could be seen to have got it wrong. At first sight, the polls' debacle may seem relatively trivial—Who cares if the pollsters have got egg all over their faces (except, of course, the pollsters)?—but in fact the debacle could be important. The polls' 1992 debacle means that, at least until the time of the next election, the polls' findings will no longer be taken as seriously as they once were. To express a view about the state of public opinion, and to base that view on opinion poll findings, will be to invite ridicule. If that happens, given that the polls provide virtually the only source of information about public opinion, then public opinion itself—the views of the general public—will be at a discount. Every politician will claim to know what public opinion is. In an odd way, the polls' discomfiture may make Britain a very slightly less democratic country.

The election had less bearing on the issue of Britain's future relations with Europe. Whatever the outcome of the election, Britain's negotiating stance vis-à-vis the rest of the European Community would have remained much the same (though a Labour government would have been keener on the Maastricht treaty's social chapter). Indeed the circumstances of the 1992 election hold out the prospect, in other European countries as well as in Britain, that a European Community negotiating cycle will develop independently of the individual electoral cycles of the member states and that the two cycles will impinge on one another scarcely at all. If so, and in the absence of genuinely democratic institutions covering the whole of Europe, the people of the Continent may participate scarcely at all in the building of Europe. They may erupt into the process only sporadically, and possibly damagingly, as in the case of the Danes' referendum on the Maastricht agreement. If ordinary parliamentary elections are seen to be increasingly irrelevant to wider European politics, the pressure in member states for special elections or referendums may become irresistible.

It remains to be seen what bearing the 1992 election has on the future of the United Kingdom. Before the election, it was widely believed that the Conservatives would lose most of their few remaining seats in Scotland, that the Scottish National party (SNP) would make sweeping gains, and that a major constitutional crisis might therefore ensue if the Conservatives retained power at Westminster. The union might not hold if the Scots once again found themselves forced to submit to an "alien" political regime. In the event, the SNP failed to gain seats (though it gained votes), and the Conservatives, far from being eliminated, gained both seats and votes. The effect in the short term was to remove Scotland from the Whitehall and Westminster, if not the Glasgow and Edinburgh, political agenda. But the fact remains that non-Conservative parties still hold 74.3 percent of the votes in Scotland and sixty-one of Scotland's seventy-two parliamentary seats, and the pressure north of the border for devolution or separation remains strong. The issue of the future relations of Scotland and England, though quiescent in London for the moment, is unlikely to go away. As in the case of Europe, the politics of British general elections and the more fundamental politics of constitutional development seem to have got seriously out of phase.[39]

The future of the Conservative party and of one-party government in Britain depends partly on how the Conservatives comport themselves in office between 1992 and 1996–97 but also on the performance during that time of the British economy. Having won an election in 1992 in the midst of a deep recession, the Conservatives hope to do even better in 1996 or 1997 when the country has come out of recession and the economy is growing strongly. Their hope is to repeat, not the triumph of 1992, but the far greater triumph of 1987. Most Conservatives believe that Britain, having gone into recession first, may be among the first to come out of recession and that, with leaner and fitter industries and a low inflation rate, Britain may be even better placed to compete in world markets in the mid-1990s than it was in the mid-1980s. Be that as it may, the Conservative government, within weeks of the 1992 election, was trying to ensure—by imposing tight controls on public spending—that the economic and electoral cycles did not get out of phase in the mid-1990s as they had in the early 1990s. The Conservatives had a bad fright in April 1992. They do not want to repeat the experience.

The Conservatives' future also depends, of course, on the future of the Labour party—on whether Labour can make itself more electable in the voters' eyes in 1996–97 than it was in 1992. The obstacles to be overcome are formidable, consisting as they do of the party's narrowing social base, of its ties to the declining and now largely discredited trade union movement, of an ideology and set of social attitudes that seem firmly anchored in the past, and, perhaps above all, of voters' accumulated suspicion of a party associated in their minds, fairly or unfairly, with high taxation, high inflation, numerous strikes, the endless disruption of public services, and hopelessly incompetent economic management. Labour elected a new leader, John Smith, and a new deputy leader, Margaret Beckett, in mid-July 1992, but the debate in the party about its future that followed the April defeat did not give the impression that more than a handful of people in the party had fully grasped the enormity of what had happened. Labour, as so often in the past, seemed determined to go on playing its own internal game according to its own internal rules, rather than engage in the much more difficult task of adapting itself to a radically changed political and social environment. Labour's electoral prognosis in the summer of 1992 was not good. If this prognosis proves correct, British government will remain one-party government into the next millennium.

Notes

1. Details of the British election results between the turn of the century and 1983 can be found in David Butler and Gareth Butler, *British Political Facts 1900–1985*, 6th ed. (London: Macmillan, 1986), 224–28. Labour's share of the popular vote at the general elections since the mid-1970s has been February 1974, 37.1 percent; October 1974, 39.2 percent; 1979, 37.0 percent; 1983, 27.6 percent; 1987, 30.8 percent; 1992, 34.2 percent.

2. Anthony King, "Tory 'Super-Party' Born out of Last-Minute Switching," *Daily Telegraph*, 13 April 1992.

3. Giovanni Sartori, *Parties and Party Systems: A Framework for Analysis* (Cambridge: Cambridge University Press, 1976), 196.

4. Writers about British politics between the end of the war and the 1960s (especially American writers) stressed the extent to which Britain's political culture was suffused with pragmatism and moderation. It is therefore worth making explicit the point that the tone and taste of British politics in recent years have become much more partisan and ideological. In her approach to politics, and in her use of patronage, Thatcher was probably the most partisan prime minister of this century.

5. See, for example, the chapters on Britain in Samuel H. Beer and Adam B. Ulam, eds., *Patterns of Government: The Major Political Systems of Europe*, 2d ed. (New York: Random House, 1962).

6. One of the few writers to note that a closely fought party battle might lead to immobilism was Ian Gilmour, later one of Thatcher's cabinet ministers. See Ian Gilmour, *The Body Politic* (London: Hutchinson, 1969), 60–61.

7. Hugh Heclo and Aaron Wildavsky, *The Private Government of Public*

Money: Community and Policy inside British Politics, 2d ed. (London: Macmillan, 1981), 76–128.

8. The ministers who spoke in these terms said they were afraid that a low standard of parliamentary opposition could lead to carelessness and mental slackness on the part of ministers and officials—on the analogy of a firm that becomes slack because of a lack of competition.

9. There were hardly any exceptions to this general rule. Either the Conservative party or the Labour party might be internally divided on a specific issue, but there were almost no issues on which a section of the Conservative party found itself allied with (or even in political sympathy with) a section of the Labour party. The Suez crisis of 1956 was a rare instance when a significant minority in the Conservative party favoured Labour's stand on the issue; and the question of British membership of the Common Market had this capacity right from the beginning. In retrospect, it is the symmetry and neatness of postwar political debate, rather than the comparative messiness of 1990s debate, that seems puzzling.

10. The ritual becomes more than a ritual, and the form more than a form, in the run-up to a general election. Prime minister's question time, in particular, is televised, and both the prime minister and the leader of the opposition are keen to use this opportunity to impress voters. Both sides prepare carefully for the parlimentary jousting.

11. Samuel Lubell, *The Future of American Politics,* 2d ed. (Garden City, N.Y.: Doubleday Anchor, 1956), 212.

12. Bagehot (Andrew Marr), "Pressure Politics," *The Economist,* 30 May 1992, 36.

13. The following account is based largely on Neil Elder, *Government in Sweden: The Executive at Work* (Oxford: Pergamon, 1970); and M. Donald Hancock, *Sweden: The Politics of Postindustrial Change* (Homewood, Ill.: Dryden Press, 1972).

14. Elder, *Government in Sweden,* 20, 187.

15. Ibid., 188.

16. Thomas J. Anton, "Policy-Making and Political Culture in Sweden," *Scandinavian Political Studies* 4 (1969): 99.

17. Elder, *Government in Sweden,* 186-87.

18. Hancock, *Sweden,* 68.

19. Ibid., 96.

20. See the descriptions in Elder, *Government in Sweden,* 119–37; and Hancock, *Sweden,* 170–97.

21. Elder, *Government in Sweden,* 154. The phrase "on remit" refers to one of the commonly used methods of prelegislative consultation in Sweden.

22. The phrase is that of Lord Hailsham, Margaret Thatcher's first lord chancellor. He used it to refer to the concentration of political power in Britain, especially in the absence of any formal constitutional checks. He expressed his doubts about the state of Britain's constitution when the Labour party was in power in the late 1970s. His doubts seem to have evaporated when the Conservatives came to power; or at any rate, little was heard of them publicly. See Lord Hailsham, *The Dilemma of Democracy: Diagnosis and Prescription* (London: Collins, 1978), 125–32.

23. See the brief account in J.A.A. Stockwin et al., *Dynamic and Immobilist Politics in Japan* (London: Macmillan, 1988), 26–28.

24. T.J. Pempel, *Policy and Politics in Japan: Creative Conservatism* (Philadelphia: Temple University Press, 1982), 40–41.

25. Bradley M. Richardson and Scott C. Flanagan, *Politics in Japan* (Boston: Little, Brown, 1984), 377–78.

26. Ibid., 185.

27. Ibid., 182.

28. Stockwin et al., *Dynamic and Immobilist Politics*, 39.

29. Pempel, *Policy and Politics in Japan*, 36.

30. Ibid., 23.

31. Elder, *Government in Sweden*, 137.

32. Edwin O. Reischauer, *The Japanese*, 2d ed. (Cambridge, Mass.: Harvard University Press, 1981), 297.

33. Pempel, *Policy and Politics in Japan*, 18.

34. Richardson and Flanagan, *Politics in Japan*, 354–55, 364–65.

35. Ibid., 354–55.

36. Reischauer, *The Japanese*, 293–94.

37. Bagehot (Andrew Marr), "A Not So Funny Old World," *The Economist*, 25 April 1992, 40.

38. See, for example, John Meisel, *The Canadian General Election of 1957* (Toronto: University of Toronto Press, 1962), 4–12. Meisel quotes one contemporary observer as saying, "Political historians may well conclude that the Liberals fell, not because of any one policy, and certainly not a pipeline policy of which the average voter knew little and cared less, but because they failed to observe the proper limits of power" (p. 10).

39. For an up-to-date account of Scottish politics and Scottish-English relations, see Andrew Marr, *The Battle for Scotland* (Harmondsworth, Middlesex: Penguin Books, 1992).

Appendix

Results of British General Elections, 1945–92

	Percentage of popular vote					Seats in House of Commons					
	Con.	Lab.	Lib.[a]	Nat.[b]	Other	Con.	Lab.	Lib.[a]	Nat.[b]	Other	Government majority
1945	39.8	48.3	9.1	0.2	2.5	213	393	12	0	22	146
1950	43.5	46.1	9.1	0.1	1.2	299	315	9	0	2	5
1951	48.0	48.8	2.5	0.1	0.6	321	295	6	0	3	17
1955	49.7	46.4	2.7	0.2	0.9	345	277	6	0	2	60
1959	49.4	43.8	5.9	0.4	0.6	365	258	6	0	1	100
1964	43.4	44.1	11.2	0.5	0.8	304	317	9	0	0	4
1966	41.9	47.9	8.5	0.7	0.9	253	363	12	0	2	95
1970	46.4	43.0	7.5	1.3	1.8	330	288	6	1	5	30
Feb. 1974	37.8	37.1	19.3	2.6	3.2	297	301	14	9	14	–34[c]
Oct. 1974	35.8	39.2	18.3	3.5	3.2	277	319	13	14	12	3
1979	43.9	37.0	13.8	2.0	3.3	339	269	11	4	12	43
1983	42.4	27.6	25.4	1.5	3.1	397	209	23	4	17	144
1987	42.3	30.8	22.6	1.7	2.6	376	229	22	6	17	102
1992	41.9	34.4	17.8	2.3	3.5	336	271	20	7	17	21

a. Liberal party 1945–79; Liberal/Social Democrat Alliance 1983–87; Liberal Democrat party 1992.

b. Combined vote of Scottish National party (SNP) and Welsh National party (Plaid Cymru).

c. Following the February 1974 election, the Labour party was 34 seats short of having an overall majority. It formed a minority government until it obtained a majority in the October 1974 election.

Index